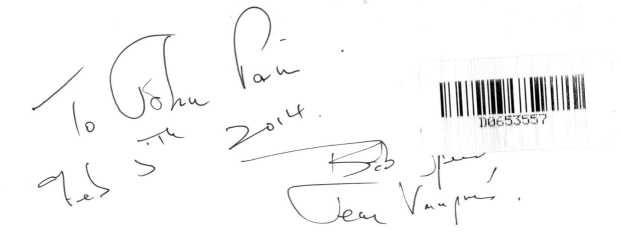

To John Paul.
Feb 5th 2014.

Best Wishes,
Jean Vanpres.

Wessex

A
Literary
Pilgrimage

Peter Tolhurst

Peter Tolhurst

Foreword by
Ronald Blythe

Black Dog Books

First published in England 1999
by Black Dog Books
11 Trinity Street, Norwich, Norfolk, NR2 2BQ

A CIP record of this book is available from the British Library.

ISBN 0 - 9528839 - 1 - 0

Typeset in 10 point Times

Printed in Great Britain
by St Edmundsbury Press, Bury St Edmunds, Suffolk
Bound by T J International, Padstow, Cornwall

*Where man and nature have dwelt side by side time out of
mind there is a presence, a genius of the spot, a haunting
sweetness and loveliness not elsewhere to be found.*

Richard Jefferies

Acknowledgements

I owe a particular debt to the following for dealing so patiently with my enquiries, for allowing me access to archive material and the use of illustrations from private collections: Amanda & Tristan Allsop; Nathalie Blondel; Dorset Record Office; Jonathan Gaunt; Tim Hawkins; Cedric Hentschel; Morine Krissdottir of The Powys Society; the National Portrait Gallery picture library; the National Trust photographic library; Richard de Peyer, curator of the Dorset County Museum and his staff; Susanna Pinney; Tate Gallery picture library; Wiltshire Record Office.

My warmest thanks go to the following for helping nurse the book through to completion: to Rebecca Goff who transformed my handwritten manuscript into something legible; to Sally Greenhill for proof reading the text; to Angela & David Rice for their hospitality; and above all to Magdalen Bear for her invaluable help with the design.

*   *   *   *   *

Every effort has been made to identify the owners of copyright material and obtain the necessary permissions, but the author would be grateful if any inadvertent errors or omissions could be brought to his attention.

The author would like to thank all those for permission to reproduce the following illustrations: Kitchenham Ltd, front cover, 246; Tim Hawkins, 10, 87, 93, 94a, 100, 133, 137, 169, 180a, 235, 250, 258; Jonathan Gaunt, 14, 28, 31, 36a, 37, 39a, 41, 45, rear cover; Bowood Estate, 19a; The Ashmolean Museum, Oxford, 29, 112; Pamela Colman, 36b; Marlborough College, 39b, 40; Cambridge University Aerial Photography, 52a; Frank Regan / The Women's Press Ltd., 52b; National Portrait Gallery, 26, 42b, 62, 65b, 97b, 113, 141, 257; Jonathan Gaunt & H Hyams, 41; R S P B, 68b; Dorset County Museum, 69, 95a & b, 99, 105a & b, 106, 110a, 118, 129a, 145, 148-51, 152b, 153, 158, 162a & b 163, 165, 166, 174, 176a & b, 179, 194, 201, 205, 219, 224, 230, 251, 253, 254; Dorset County Record Office, 74, 142, 182; The National Trust, 78; The Powys Society, 79a & b, 161, 203, 210, 229, 225; The National Trust / Rupert Truman, 85; Peter Reddick, 88; Magdalene College, Cambridge, 97a; John Nash estate, 102, 198; Gregory Stevens-Cox, 108; News International, 120; Mark Douet / Picador, 126; The National Trust / Mike Williams, 128; Chatto & Windus, 129b; Amanda Allsop, 135, 140; Colin Varndell, 139; Morine Krissdottir, 156, 216, 222, 231; Simon McBride, 159; The National Trust / David Noton, 199; Richard Garnett, 215; Janet Pollock, 220; Susanna Pinney, 221a & b; David Burden, 226; Chris Gostick, 228; Mary Butts estate, 236a & b; The National Trust / Ian West, 239; The Tate Gallery, 240, 244; The National Trust / Joe Cornish, 246; Dr Philip Mansel, 248; Nathalie Blondel, 255.

The author would also like to thank the following for permission to quote from copyright material: for the works of Edward & Helen Thomas, Myfanwy Thomas; for the works of John Betjeman, John Murray Ltd.; for the works of William Golding, Faber & Faber Ltd.; for the works of E M Forster, The Society of Authors & King's College, Cambridge; for the works of Mary Butts, the estate of Mary Butts; for *Boy Blue* by Stevie Davies, The Women's Press Ltd.; for *A Passionate Apprentice* by Virginia Woolf, Random House UK Ltd.; for the works of Sylvia Townsend Warner, Susanna Pinney; for the works of John Cowper Powys, Laurence Pollinger and the estate of John Cowper Powys; for *The Kingdom By The Sea* by Paul Theroux, Penguin Books Ltd.; for the works of Llewelyn Powys, Laurence Pollinger & the estate of Llewelyn Powys; for *The French Lieutenant's Woman*, John Fowles; for *Ever After* by Graham Swift, A P Watts Ltd.; for *First Light* by Peter Ackroyd, Penguin Books Ltd.; for *In The Country* by Kenneth Allsop, the estate of Kenneth Allsop; for the works of T F Powys, Laurence Pollinger & the estate of T F Powys; for *A Shell Guide to Dorset* by Paul Nash, David Higham; for *The Black Tower* by P D James, Greene & Heaton Ltd, for *Notes From a Small Island,* Bill Bryson & Greene & Heaton Ltd.

Foreword

Where the West Country was concerned, Thomas Hardy was an audacious empire builder, eventually laying claim to all the territory from Oxford to north Cornwall - 'Farthest Wessex'. This delightful peregrination stays within the bounds of Wessex proper as it were, Dorset and Wiltshire, those wide open yet often dark and mysterious highlands which have been inhabited since Neolithic times and which remain full of myth and drama. Here, as well as Hardy, worked many other poets, novelists, naturalists and travel writers, and it is Peter Tolhurst's task to guide the reader to them via the places which inspired their work. The accounts vary according to the local status of the writer. Hardy, of course, possesses the indigenous eye at its most far-seeing, most ruthless, most artistically and purposefully limited. He sees what both men and women see, what the unlettered see, and what genius alone sees, and he brings all these visions together in a powerful mix. So do the Powys brothers. But literature, especially novels, benefits from incomers to a particular region, and Wessex has had no shortage of these. And it also benefits greatly from the writer on the hoof, and as Dorset and Wiltshire contain some of the best walking country in the whole of Britain, they have over the years prompted much fine travel-writing.

This is a devoted bookworm's companion. By taking the reader's literary passion for granted, Peter Tolhurst is able to explain and extol at length as he leads us through some of the most celebrated scenes in English fiction, and some of the least known. Hardy dominates, though a Hardy witnessed afresh, so that if we have been here before - Flintcomb-Ash, 'haggard Egdon', Casterbridge itself - new views emerge, which is as it should be when a reader goes over old but ever fertile ground. Today's understanding of ecology adds its own revelation to Hardy's setting of his novels, making it plain why furze or Portland stone, or simply the toil-hungry fields themselves could have made it impossible for those who dwelt among them to escape. In the soap opera characters have to be artificially cooped up in order to provide friction. In Hardy there is much 'geographical' cooping-up which Peter Tolhurst shows us during many enlightening journeys across his terrain. The great writer himself had spent his early years in a London architect's office, working on his first poems and stories in the evening. But he returned to Bockhampton when he felt able to make his initial statement about the literary territory which he intended to occupy. Sitting at the window of the little room which he shared with his brother, he wrote 'Far from the Madding Crowd', the book which immediately placed him on the Victorian's equivalent to a best-seller list and launched his career as a novelist.

For Thomas Hardy, indeed for many writers and artists who stay at home, it is not just the comfort of possessing the authority to say what they really feel about their native scenery, but the uncomfortable personal pressures animated by their being the curious people they are in the place where they were born, which gives their work a unique depth and importance. Some of the extracts chosen by Peter Tolhurst illustrate the tensions of being a local author.

Certainly we who like to look around some celebrated literary countryside or city are most moved when the writer who made it famous was native to it. It is one of the things which this guide understands. It is reflective and unhurried, making clear how essential it is to read the writers whose landscapes have become so fascinating from having been 're-drawn' by them.

The Powys brothers too were rooted in Dorset. John Cowper (his mother belonged to the same family as the poet) possessed vast creative energy, so that reading him is like being half torn apart by the winds which lash Maiden Castle, or like being with someone who is a contemporary of menhirs and stone circles. Llewelyn deals successfully, if dangerously, like D H Lawrence, with the sensuality of earth and sky. And Theodore Powys, in his funny-profound masterpiece 'Mr Weston's Good Wine', brings God on a tour of inspection to a 1920's parish, properly chauffeured, of course, by an archangel. Theodore's address was Chaldon - *possibly the most hidden village in Dorset* - according to Llewelyn. The enchanting novelist and short-story writer Sylvia Townsend Warner lived there too with her lover the poet Valentine Ackland. Both Sylvia and Theodore are brilliant at introducing misrule and disturbance into apparently quiet, dull scenes. Living in remote Chaldon allowed Sylvia her sharp view of the East Anglian fens in a wonderful historical novel called 'The Corner That Held Them' - a title which would have suited this literary ramble.

Netherhampton House near Wilton where Virginia Woolf stayed in the summer of 1903.

Writers often research some distant location for a book. Or they set it where they have briefly been, having retained its strange or beautiful or just compellingly ordinary atmosphere. Or sometimes a particular house demands certain characters and happenings. And sometimes such writers encounter those authors to whom these corners belong by birthright. Was it when E M Forster set his novel 'The Longest Journey' partly in the West Country that he began to read the wonderful Dorset dialect poet William Barnes? Forster said, *It is impossible to read a poem like 'Woak Hill' by Barnes without tears in one's eyes. Or rather, if one has not tears in one's eyes at the end of 'Woak Hill' one has not read it.* Among the Wiltshire writers we have the diarist Francis Kilvert whose account of his visit to Barnes is a perfect example of the pleasure we all get from making literary pilgrimages.

In this Wessex anthology Peter Tolhurst's choice is selective and personal, as it should be. By journeying to any of his writers the bookish traveller cannot fail to find others on the way. Wiltshire can lay claim to much of Barsetshire but has as its centrifugal centre, marked by Salisbury cathedral spire, William Golding. To spend much of one's working life, as he did, in the shadow of some towering glory, man-made or natural, can be a lasting influence. Golding was both exalted and cast down by his tower which bears the tallest spire in England. In spite of their architectural splendour, when we see either this or Stonehenge from a distance our thoughts go to the novels as much as to Pevsner, to 'The Spire' and 'Tess of the d'Urbervilles'.

The passages on Richard Jefferies make one long to see the country south of Swindon whose every aspect he recorded. He was a young writer in a hurry, the dreaded but then all too common tuberculosis urging him on. Marvellous essays, social history, matter-of-fact farming, and then the mystical 'Story of My Heart' which many people could not take but which to us is a remarkable part-psychological, part-dream confession, touchingly intimate and still redolent of the grassy hill on which Jefferies (as did William Hazlitt in Wiltshire) liked to sprawl looking up at the clouds as they and he drifted towards infinity.

Peter Tolhurst has chosen the best method of all to entice us to his expanded literary Wessex - by letting us enjoy once again so many Wiltshire and Dorset writers' views of it.

Ronald Blythe

9

Marshwood Vale, Dorset with Gerrard's Hill in the middle distance, one of Hardy's many *Wessex Heights.*

Introduction

The subtle contours of scarp and vale that define the topography of southern England rise to a grander scale, inscribe a more intricate pattern across the face of Wessex. The old ridgeway track running from the Berkshire Downs to the coast at Lyme Regis marks the great sinuous divide between two very different landscapes. On one side the bare chalk hills stretch away, an ancient land of earthworks and sarsen stones. In the other direction the rich clay vales, a gentler, more secretive country of butter pastures and stone manor houses spread themselves comfortably at the foot of the downs. Rising to 964 feet Tan Hill overlooking the Vale of Pewsey is the highest point, but for dramatic effect the contorted projections along the edge of Blackmore Vale remain unsurpassed, crowned by a succession of majestic hillforts that stand out like teeth in an old jaw.

Throughout history people living in the shadow of these lofty hills have gathered there to worship the old gods, to celebrate the seasons or attend the great sheep fairs and in this way the lonely summits have become sacred places lodged deep in the folk memory of successive generations. Tribes of semi-nomadic Celts first recognised the defensive possibilities of the steepest slopes. Encircled by a complex succession of ditch and rampart, these earthworks became an outward expression of an inner need for refuge and renewal. Well into the last century, bonfires to mark the onset of winter or beacons lit in times of danger flared in the night sky, while ravens circled above the gibbet at some remote crossroad. The hills of Wessex have always been places of ritual and retribution with their own peculiar mythology. To isolated country people suspicious of more rational explanations, they had been raised by the devil or by some race of giants, and hoards of treasure awaited those brave enough to venture below ground and do battle with the fiery dragon.

In this century the 'Wessex Heights' as Hardy called them, have acquired new meaning for writers and a special place in the literary landscape of the region. For Richard Jefferies the hillforts at Barbury and Liddington on the Marlborough Downs became charged with a mystical energy, an almost palpable force that inspired 'The Story of My Heart' and the poetry of disciples like Edward Thomas, Alfred Williams and Charles Sorley. The journalist Kenneth Allsop lived for many years in a watermill near the foot of Eggardon Hill, the most dramatic of all the Dorset hillforts. The ramparts, with buzzards soaring overhead and views across Marshwood Vale, were a constant joy throughout his last difficult years.

Other earthworks less impressive in scale or situation, have come to exert an equally powerful influence on the creative process. Figsbury Ring near Salisbury provided E M Forster with a symbol of redemption in 'The Longest Journey', and in John Cowper Powys' 'Maiden Castle', the majestic sequence of bank and ditch near Dorchester became the most pervasive force in the novel. Equally alive to the magic of place, Paul Nash discovered *nothing so beautifully haunted as the wood in Badbury Rings* between Wimborne and Blandford. A year earlier the response of the Dorset writer Mary Butts had been both immediate and lasting: *I lay stretched out on the ground and understood that the Rings' signature is written in its quiet .... made audible by the sound in the grove.* With each solitary visit she felt the place charged with a mystical force that was to inspire much of her work, notably 'Ashe of Rings'.

For Hardy too the hills of Wessex had a dramatic quality beyond mere scenery. In 'The Return of The Native' it is the brooding presence of Rainbarrow that presides over the fate of his characters. Relocated in the centre of Egdon Heath it becomes the fixed point around which events revolve. High Stoy overlooking the Vale of Blackmore, occupies a similar position in 'The Woodlanders', *the axis of so many critical events* in the life of Little Hintock and a meeting place between old beliefs and new ideas. Standing alone on the summit Grace Melbury and Giles Winterborne gaze into the evening sky, their eyes travelling on *under a species of golden arcades, and past fiery obstructions, fancied cairns, logan stones, stalactites and stalagmite of topaz.* This dazzling spectacle becomes a momentary escape from the burden of life and ends as a place of refuge in *a bottomless medium of soft green fire.* The view becomes a vision of release soothing the pain of unrequited love in a world of rigid divorce laws.

At the beginning of Hardy's most popular novel the reader is invited to stand on the rounded summit of Norcombe Hill, *far from the madding crowd,* and feel the immensity of the universe when *the twinkling of all the stars seem to be but throbs of one body, timed to a common pulse.* On a clear midwinter eve this lonely spot is more like an observatory designed to study the galaxy or a platform from which to travel through the night sky:

the roll of the world eastward is almost a palpable movement. The sensation may be caused by the panoramic glide of the stars past earthly objects, which is perceptible in a few minutes of stillness, or by the better outlook upon space that a hill affords, or by the wind, or by the solitude; but whatever be its origin the impression of riding along is vivid and abiding .... having first expanded with a sense of difference from the mass of civilized mankind, who are dream-wrapt and disregardful of all such proceedings at this time, long and quietly watch your progress through the stars. After such a nocturnal reconnoitre it is hard to get back to earth, and to believe that the consciousness of such majestic speeding is derived from a tiny human frame.

Hardy was a poet by inclination but with the rejection of his early verse he turned to fiction and, encouraged by the success of 'Far From The Madding Crowd' and the need to support a wife, he decided to abandon architecture and become a professional writer. Although he always felt he had simply exchanged one trade for another, his novels often express feelings in images that are essentially poetic and he continued writing poetry throughout his early career. In **Wessex Heights** (1897) the Dorset hills are a symbol of retreat from an increasingly hostile public. With the savage reviews that had followed the publication of 'Jude the Obscure' the previous year, Hardy vowed it would be his last novel. In this sense Hardy is part of the Romantic tradition where remote elevations have always been realms of the imagination, places of inspiration far removed from the time / space constraints of the world below.

Wessex Heights

There are some heights in Wessex, shaped as if by a kindly hand
For thinking, dreaming, dying on, and at crises when I stand,
Say, on Ingpen Beacon eastward, or on Wylls-Neck westwardly,
I seem where I was before my birth, and after death may be.

In the lowlands I have no comrade, not even the lone man's friend -
Her who suffereth long and is kind; accepts what he is too weak to mend:
Down there they are dubious and askance; there nobody thinks as I,
But mind-chains do not clank where one's next neighbour is the sky.

In the towns I am tracked by phantoms having weird detective ways -
Shadows of beings who fellowed with myself of earlier days:
They hang about at places, and they say harsh heavy things -
Men with a wintry sneer, and women with tart disparagings.

Down there I seem to be false to myself, my simple self that was,
And is not now, and I see him watching, wondering what crass cause
Can have merged him into such a strange continuator as this,
Who yet has something in common with himself, my chrysalis.

I cannot go to the great grey Plain; there's a figure against the moon,
Nobody sees it but I, and it makes my breast beat out of tune;
I cannot go to the tall-spired town, being barred by the forms now passed
For everybody but me, in whose long vision they stand there fast.

There's a ghost at Yell'ham Bottom chiding loud at the fall of the night,
There's a ghost in Froom-side Vale, thin-lipped and vague,
                                        in a shroud of white,
There is one in the railway train whenever I do not want it near,
I see its profile against the pane, saying what I would not hear.

As for one rare fair woman, I am now but a thought of hers,
I enter her mind and another thought succeeds me that she prefers;
Yet my love for her in its fullness she herself did not know;
Well, time cures hearts of tenderness, and now I can let her go.

So I am found on Ingpen Beacon, or on Wylls-Neck to the west,
Or else on homely Bulbarrow, or little Pilsdon Crest,
Where men have never cared to haunt, nor women have walked with me,
And ghosts then keep their distance; and I know some liberty.

The lowlands are a place of painful isolation haunted by ghosts from his past life as a novelist and the characters he created. *The ghost in Froom-side Vale* is Tess d'Urberville and the *figure against the moon* appears like Eustacia Vye on Egdon Heath.

For so long Hardy had been working *down there* at what he regarded as the inferior craft of novel writing, but now with the financial security it offered he could escape the *mind chains* of hostile criticism and devote himself entirely to poetry. In order to assume the poet's mantle and the *simple self* Hardy realised that, like a chrysalis, he must shed his old self and relinquish old attachments. The poem was written at a time of intense personal unhappiness and with the end of his *impossible love* for Florence Henniker, his *one rare fair woman*, he was left to reflect on a marriage that had gone disastrously wrong. He knew he would remain a prisoner of the past unless he could grow as a poet and that only through the pain of leaving would he be able to sustain the imaginative intensity necessary to write poetry. In his fiction Hardy used the subtleties of landscape to mirror the fate of his characters, especially in 'Tess of The d'Urbervilles' where the lowlands are equated with personal happiness and the uplands with the predations of a modern world. In 'Wessex Heights', his farewell to fiction, Hardy reversed the analogy to mirror his own predicament.

Cherhill Down west of Avebury, adorned by Lansdowne obelisk (1845), a white horse cut in 1780 by Dr Allsop of Calne and the remains of Oldbury Castle hillfort.

1

Sacred Ground

North
Wiltshire

So Bevis sat down, and the wind began to sing, so low and sweet and so strange an old song, that he closed his eyes and leaned on his arm on the turf. There were no words to the song, but Bevis understood it all, and it made him feel so happy. The great sun smiled upon him, the great earth bore him in her arms gently, the wind caressed him, singing all the while. Now Bevis knew what the wind meant .... something seemed to come to him out of the sunshine and the grass.

From *Bevis* by **Richard Jefferies**

Langley Burrell

On September 2nd 1872 Francis Kilvert *left Clyro forever.* The young curate had lived in Radnorshire for six years and although he only began his now famous diary two years before returning to Wiltshire, the time was, by his own account, the happiest of his life. This may help explain why Kilvert is more readily associated with the Welsh border than the gentle countryside of the Wiltshire Avon. Kilvert was born and brought up in the rectory at Hardenhuish on the northern outskirts of Chippenham and in 1872 he returned to spend four years as curate to his father in the neighbouring parish of Langley Burrell, an unremarkable village strung out between the Chippenham highway and the Great Western railway. Today the few interesting houses include Langley Lodge, the home of Kilvert's friends the Dallins, but the church and manor house are hidden away among trees nearly a mile distant on the main road. St Peter's with its Norman arcade, Early English work and pretty 18th century wall monuments, is much as Kilvert would have known it although the oil lamps and internal plasterwork have been removed. The headstones and table tombs would also have been a familiar sight as he wandered in the churchyard:

The ivy-grown old church with its noble tower stood beautiful and silent among the elms with its graves at its feet. Everything was still. No one was about or moving .... It seemed to be given up to the birds and their morning hymns. It was the bird church, the church among birds .... The hour for service drew on. The Clerk coughed in the church. Two girls in grey dresses passed quietly through the church and moved about among the graves .... Then a woman in deep mourning moved slowly down the path of the churchyard and the clerk began to ring the bell for service.

The late Georgian manor house, *ashlar faced and dignified if not particularly eventful,* was home to the Ashe family who ruled the village from a safe distance. When Robert Ashe succeeded as 'squarson' of Langley Burrell he immediately relinquished his clerical duties to manage the estate and appointed Kilvert's father to the living. Shortly after, the squire decided to isolate himself still further by demolishing the rectory and removing the Kilverts to a gentrified farmhouse nearer the village. Having re-mapped the social geography to his satisfaction Robert Ashe continued to meddle in village affairs. The Victorian Gothic school near the church had been built by his father and not surprisingly, when asked who make the world, one of the class replied 'Mr Ashe'. One November day he marched into the classroom and, oblivious to the cries of cold children and indignant parents, reminded the school mistress that windows and doors were to be left open at all times. The squire clearly felt able to exercise his authority here more effectively than in church. The outburst came soon after he had reluctantly agreed to the installation of a harmonium, but he refused to contribute towards its cost on the grounds that he *disapproved of any music in a church beside the human voice.* This display of mean-spirited disapproval matched that of his grandfather, the Revd Samuel Ashe, who had attempted to put an end to Sunday football by lurking among the trees on the edge of the common until the ball came close enough for him to puncture it with a knife.

Kilvert's Wiltshire churches from a drawing by Robin Tanner for the Kilvert Society.

16

Reading Kilvert, one is struck by the man's disarming honesty. He was occasionally *greatly troubled by the licentiousness of the school children* but elsewhere in his record of daily life there is remarkably little moral condemnation. He took an innocent pleasure in the gossip picked up on his parish rounds, describing the more dramatic events with evident good humour and a journalist's eye for detail. The more memorable incidents include the sight of the 13th Hussars marching through Chippenham, a hot air balloon drifting over the Rectory and the bloody confrontation between rival gangs from Chippenham and the Langleys in which two Chippenham men were killed. Kilvert made no attempt to denounce the violence that, according to his informant, had been started by a group of Chippenham thugs, and stories are often retold without verification. When graves in Chippenham churchyard were disturbed by foundations for the north aisle, an assistant at the chemist's shop told the young curate that *scalps with hair still on them were left lying about and that he himself had seen a hedgehog tearing at the arm of a body which still had flesh upon it.*

As an eligible young bachelor Kilvert was much in demand at society gatherings and his susceptibility to female beauty is one of the curate's most endearing qualities. At the Twelfth Night party given by Sir John Audrey he was much taken with Francie Rooke and as the evening turned into a jolly romp everyone danced *wildly and promiscuously with whoever came to hand.* Soon after, Kilvert was captivated by the gypsy beauty of Ettie Meredith Brown and he often walked across the water meadows to Spye Park and the manor house where she once lived. When Ettie's mother finally put an end to the affair, the young curate was so heart-broken that two months later he gladly accepted the living at St Harman's and returned to his beloved Radnorshire.

The Ashe family crest and the date 1844 are still clearly visible on the gable end of Langley Burrell school.

Any suggestion that Kilvert was just a gay socialite or love-stricken poet is quickly dispelled. As a country priest he displayed abundant compassion moving easily from the squire's drawing room to the labourer's kitchen and he never once neglected his moral duty to either the sick or the destitute. His concern for the motherless boy he met one afternoon on the high road is especially touching and on most days he could be seen about the lanes bringing comfort to his more isolated parishioners. Regular visits like those to his *dear little lover Mary Taverner, the deaf and half dumb child,* were keenly awaited and warmly received:

When I opened the door of the poor old crazy cottage in the yard the girl uttered a passionate inarticulate cry of joy and running to me she flung her arms round my neck and covered me with kisses. Well, I have lived and I have been loved, and no one can take this from me.

Filled with fresh, evocative descriptions of mood and landscape, Kilvert's diary is an appreciable literary achievement as well as a fascinating historical document. He liked nothing better than to escape the noise and *tawdry finery* of Chippenham market to wander on his own along footpaths where generations of his forefathers had trodden, and in this reflective mood the most familiar scenes take on an Arcadian glow. He went down to *Greenway Lane Farm by the quiet meadows fragrant with the incense of evening prayers* to where Fair Rosamund was *making up the sweet rolls of rich golden butter* while he drank *warm whey* from a jug. He enjoyed walking at all times, but was in most rapturous mood on those warm summer evenings when *a soft moonlight was flooding the common as the moon sailed out from behind a net of heavy clouds and the cattle looked ghostly in the weird silver light.* Autumn was his favourite time when he would often walk across the watermeadows of the Avon to wander round by the lake in Bowood Park, his senses alert to every new sound:

... the fluttering of the coot as she skimmed the water with her melancholy note, the cry of the swan across the lake .... the quiet rustle of the red and golden drifts of beech leaves, the rush of the waterfall, the light tread of the dappled herd of deer .... and the merry voices of the Marquis's children at play.

Some of Kilvert's finest prose was inspired by atmosphere in the presence of a beautiful young woman. After a visit from Ettie Brown when the sun had lit up her *graceful crimson figure*, Kilvert's heightened awareness re-creates an early morning landscape of magical intensity:

All night the heavy drenching fog brooded over the land, clinging to the meadows long after the sun was risen .... Then the morning suddenly became glorious and we saw what had happened in the night. All night long millions of gossamer spiders have been spinning and the whole country was covered as if with one vast fairy web. They spread over lawn and meadow grass and gate and hawthorn hedge, and as the morning sun glinted upon their delicate threads drenched and beaded with the film of the mist the gossamer webs gleamed and twinkled into crimson and gold and green like the most exquisite shot-silk dress in the finest texture of gauzy silver wire .... 'the Virgin's webs' glowed with changing opal lights ....

The lake in the park at Bowood.

It is remarkable that any of Kilvert's diary should have survived. On his death Kilvert's wife destroyed several volumes and most of the remaining twenty two notebooks were later disposed of by an elderly niece. With some obvious gaps, the three extant volumes covering the last nine years of his life now form part of that peculiarly English literary genre, the 'View from the Parsonage'. His insight into Victorian rural society is a welcome antidote to Parson Woodforde's bloated vision of country life begun in Somerset a century earlier, and since its publication in 1939 Kilvert's diary has achieved the status of a minor classic.

Richard Jefferies
(1848 - 87)

Coate

The work of **Richard Jefferies**, much of it inspired by childhood memories of the north Wiltshire countryside, continues to arouse strong and often conflicting emotions. From his early essays on country life to the nature mysticism of his later years, much of Jefferies' writing is an uncomfortable mix of politically reactionary opinions and intense spirituality. These contradictions were, according to Richard Mabey, expressive of a rare honesty as the young writer struggled to rethink his ideas on issues such as the role of the landowner, country sports and the agricultural labourer, at a time of great social and economic change. In his last years he managed to embrace many of the arguments that still rage about the role of the countryside.

The manner of Cobbett's interviews with local farmers, the gossip endemic in Mitford's village and the conversational style of Borrow's gypsy encounters suggest a sense of community and an engagement with life in the countryside more prevalent among Jefferies' predecessors. As the critic W J Keith points out, his pivotal position in the rural tradition stems largely from the fact that he was its first non-believer. His spiritual autobiography **The Story of My Heart** (1883) marked a real turning point in Jefferies' work from the traditional realism of his journalistic essays to the visionary introspection of his last years. Jefferies inspired a whole generation of writers most notably Alfred Williams, W H Hudson, Edward Thomas and Henry Williamson; men who were to experience the horror of war and remain agnostics. Their preference for long, solitary walks reflected a sense of loss and alienation that, according to Keith, inevitably followed the destruction of Massingham's God-Man-Earth trilogy.

Brought up just south of Swindon, Jefferies was never really part of a working landscape and the tenuous status of Coate Farm as an agricultural unit is reflected in the ambiguity of his writing. The growing tensions of rural life, exacerbated by proximity to a large urban area, are exemplified by Jefferies background and early life. Although he was ready to use the address 'Coate Farm' to further his literary career, the place was no more than a 40 acre small holding purchased by his grandfather in 1800. Jefferies' father had given up his job with a Fleet Street printer in 1816 and moved with some reluctance into the house at Coate in order to manage the family's Swindon bakery. Like most urban dwellers he soon adopted country manners, proved adept with a gun and was, according to one contemporary account, an imaginative gardener who:

... rooted up the rough old cider apples and stocked the orchard with sweet, delightful codlins and russets .... he planted pear trees on the walls, the Siberian crab and the yew-tree on the lawn, and the luscious and then little known egg-plums .... He scattered the musk-seed, so that each year the delicate, scented little plant would crop up between the paving and under the 'parlour' window.

Jefferies' indulgent father was also, according to Edward Thomas, *a lover of books and curious things*, and it was the family connections with the book trade that helped shape the boy's literary aspirations. Jefferies was never a farmer's boy and, preferring the company of his London relatives, was sent to live in Sydenham at the age of four. Under the attentive eye of Aunt Harrild he soon learnt to read and his admiration for Fred Gyde, the gifted uncle who taught Jefferies to draw, is evident from his affectionate portrait of the man as Alere Flamma in **Amaryllis at the Fair** (1887). Rural writers like Hardy and W H Hudson sharpened their view of the countryside by spending time in London and Jefferies' years in Sydenham gave him the critical perspective necessary to write about rural life for a largely urban readership.

On his return to Wiltshire five years later, armed with a good selection of reading material, Jefferies was left to indulge his passion for nature and solitary reflection. He could often be found with a book in some sunny corner of the garden or in a boat on Coate reservoir reliving the adventures of Ulysses. The vitality and atmosphere of his idyllic boyhood were recaptured years later in **Wood Magic** (1881) and more especially in **Bevis** (1882), his best loved work. Here he re-enacts the more blood thirsty episodes from 'Treasure Island', admits to the pleasures of egg collecting and the thrill of shooting rabbits with his father. Published the year before 'The Story of my Heart', intimations of mystical experience had already begun to creep into 'Bevis'. Most memorable was the young boy's sensation of lying on the grass watching the new moon rise above the mulberry bush and feeling the presence of the stars, as tangible as the elms in the garden: *The green path by the strawberries was the centre of the world, and round about it by day and night the sun circled in a magical golden ring.*

Coate Farmhouse, the childhood home of Richard Jefferies, is now a museum dedicated to the writer's life and work.

While still at home Jefferies began work on the North Wilts Herald but after the serialisation of his history of Swindon, the ambitious young reporter found the discipline of regular work increasingly irksome. The breakthrough came in 1872 with the publication of his letters in 'The Times' on the life of the Wiltshire labourer in which he argued the case for the landowner faced with the threat of worker unrest. This piece of opportunism carried the weight of observation rather than personal experience and was calculated to appeal to the paper's readership. Jefferies' real feelings, set out at the same time in 'A True Tale of the Wiltshire Labourer', proved too radical and the article was never printed. Years later with the confidence of an established writer, Jefferies reworked the essay for the Manchester Guardian of a farm labourer trapped in a cycle of grinding poverty and long hours of arduous toil, set against the background of a bountiful harvest. The author's assertion that *the wheat is beautiful, but human life is labour* demonstrates how far Jefferies had progressed as a social commentator.

'The Times' correspondence attracted much attention and rescued Jefferies from the obscurity of romantic fiction. He began to receive requests for articles on agricultural subjects and soon found himself a regular contributor to publications as diverse as The Livestock Journal and The Pall Mall Gazette. His love of field sports and respect for property endeared him to a wide readership. London editors were also impressed by his unpolished style and he soon came to be regarded as the authentic voice of the countryside. Jefferies could now afford to marry his sweetheart Jessie Baden, and in 1877 they decided to leave for London where he could more easily further his career.

Burderop House, centrepiece of the estate that inspired some of Jefferies' finest essays.

The move suited Jefferies and once in Surbiton he never returned to Wiltshire but continued to draw heavily on memories of the Wiltshire countryside. His prodigious output of over 400 articles in a working life cut short by tuberculosis, provided material for several collections of essays, the first being *The Gamekeeper at Home* (1878). Subtitled 'Sketches of Natural History and Rural Life', it established the pattern and content of Jefferies' non-fiction right through to his finest achievement *The Life of the Fields* (1884), *The Open Air* (1885) and the posthumous anthologies *Field and Hedgerow* (1889) and *The Toilers of the Field* (1892). *The Amateur Poacher* (1879) and *Round About a Great Estate* (1880) were inspired by his friendship with the head keeper in Burderop Wood while the essays in *Wildlife in a Southern County* sprang directly from observations of the natural world recorded in one of the leather-bound notebooks Jefferies always carried with him.

The essays represent a considerable body of work, a coherent picture of the countryside constructed from accurate details that give Jefferies' writing its distinctive flavour. Unlike Gilbert White who saw only the wild creatures of Selborne, Jefferies provided an inclusive vision of man and nature that was perhaps his greatest achievement. The pursuit of field sports and the art of poaching were, for him, a part of the rural economy and the mark of a true countryman that brought him to a closer understanding of nature. This view relied on maintaining the established order and in his early essays Jefferies argued in favour of the game laws as a necessary measure to protect landowners from the *semi-bohemian trespassers* who roamed the countryside. In *Hodge and his Masters* (1880) he celebrated the sober virtues of the yeoman farmer identifying *moral apathy and contempt for property* as the greatest threats to rural society. In later years he recognised the importance of the village as an economic and social institution but stressed its need to adapt. He supported the provision of facilities such as cottage hospitals, libraries and allotments and his idea of the village as an organic community was taken up by his immediate successor George Sturt.

Jefferies' retreat into the fantasy world of 'Wood Magic' and 'Bevis' was in part a response to deteriorating health, but there was still little to suggest the sensations of *Soul-Life* stored up in his mind since adolescence. It was eventually the appearance of his celebrated essay 'The Pageant of Summer' alongside Hardy's 'The Dorsetshire Labourer' in 1883 that led directly to the publication of his poetic autobiography later that year. The book came as something of a shock to many readers and *The Story of My Heart* has continued to divide critics ever since. Admirers of his nature essays found the shallow mysticism painfully embarrassing. W H Hudson's initial enthusiasm soon turned to revulsion, and H J Massingham found it *a very bad and tawdry book*. For others it placed Jefferies in the tradition of nature mysticism that stretched back to Wordworth's 'Prelude', but its uncomfortable quality was summed up by the poet Richard Church for whom reading it was *like holding a fast breathing bird in one's hand*.

The great elm at Coate with its view towards Liddington Hill or the ivy-covered crab tree along the lane were just two of the many *thinking places* where Jefferies experienced brief moments of exaltation, but his soul-life took

shape among the *pleasant ambulatory* spaces between the cartsheds and alongside the garden wall where observation became insight through the gradual process of reflection. The source of Jefferies' vivid revelations lay in the boy's remarkably strong eyesight that enabled him to transform the image into Blake's *eternal moment*. At first the experience, *the unconscious happiness in finding wild flowers* before the conscious pleasure of discovering their names, was sufficient:

> But though I can recall every item of such times, the very spots on the rude wall where the mortar had fallen, the peeled willow poles stored across the beams, the angle where there was a swallow's nest, the green decayed board of the palings .... the rusted iron bar of the cow-shed windows, the very colour and aspect of the rain .... though I remember so exactly, I do not think I noticed it any more than the swallows themselves did. The entire absence of the conscious mind left the retina to receive a vivid and complete delineation.

There are few topographical references in Jefferies' work, but just south of Coate the great chalk amphitheatre is guarded by the twin hillforts of Barbury Camp and Liddington Castle. Jefferies was just 18 when he first experienced the full intensity of soul-life that had been welling up within him. Leaving the *petty circumstances* of daily life he began to breathe the clear, pure air on top of Liddington Hill and felt, in the exhilaration of sun and sky, the desire to break through to a new level of consciousness. The long, slow ascent became a spiritual journey and the initial experience, repeated elsewhere in his life, became enshrined in the earthworks. In *Restless Human Hearts* (1875), one of Jefferies' early romantic novels, the heroine underwent a similar experience:

Liddington Hill where Jefferies' *Soul-Life* took shape and found lasting expression in *The Story of My Heart.*

She climbed up the steep-sided downs, and choosing a hollow sheltered from the wind, lay down upon the soft, thymey turf; while the bees flew overhead and the lark sang high above her, and dreamt day-dreams, not of heaven, but of something - she knew not what; of a state of existence all and every hour of which should be light and joy and life. It was one of her fancies, thus lying on the broad earth, with her ear close to the ground, that she could hear the heart of the world throb slowly far beneath.

Written shortly after his marriage, the passage suggests a sexual basis for the author's adolescent revelation. By using the more measured language of the novel Jefferies managed to convey succinctly the state of bewildered delight he struggled so hard to understand in 'The Story of My Heart', where at one point he cries out *who could have imagined the whirlwind of passion that was going on within me as I reclined there!* The fervent pulse of the book owes much to the pain and despair of Jefferies' last few years but at times the more lucid passages acquire a mantra-like insistence:

I cannot understand Time .... it is eternity now. I am in the midst of it. It is about me and in the sunshine; I am in it, as the butterfly floats in the light-laden air. Nothing has to come .... Now is eternity; now is immortal life.

Jefferies craved revelation but, having rejected the idea of a personal deity, he was left with the nebulous concept of *Beyond*. The problem was that Jefferies had no clear philosophical basis for his ideas. He knew the essence of his soul-life but like many before him his inability to express it adequately did not prevent him from trying to articulate the *meaning waiting in the grass and water.* Given the vague nature of Jefferies' quest 'The Story of My Heart' is for many a necessary, if glorious, failure. The book had a profound influence on the work of both Llewelyn Powys (see p 224) and D H Lawrence. All three men chose to draw their strength from an elemental life-force and, according to W J Keith, *all were consumptives whose love of nature had the feverish, ecstatic quality of those who know themselves condemned to an early death.* For others like Henry Williamson, whose impassioned prose also bore the mark of Jefferies, 'The Story of My Heart' was *one of the most beautiful and most noble books in the world.*

Jefferies' soul-life began to glow from repeated exposure to *the intense life of summer days* on Liddington Hill until it burst into the *Sun-Life* of his last few bed-ridden years. Eventually discarded as the title for his autobiography, *Sun-Life* remained the *life which burned around us as if every grass blade and leaf were a torch*, but in his attempt to locate the source of this golden grail, the bearded prophet of Liddington Hill came nearest the truth whenever his attention was arrested by a single object of vibrant beauty. The golden crested wren and the *citron-tinted head of the yellow hammer* were transformed into images of golden light but one diminutive downland flower above all others, *a delicious suffusion of egg-yolk orange and yellow*, symbolized for Jefferies the eternal youth of his Wiltshire heartland:

The bird's-foot lotus is the picture to me of sunshine and summer, and of that summer in the heart which is known only in youth and then not alone. No words could write that feeling: the bird's-foot lotus writes it.

On leaving Oxford, **Edward Thomas** and his young wife chose to live deep in the countryside, firstly in the Kentish Weald and later on the edge of the Hampshire downs, but through his love of Richard Jefferies the young Welshman always regarded Wiltshire as his spiritual home. Holidays spent exploring Jefferies' countryside were, as Helen Thomas recalled, *the most treasured memories of his boyhood .... The Downs about Swindon he knew and loved as no other part of England.* Throughout his short life Thomas was always searching for the elusive heart of England immortalised by Jefferies but, unlike his mentor, Thomas had been brought up in a succession of dreary south London suburbs. He yearned for the outdoor life but always felt cut off from the long tradition of country writers he most admired by his rootless middle class background. Conscious that his prose work lacked their vitality, his own verdict on **The Heart of England** - *Borrow and Jefferies sans testicles and guts* - summed up an attitude to much of his writing.

When Thomas discovered a copy of Jefferies' 'The Amateur Poacher' in his father's library, the familiar territory of woods and streams where he had first learnt to climb trees with his brothers, catch minnows and build dens, was even then being destroyed by development. The impact of the book was immediate and lasting and the concluding words, copied neatly into each of his books, became his personal creed: *Let us go out of these indoor narrow, modern days, whose twelve hours somehow have become shortened, into the sunlight and the pure wind. A something that the ancients thought divine can be found and felt there still.* Encouraged by the Unitarian minister at his Sunday school, Thomas was soon writing imitative nature essays while reading 'Bevis', 'Round About a Great Estate' and anything else by Jefferies he could lay his hands on. As he later recalled :

What I liked in the books was the free open-air life, the spice and illegality and daring, roguish characters - the opportunities so far exceeding my own - the guns, the great pond, the country house, the apparently endless leisure - the glorious moments that one could always recapture by opening the Poacher .... Obviously Jefferies had lived a very different boyhood from ours, yet one which we longed for and supposed ourselves fit for. He had never had to wear his best clothes for twelve or fourteen hours on Sunday.

By an extraordinary coincidence Thomas had a grandmother in Swindon, just a mile or two from Jefferies' birthplace. Each holiday, anticipated with growing excitement, brought him in touch with a world remote from that of his cramped suburban house. Swindon was then still a small country town and on market days the place was alive with Jefferies' Wiltshire peasants:

Curious wizened old men with old hats, enormously stout with shawls and black bonnets, smiling rosy ones with feathers drove by. Their little carts were laden with eggs, butter, fowls, rabbits and vegetables, from Lydiard and Shaw and Purton and Wootton Bassett. One or two always stopped at our gate, and the woman came to our door with a broad flat basket of eggs or butter under a cloth and, very rarely, some mushrooms .... She with her cheerful and shrewd slow way was as strange and attractive to me as any poet's or romancer's woman became afterwards.

Edward Thomas
(1878 - 1917)
Linocut by Robin Guthrie

Of all the people Thomas met on these holidays, his friendship with the old poacher David Uzell proved most influential. This ex-militia man, whose wild youth and itinerant life had all the romance of a George Borrow character, was an inexhaustible fund of country lore. He showed Thomas where to find the best nesting sites, how to skin a rabbit and taught him the medicinal properties of wild plants. Thomas eagerly wrote up much of this practical advice in the notebooks he always carried with him. They provided the groundwork for his nature writing, notably **The Woodland Life** (1897), his first collection of essays about Wiltshire published when he was just 19. Before going up to Oxford he and Helen Noble had become lovers and, anxious to show her his adopted county, Thomas arranged a few precious days together as the guests of Uzzel and his wife. Years later Helen could recall every detail of the place:

In his biography of Jefferies, Edward Thomas wrote *The keeper lived in the cottage with three-scalloped thatch in Hodson Bottom; sweet chestnut behind it ... date 1741.* Years later Thomas and Helen Nobel stayed here as the guests of David Uzell.

It had a deep thatched roof almost hiding the little windows of the bedrooms with its deep eaves and a porch with a little bench on either side, covered with travellers' joy and briar roses that filled the air with musky scent. It belonged to the wood and the wood to it, as if it has been in reality the brown fur-covered creature that it looked, whose eyes peered out from under its overhanging brows shyly and kindly. All along under the thick untrimmed hedge of the garden was a row of beehives, one or two of the painted wooden new kind, but half a dozen or more of the old-fashioned skeps with earthenware pans inverted over them .... I had never seen anything so lovely, so exactly what I should have chosen for my honeymoon.

The young couple found the cottage interior equally charming. The living room had a stone floor and a large open range. The walls were adorned with guns and traps and bunches of herbs hung from the ceiling. Their tiny bedroom with its four poster bed and thick horsehair mattress was *just as right as all the rest of the cottage* and they fell asleep listening to the sounds of the wood at night, lulled by a sweet-smelling breeze that blew in through the open window. The two lovers spent all next day walking in the woods, returning exhausted to Granny Uzell's delicious high tea and an evening of songs round the fire with glasses of home-made mead. Edward and Helen enjoyed several other holidays in Wiltshire, notably in preparation for his biography of Jefferies, published in 1909, but they were never again so unimpededly happy. Although in later years Helen was unsure about the exact location of that fairy-tale cottage, the reservoir where Edward bathed could only have been at Coate on the edge of Burderop Wood. And so in that enchanted spot, they touched the 'Wood Magic' of Jefferies' own boyhood.

After a secret marriage in 1899 with Helen expecting their first child, Thomas threw himself into a punishing regime of hack work; endless reviews and topographical books written to increasingly tight deadlines. Attacks of depression were never far away, aggravated by poverty, overwork and frequent moves as he struggled to support a growing family. Even his best work like **The South Country** (1909) is too rhetorical and despite its title, conveys no real sense of locality. Few places are mentioned by name and the reader is offered a series of composite pictures that are curiously unsatisfying. For years he had been struggling in the wrong medium to define *an ideal country belonging to itself and beyond the power of the world to destroy*. Ironically it was his decision to enlist that finally released Thomas from the drudgery of prose writing. This, and his meeting with the American poet Robert Frost, gave him a confidence to write verse and it produced a remarkable body of work; 141 poems in his last two years.

Beech clumps between Hackpen Hill and Barbury Castle, a length of the Ridgeway well known to Edward Thomas.

In April 1915, Thomas finished **Lob**, his longest and most patriotic poem. Asked once by Helen what he was fighting for Thomas, picking up a handful of earth, had answered *literally this*. The poem is no mere lament for the passing of Merrie England, but his finest expression of that search for the true spirit of the countryside that foundered in his prose. It stands as a tribute to the memory of David Uzell and to the wisdom of all countrymen:

> *At hawthorn-time in Wiltshire travelling*
> *In search of something chance would never bring,*
> *An old man's face, by life and weather cut*
> *And coloured - rough, brown, sweet as any nut, -*
> *A land face, sea-blue-eyed, - hung in my mind*
> *When I had left him, many a mile behind.*

'Hedge Flowers' by Robin Tanner from **Wiltshire Village.**

The search begins in a particular landscape, the Vale of Pewsey, but even here the old man soon becomes lost in the network of country lanes and villages: *And whether Alton, not Manningford, it was, / my memory could not decide.* Lob is everywhere and Everyman, Jefferies' Hodge and Shakespeare's Tom, a folk tale hero as old as man himself. Down through the ages he named the fields, the hills and wayside flowers:

> *He is English as this gate, these flowers, this mire.*
> *And when at eight years old Lob-lie-by-the-fire*
> *Came in my books, this was the man I saw.*
> *He has been in England as long as dove and daw,*
> *Calling the wild cherry tree the merry tree,*
> *The rose campion Bridget-in-her-bravery;*
> *And in a tender mood he, as I guess,*
> *Christened one flower Love-in-idleness,*

Lob is both real and mythical green man, the strength and continuity of country life, and the poem ends where it began with his elusive figure disappearing once more:

> *In hazel and thorn tangled with old-man's-beard.*
> *But one glimpse of his back, as there he stood,*
> *Choosing his way, proved him of old Jack's blood,*
> *Young Jack perhaps, and now a Wiltshireman*
> *As he has oft been since his days began.*

Given his deep love for the county, it was fitting that Thomas should spend his last days on English soil in Wiltshire. Stationed in the Wylye valley, Thomas walked over the hills from Codford to lunch with the Newbolts at Netherhampton House in the Nadder valley (see p66). His diary entry for January 21st 1917 describes a winter landscape full of disturbing images:

Freezing drizzle - freezes on the ground, white grass and icy roads. 2 families of vagrants in green road roasting a corpse of something by slow woodfire. Beautiful downs, with one or two isolated thatched barns, ivied ash trees, and derelict threshing machines. Old milestones lichened as with battered gold and silver nails.

A week later, on the eve of his return to France, Thomas took one last walk *over the downs by Chicklade Bottom and the Fonthills to Hatch*, to spend the night with his youngest daughter Myfanwy at the home of Arthur Ransome. East Hatch is a hamlet in the parish of Tisbury and here the sense of foreboding is etched more graphically on the headstone to Kipling's parents in the village churchyard. Kipling, once an advocate of the war with Germany, had already lost his only son at the battle of Loos. Three months after his visit Thomas lay dead on the battlefield at Arras but like Lob, who was *seen dying at Waterloo, / Hastings, Agincourt, and Sedgemoor too* - Edward Thomas *lives yet* in the two slim volumes of poetry published after his death. His memorial on the hillside at Steep in Hampshire is, like Jefferies' memorial at Barbury Castle, a sarsen stone from the Marlborough Downs; a symbolic link with his adopted county and the man who remained his greatest inspiration.

A gate 'harr' with burdock
by Robin Tanner.

Sarsen stones, known locally as 'grey wethers', litter the downs at Overton and Fyfield.

South Marston

Apart from a short spell in India during the Great War, Alfred Williams lived all his life just outside Swindon. He wrote about the English countryside and the corrupting influence of towns with the authority of one who had experienced both ways of life. For a man who taught himself the classics after long hours of factory work and who suffered from poor health and penury all his life, his literary achievements were, according to the Poet Laureate Robert Bridges, *an abiding spiritual example to the workmen of this country.* Williams was no stranger to poverty. His father had abandoned the family when Alfred was only three, leaving a wife crippled with debt to bring up eight young children. They were soon put to work in the fields and at the age of eight Alfred became a *half timer* on a local farm while attending the village school each morning. Roaming the meadows around South Marston or by the banks of the river Cole, *clear companion of my boyish years*, he soon developed an untutored delight in the countryside that shaped his literary preoccupations. Blessed with an enquiring mind Williams spent long summer evenings investigating the myriad creatures in the murky waters of the Wilts and Berks canal. It was here beside the towpath at Longleaze Farm where he began work at the age of 11 that Williams first became aware of the rich folksong tradition he later did so much to record. To the south stretched the bare outline of the Wiltshire downs crowned by Liddington Castle, its contours brought into sharp focus by the second-hand telescope he had acquired to observe the stars. The chalk hills presented an intriguing prospect to a young lad from the lowlands restless to explore beyond the confines of his native parish, and years later they inspired several poems in his first collection.

The canal had fallen into disuse with the opening of the Great Western Railway and it was the sight of steam trains thundering past the farm that gave Williams his greatest thrill. Engines with names like Ajax, Achilles and Agamemnon fired his imagination and introduced him to the world of ancient Greece. The way ahead seemed clear and at 15 he joined the rural exodus in search of higher wages to begin work alongside his elder brothers as a furnace boy in the GWR factory at Swindon. The next few years were a period of intense activity. Encouraged by the vicar of Stanton Fitzwarren who made available his library, Williams embarked on a punishing regime of academic study. In 1900 he enrolled on a correspondence course in English Literature at Ruskin College and, and on discovering a gift for languages, taught himself Latin and Greek. He read Shakespeare during his lunch break and having walked back to South Marston, resumed his studies late into the night. By the time he married Mary Peck in 1903, Williams had been promoted to the position of hammerman and a few of his early Wordsworthian poems began to appear in anthologies. With the support of his wife and the small group of working class poets with whom he corresponded, Williams continued his search for a publisher but it was the dedication of two sonnets to Lord Fitzmaurice, a leading figure in Wiltshire society, that produced a more encouraging response. Fitzmaurice agreed to underwrite the cost of publishing **Songs in Wiltshire** (1909) although as a result of the poet's strenuous efforts to sell copies this eventually proved unnecessary.

While distributing the book Williams discovered 'The Story of My Heart' and realised that in Jefferies he had found a true kindred spirit. Here, just a short distance from South Marston, was a man who had walked the same woodland paths, who knew the beauty of the skylark's song and the silence of those ancient earthworks. Williams' second volume, **Poems in Wiltshire** (1911), was a familiar mixture of love sonnets, nature poems and translations from the Greek but, dedicated to the memory of Jefferies, it revealed a growing interest in archaeology and a deeper, more religious tone. With its abundant evidence of classical scholarship and a more individual style **Nature and other Poems** (1912) was received more enthusiastically and critics singled out several of the longer poems for special praise. Conceived during periods of quiet reflection beside the river Cole, 'The Testament' is a message of hope in which the poet's mind takes flight from the degradation of factory life to find solace in *the old forked willow* and *the long sloping hill*. In the last stanza the poet, *full of strong rumour,* offers himself as *the prophet of deliverance* in a manner reminiscent of Walt Whitman. In 'The Hill', by celebrating the abiding strength of the *quiet contemplative* and *tender compassionate* chalk downs, Williams again acknowledges his debt to Jefferies.

Alfred Williams
(1877 - 1931)
The 'Hammerman Poet' in the
GWR works at Swindon.

The accumulative effect of hard physical labour and long hours of study had already begun to affect Williams' health when, despite favourable reviews, he decided to turn his attention from poetry to topographical prose. The practical wisdom of the move, prompted largely by the need to earn money, was soon justified by Duckworth's agreement to publish *A Wiltshire Village* (1912) without financial penalty. In this unadorned account of South Marston, Williams is not uncritical of local landowners but, as he wrote to a friend, *after all, the rustic life is the ideal life. I have tried to emphasise the fact that the greatest serfdom is in the towns.* Despite his condemnation of conditions on

The river Cole, *clear companion of my boyish years* flowing beneath the GWR railway on the Wilts / Oxon border.

the shop floor he refused to become a mouthpiece for radical socialism, preferring to argue the rights of his fellow workmen with an independent voice. His failure to embrace the class struggle reflected the moderating influence of Lord Fitzmaurice, without whose generosity Williams would never have been published. Encouraged by the success of 'A Wiltshire Village' and attracted by the idea of tackling a more coherent stretch of countryside, he launched into **Villages of the White Horse**. Whereas his first prose work had drawn on years of personal experience, this next project involved excursions into less familiar territory but he never lost sight of the grand picture:

In the distance lie the downs, ranged along with graceful and exquisite ease, green and golden, or faint blue, rising and falling in a series of lovely lines, softly blending and intermingling, while below is a panorama of fertile cornfields, studded with farms and ricks and numerous clumps of beeches dotted about, and the long white road winding through the middle of the hollow towards Liddington Castle, visible on the skyline.

Williams worked in the Swindon factory for twenty years until a bout of acute dyspepsia, brought on by constant exposure to smoke from the furnaces, forced his retirement in 1914. One result of this was the release of **Life in a Railway Factory** (1915), the critical account of conditions in the GWR works that, until then, Williams had felt unable to offer for publication. The book, begun as a survey of work practices, became a treatise on the iniquities of the Victorian factory system. At work he was always alert to signs of the natural world and the comfort he took from seeing hares in the factory yard and a profusion of wild flowers beyond the boundary fence helped him to endure the nightmare world of the stamping shed. He witnessed the degradation of work and the arrogance of officialdom that broke or brutalised all those who walked through the gates. His survival was a tribute to both his determination and a poetic vision kept alive by the distant prospect of Liddington Hill between the engine sheds. 'Life in a Railway Factory' is a unique social document, an impassioned plea for human dignity and individual rights that shocked many of its readers.

The memorial stone to Richard Jefferies and Alfred Williams on Burderop Down with Liddington Hill in the distance.

Back in South Marston digging his allotment, Williams' health gradually returned and with it the idea for another book. Following the course of the river Cole northward to its appointment with the Thames at Inglesham he began to map out the territory for a sequel to 'Villages of the White Horse'. Entitled **Round about the Upper Thames** (1923), the field work took him on long cycle rides deep into the countryside. Williams was also fascinated by traditional ballads and as a local man he had little difficulty persuading country people to share their songs. He saw them as an important expression of that same folk culture he was attempting to record and in 1915 he embarked on a remarkable salvage operation that culminated in **Folk Songs of the Upper Thames** (1923), a companion volume to his topographical survey. In his introduction Williams recalled the many journeys he made in all weathers to collect songs; returning from a visit to an octogenarian in some remote cottage to the sound of the nightingale and a late moon rising above the Cotswolds, or the occasion he was almost swept away by floods in the *stygian darkness* of a winter's night. The value of his collection, over 800 songs, was marred by the

South Marston churchyard where
Alfred Williams is buried.

discovery that many were derived from the music hall tradition. His mission
had come a generation too late but the collection, less diligently transcribed
than the work of his more illustrious contemporaries Cecil Sharp and Vaughan
Williams, remains an important contribution to folk-life studies.

The publication of his Thames books was interrupted firstly by military
service and then, on his return, by the discovery that the South Marston cottage
had been sold by the estate. Williams and his wife then threw their
considerable energy into building a house with stone salvaged from a derelict
cottage and bricks from the lock walls of the canal. The plain box-like
structure, a grim reminder of their struggle, took all their strength and every
penny of their savings. Attempts to expand their allotment into a market
garden, made possible by a grant from the Royal Literary Fund, were thwarted
by a succession of disastrous late frosts. Williams continued writing articles
and one last book on the Thames but by now his interests lay elsewhere.

With a mixture of perversity and dogged persistence, he set himself the huge
task of learning Sanskrit, often cycling to Oxford to consult obscure texts in
the Bodleian library. For a writer concerned with the virtues of rural culture
his translation of Indian folk tales, *Tales from Panchatranta*, represented a
curious but logical extension of his work in the Wiltshire countryside. His last
years continued to be dogged by poor health and bouts of depression induced
by a growing sense of failure. The publication of his *Selected Poems* in 1925
brought some pleasure but 'Life in a Railway Factory' had sold only a handful
of copies in Swindon and none of his books were reprinted in his lifetime. The
knowledge that his wife lay dying of cancer provoked a fatal heart attack only
weeks after the belated award of a Civil List pension.

Marlborough

The town's distinguished literary tradition began with society gatherings held by Countess Hertford in the mansion built by the Duke of Somerset in 1700 near the site of the old Norman castle. Among her guests were Stephen Duck, the 'thresher poet', and James Thomson who completed the 'Spring' section of his long and hugely successful pastoral poem 'The Seasons' while on a visit in 1728. The house was later converted into the Castle Inn, one of the most elegant coaching establishments on the London to Bath road, before its acquisition by Marlborough College in 1843. Surrounded by austere Victorian school buildings, it became familiar to a succession of aspiring young writers.

The Duke of Somerset's mansion, the centrepiece of Marlborough College for the last 150 years.

Most notable among a group of popular novelists were Anthony Hope Hawkins who achieved success with 'The Prisoner of Zenda' (1894); J M Falkner, best known for his smuggling yarn 'Moonfleet' (1898 see p179) and E F Benson whose story 'David Blaize' (1915) drew on his time at Marlborough. The list of poets who survived the rigors of college life is more substantial. The college magazine nurtured the diverse literary talents of William Morris, Siegfried Sassoon and John Betjeman, who was here with Louis MacNiece in the 1920s. But it is **Charles Sorley** and his single volume, ***Marlborough and Other Poems*** (1915), who is most readily associated with the area.

At college on the eve of the First World War, the young Scotsman discovered the works of Richard Jefferies and, through his admiration for the Wiltshire writer, came to regard the Marlborough Downs as his spiritual home. Here, revelling in a new sense of freedom, he soon rejected orthodox Christianity for the pagan, outdoor life. Strenuous cross-country runs in the rain gave him a mystical sense of belonging to the earth:

Charles Hamilton Sorley
(1895 - 1915)

The earthworks at Barbury Castle on the crest of the downs became endowed with sacred meaning for a whole group of Wiltshire writers inspired by the natural world.

There is something in the rain
That would bid me to remain:
There is something in the wind
That would whisper, 'Leave behind
All this land of time and rules
Land of bells and early schools.

In his poem 'Barbury Camp', named after the other great hillfort haunted by Jefferies, Sorley's ascetic voice rises in exultation to the sound of men as they struggle to raise the first ramparts in the bitter cold; *And here we held communion with the rain / That lashed us into manhood with its thong, / Cleansing through pain. / And the wind visited us and made us strong.* Years later Robert Graves' poem 'Sorley's Weather' recalled the young poet's Laurentian delight in wild nature: *Yet rest there, Shelley, on the sill, / For though the winds come frorely / I'm away to the rain-blown hill / And the ghost of Sorley.* As Sorley admitted, *in the midst of* (his) *setting up and smashing of deities* he could always turn to Jefferies for inspiration. He would often walk the nine miles from college up to Liddington Castle for the pleasure of reading 'Wildlife in a Southern County' on the same *rampart down* where the author had sat and made field notes for the book. In 1913, returning to college at the beginning of term, Sorley walked along the ridgeway from his parents' home in Cambridge. The journey inspired several new poems including his homage to Jefferies and, in ***Return***, his delight in the familiar scenes:

> *Still stand the downs so wise and wide?*
> *Still shake the trees their tresses grey?*
> *I thought their beauty might have died*
> *Since I had been away.*

On leaving Marlborough Sorley studied for a time in Germany while waiting to go up to Oxford, only to return to Europe shortly after as an officer in the Suffolk regiment. Poems from the front were written in a curiously detached style with little of Rupert Brooke's youthful idealism or the patriotic fervour of Edward Thomas. They continued to display the same deep affection for the one corner of England he knew intimately and the belief that he would return, not in army uniform but *in grey bags, an old coat and a knapsack, coming over the downs from Chiseldon*. As he reminded a friend, 'Sorley' is Gaelic for 'Wanderer'. Faced with the horrors of trench warfare the theme of return becomes more insistent and more ambiguous:

> *And soon, o soon, I do not doubt it,*
> *With the body or without it,*
> *We shall all come tumbling down*
> *To our old wrinkled red-capped town.*
> *Perhaps the road up Isley way,*
> *The old ridge track, will be my way.*

By December 1914, having struggled to express his feelings for the chalk landscape, Sorley was convinced he had at last found the right poetic form; *simplicity, paucity of words, monotony almost, and mystery are necessary.* In the following April he sent home the last of his Marlborough verse, including *Lost*, in which memory is obliterated and the future ominously uncertain:

> *Across my past imaginings*
> *Has dropped a blindness silent and slow.*
> *My eye is bent on other things*
> *Than those it once did see and know.*
>
> *I may not think on those dear lands*
> *(O far away and long ago!)*
> *Where the old battered signpost stands*
> *And silently the four roads go*
>
> *East, west, south and north,*
> *And the cold winter winds do blow.*
> *And what the evening will bring forth*
> *Is not for men nor you to know.*

The signpost referred to was an isolated landmark a few miles north east of Marlborough at a point where several old drove roads converge, but in his sonnet *Death on the Downs*, Sorley sees it everywhere and, like the roadside gibbet, it points in one direction only. His death six months later at the Battle of Loos deprived England of a most gifted young poet, his reputation based on the one slim volume of 37 poems published posthumously to both popular and critical acclaim.

Four Mile Clump and Sorley's *old ridge track* from Marlborough up to Barbury Castle.

Upon Philistia will I triumph.

From School in Oxford **John Betjeman** went to Marlborough in 1920 when he was just fourteen. His time there was recalled years later with some affection and rather more bitterness in his long autobiographical poem **Summoned By Bells** (1960). Life in Junior House, haunted by the fear of punishment and ritual humiliation, was typical of most public schools at that time. *The dread of breaking rules* was followed by *The dread of beatings! Dread of being late! / And the greatest dread of all, the dread of games!* It was, according to one of his comtemporaries, *the most awful barbarous place.* At the end of his first year Betjeman was assigned to one of Blore's barrack-like wings where all was *Doom, shivering doom.* He only really felt at home in the Victorian Gothic splendour of the college chapel. *The Chapel was the centre of my life / The only place where I could be alone* with the Pre-Raphelite paintings of Spencer-Stanhope.

He was ridiculed mercilessly by the Classics master and the emotional scars remained for years after, but it sharpened his own mocking wit into a powerful weapon with which to defend himself against the school hearties. He felt naturally drawn to the group of aesthetes that included Anthony Blunt and Louis MacNiece. Together they formed the Anonymous Society and published 'The Heretick', a subversive rival to the official school magazine used to ridicule the powerful athletic clique, the Officer Training Corps and the *intellectual discomfort of school.* The journal was banned after two memorable editions but by this time Betjeman was beginning to enjoy his role as a *triumphant misfit.* His reputation as a brilliant mimic made him a great success

39

in the Dramatic Society and the inclusion of his poem ***The Song of a Cold Wind*** in 'Public School Verse' signalled the emergence of a distinctive style:

> *The song of the wind in the telegraph wires,*
> *The breathing wind of the downs,*
> *The wind that whistles through twenty shires*
> *Of red-roofed country towns.*

Betjeman chose 'The Marlburian' to launch the first of his conservation campaigns against the school authorities for allowing Lady Hertford's shell-lined grotto to be used as a potato store. He was in scornful mood, quoting Stephen Duck in support of his claim for the building as *the culmination of polite elegance* and signing himself ALEXANDER POPE.

> *Within the Basis of the verdant Hill,*
> *A beauteous Grot confesses HERTFORD'S Skill;*
> *Who, with her lovely Nymphs, adorns the Place;*
> *Gives every polished Stone its proper Grace;*
> *Now varies rustic Moss about the Cell;*
> *Now fits the shining Pearl, or purple Shell.*

Lady Hertford's grotto at the foot of castle hill became the subject of John Betjeman's first campaign against official indifference.

More familiar with the squat granite churches of Cornwall and the delights of Cotswold vernacular, Betjeman found the bare chalk downs with their beech woods, thatched barns and dearth of interesting churches something of a disappointment, but under the influence of *that good, delightful and hospitable man Colonel Christopher Hughes* who took his students on sketching expeditions to remote hamlets along the Kennet valley, Betjeman grew to appreciate this new landscape:

And now how lovely seemed the light and shade
On cob and thatch of Wiltshire cottages.
When trout waved lazy in the clear chalk streams,
Glory was in me as I tried to paint
The stretch of meadow and the line of downs,
Putting the buttercups in bright gamboge,
Ultramarine and cobalt for the sky.

Betjeman soon developed a taste for the more sophisticated pleasures of country house architecture. One of his favourite buildings was Ramsbury Manor, *a perfect example of the moderate-sized brick mansion of about 1680* set in its landscape park on the banks of the Kennet. Undeterred by his failure to reproduce the classical proportions of Ramsbury's facade he was consoled by the poetry that *poured from* (his) *pen to keep the ecstasy* and the memory that *what the Louvre was to Anthony Blunt .... Ramsbury Manor was to me. I think the mystery of its winding drive gave me a respect for the system of hereditary landowning which I have never shaken off.*

Ramsbury Manor beside its lake in the Kennet valley.

In *First and Last Loves* (1952) Betjeman admitted that of all the unrestored village churches *the loveliest I know is Mildenhall.* Just a mile downstream from Marlborough across the watermeadows, with *the smell of trodden leaves beside the Kennet* and with *Swinburne in* (his) *brain,* he approached the building with growing excitement. *You walk into the church of a Jane Austen novel, into a forest of magnificent oak joinery, an ocean of box pews stretching shoulder high all over the church. Each is carved with decorations in a Strawberry Hill Gothic manner.* The interior with its pews, west gallery and

Mildenhall church complete with all its late Georgian woodwork.

pair of three-decker pulpits arranged on either side of the chancel arch, retains all its late Georgian fittings, and there is a memorial to the Revd Harris who built the school and was the last village 'squarson'. Betjeman enthused; *Mildenhall is a patriarchal country church. It is the embodiment of the Church of England by law established, the still heart of England, as haunting to my memory as the tinkle of sheep bells on the Wiltshire Downs.*

* * * * *

Eventually it took the achievements of a local boy to raise Marlborough from comfortable obscurity to its dubious position in the literary landscape of Wiltshire. In the late '30s **William Golding** was an outstanding pupil at the local grammar school where, because his father was a master, he always felt the family were *all the poorer for* (their) *respectability*. Brought up in a timber frame house on The Green, Golding soon came to appreciate the nuances of the town's social geography. As he later confirmed, the presence of the public school at the opposite end of the High Street *made every social interface red-hot by pressure from above*. Golding was a child of provincial England between the wars and acutely aware of his place:

In the dreadful English scheme of things at that time, a scheme which so accepted social snobbery as to elevate it to an instinct, we had our subtle place. Those unbelievable gradations ensured that though my parents could not afford to send my brother and me to a public school, we should nevertheless go to a grammar school .... In fact, like everybody except the very high and the very low in those days, we walked a social tightrope, could not mix with the riotous children who made such a noise and played such wonderful games on the Green. I did not question these contradictions.

William Golding
(1911 - 93)

The house with its ancient cellar, its blocked-off wells and *crazily gabled porch* in the lea of St Mary's church, became full of the unforeseen horrors and subconscious desires that were to resurface in many of Golding's novels. At dusk in the adjoining churchyard he knew, without daring to look, that *the stones were lengthening, lifting and peering blankly, inscrutably, over the wall.* One day he noticed how some of the headstones were laid right against the brickwork. Fascinated by the stories of Edgar Allen Poe the inference was quite clear; dead bodies extended under the Goldings' manicured lawn that *had been sunny and innocent until* (his) *deliberate exercise of logic had invited the enemy in.* Golding's favourite refuge was the horsechestnut that grew in a corner of the garden. Hidden among the branches he could spy on courting couples or travel with Odysseus on his adventures through ancient Greece, while down below in the adult world his parents began mapping out his future. Having won a place at Brasenose to read science he soon discovered there was *no place in this exquisitely logical universe for the terrors of darkness* and turned to the delights of Beowulf. After Oxford he seemed destined to teach and accepted a post at Bishop Wordsworth school in Salisbury. While there he wrote 'Lord of the Flies' (1954), the spectacularly successful novel that launched his career as a writer. For the next few years Marlborough was able to bask in the glory of its most famous protege, until Golding decided to turn his withering gaze on the hypocrisy of provincial life. As he later admitted:

I think that the pyramidal structure of English society is present and my awareness of it is indelibly imprinted in me, in my psyche, not merely in my intellect but very much in my emotional, almost my physical being. I am enraged by it and I am utterly unable to escape it.

Headstones beyond the garden wall of Golding's childhood home.

In 'The Spire' (see p57) Dean Jocelin looks northward to the *white stones of the new bridge at Stilbury* gleaming in the distance and the enclosed, quadrangular world of its nunnery. Peering down from the apex of one novel to the base of another, Golding acknowledges the place that will shortly become the centre of **The Pyramid** (1957), his most autobiographical novel. With *college gents to the East, stable lads to the West, a spread of hot, sexy woodland to the south of it* (Savernake Forest) *and only the bare escarpment to the north*, Stilbourne is unmistakably the Marlborough of Golding's youth. But in the author's world there are no wide horizons, the landscape is subdued and the language deliberately lifeless. Surrounded by chalk hills and circumscribed by a meanness of spirit, Stilbourne is a closed and sterile society operating behind locked doors and clipped hedges. Even the sky, *bright blue in a co-operative sort of way*, was cheap and tasteless. The snobbery endemic in Golding's secular Barsetshire sits firmly in the tradition of the English novel. It is no coincidence that 'The Pyramid' was published exactly 100 years after 'The Last Chronicle of Barset' or that Imogen Grantley is a grand niece of the Dean of Barchester (Salisbury).

'The Pyramid' is really three interlinked novellas that offer different perspectives on Stilbourne through the eyes of Oliver, its adolescent central character. His growing sexual awareness is tainted by the prejudice instilled in him by a rigid class structure and it soon becomes clear there is no love or generosity in a town that thrives on exploitation and suspicion. Trapped in the stifling atmosphere of Golding's crystal pyramid, a translucent Silbury Hill, the undead tomb dwellers of Stilbourne *vibrate in time* to the tick of Miss Bounce's metronome as we watch them struggle to maintain their positions in the social hierarchy. The extremes of Stilbourne society play almost no part in Golding's High Street drama. College wives are consigned to the Jolly Tea Rooms and the ragged poor are condemned to the slums of Chandler's Close but the intermediate layers, underpinned by the Babbacombe family, are exposed with a vengeance. Mrs Babbacombe, a respectable working class mother and the town's only Catholic, negotiates the main street with jerky bird-like movements to greet her social superiors:

Naturally these greetings were never acknowledged or even mentioned, since no one could tell whether Mrs Babbacombe was mad, and believed herself entitled to make them, or came from some fabulous country where the Town Crier's wife and the wife of the Chief Constable might be on terms of intimacy.

At the other extreme stands Norman Claymore, leading light in the Stilbourne Operatic Society, together with his wife Imogen, *indifferent to the fact that she could not sing.* Those like Evie Babbacombe with a good voice but a bad reputation - *Evie had none of Imogen's sacred beauty, she was strictly secular* - would never be asked to join the SOS, and so every few years, once the self-inflicted wounds from the last production had healed, the Society would be revived by *a handful of people round whom an invisible line was drawn. Nobody mentioned the line but everyone knew it was there .... With diabolical inevitability, the very desires to act and be passionate, to show off and impress, brought to full flower the jealousies and hatreds, meannesses and indignations we were forced to conceal in ordinary life.*

Brought up in a house overlooking The Green with the public school at the other end of town, William Golding became acutely aware of Marlborough's social geography.

Next door to Oliver lives Dr Ewan for whom Oliver's father dispenses medicine. The nuances of social deference are brought into sharp relief by the two sons. With a place at Cranwell, *the sort of look that kept the Empire together* and a straight left jab, Bobby Ewan was clearly officer material whereas Oliver fought dirty and looked like a milkman. Even his position as head boy of the local grammar school counts for little in a place built around the advantages of private education. After Oxford Oliver begins work as a research scientist in germ warfare (Porton Down is a few miles south of Marlborough on the edge of Salisbury Plain). But he never really escapes the stultifying effects of his upbringing where almost everyone is engaged in spreading their own lethal gossip and innuendo. The disease that grips Stilbourne is sterility and it will take more than the laxatives dispensed by Oliver's father to move the hearts of Stilbourne residents.

Both boys are rivals for the sexual favours of Evie Babbacombe and Bobby's motor bike accident affords Oliver some secret pleasure - *I felt a little of Stilbourne's excitement and appetite at the news of someone else's misfortune.* Oliver is not to be seen out with Evie and is obliged to make elaborate arrangements to meet her under the bridge or up in the woods. When Evie realises she might be pregnant, Oliver looks out over the town from their love nest knowing that *down there, the depths of my offense would be measured.* If forced to marry Evie, Oliver also knows what the shame would do to his parents: *I saw their social world, so delicately poised and carefully maintained, so fiercely defended, crash into the gutter.*

Evie, who suffers from Stilbourne's disease, is not pregnant but remains *the ripest apple on the tree*, never more than an object of desire. The motto on the cross that dangles enticingly between her breasts - 'Amor vincit omnia' - is a mockery of the way Evie is abused and Oliver's loose translation - 'Love beats everything' - is a telling reminder of her sadistic father and the demands of Capt Wilmot, a discarded war veteran reduced to living in Chandler's Close. Evie soon concludes that all men are beasts and her revenge on those who abuse her is exposure. She manoeuvres Oliver into a more prominent position on the escarpment where, like some rampant hill figure, he satisfies his lust while Oliver's father observes his humiliation through a pair of binoculars. After another transgression Evie is forced out of town but, branded by her experiences, she can never really leave and, as one critic concluded, she is condemned to *crawl on, like everyone else, up the dreadful social pyramid that is a mountain of purgatory with no heaven at its summit.*

The sloping green became The Square in Golding's novel *The Pyramid*, where from behind lace curtains Stilbourne society passed judgement on the town's more unfortunate residents.

Marlborough's ponderous town hall (c.1900) is a focal point in Golding's high street drama and home of the Stilbourne Operatic Society (the SOS).

The only person who does manage to escape is Oliver's piano teacher Miss Bounce but, starved of affection, the only means left to her are madness and death. Bullied into a lifetime of music by a demanding father who gave Stilbourne *a painless excuse to feel that it was in touch with the arts*, Bounce is a rather lonely and unattractive spinster exploited by the oily charm of Henry Williams. The young garage mechanic makes himself indispensable, insinuating himself and his family into Bounce's large house on The Square. Having built up his engineering business to the point when her hospitality is no longer required, the family move out and Bounce is left to contrive a series of mechanical breakdowns in order to attract Henry's attention. These bizarre and poignant cries for help become a rather laboured joke in Oliver's house - *I wonder what she'll do when she runs out of phone boxes?* Bounce, like Evie, is eventually driven to naked exposure in her desperation. Having burnt her father's music together with his metronome she tastes freedom for the first time. Clad only in hat and gloves she walks serenely towards Henry's garage and out of Stilbourne life.

The whole business is observed from behind lace curtains by The Square's network of spies with a mixture of contempt, mistrust and ultimately triumph at her misery. Oliver's mother, a petty-minded but perceptive woman with finely tuned antennae, is always quick to apportion blame. Henry's free driving lessons are *a sprat to catch a mackerel,* a saying which Oliver in his innocence fails to understand. As he grows older he is caught in the adult web of secrets and lies and one by one his illusions are shattered. His parents had always boasted of his devotion to Miss Bounce but, like her father, she turns out to be a failed musician and her epitaph 'Heaven is Music' is bitterly ironic, like the inscription round Evie's neck. It is not until after her death that Oliver is able to admit that he had hated Bounce as a child because he feared the severe, pipe-smoking woman with her stained frills and gloomy corridors. But he remains ignorant of Stilbourne's darker secrets, failing to grasp the significance of the director's ballerina photographs or the bruises on Evie's thighs. When he does finally realise he sees how Evie has struggled to extricate herself from the filth of Chandler's Close and admits that together they might have made music. But as he is about to follow her across The Square he sees *the shadow of* (his) *mother pass across the curtain* and the opportunity is lost.

Years later, out of mild curiosity, Oliver turns off the motorway and down into Stilbourne, a place now just like any other. He notices how Henry Williams' business has grown, how the concrete has spread slowly like a glacier over back gardens to the river bank. While Golding's spire is a monumental folly cut from stone and pointing towards heaven, his pyramid is based firmly on material success of the kind by which Henry has managed to climb the social ladder. Oliver finally acknowledges that he has climbed the same ladder, that even if he were in a position to regenerate Stilbourne it would involve great personal sacrifice and that, like Henry, *he would never pay more than a reasonable price.* Oliver can never escape his past; he will always be Stilbourne and bred.

2

Blood on the Tracks
Salisbury &
the Plain

The whole system of the country lay spread before Rickie .... He saw how all the water converges at Salisbury; how Salisbury lies in a shallow basin, just at the change of soil. He saw to the north the Plain, and the stream of the Cad flowing down from it.... He saw Old Sarum, and hints of the Avon Valley, and the land above Stonehenge. And behind him he saw the great wood beginning unobtrusively, as if the downs too needed shaving, ... chalk made the clean rolling outlines of the land, and favoured the grass and the distant coronals of trees. Here is the heart of our island: The Chilterns, the North Downs, The South Downs radiate hence. The fibres of England unite in Wiltshire, and did we condescend to worship her, here we should erect our national shrine.

From ***The Longest Journey*** by **E M Forster**

The Plain

From the infantry school at Warminster to the airfield at Upavon, round in a great arc to the barracks that sprawl between Tidmouth and Bulford, to the fighter-base at Boscombe Down and Porton's chemical warfare plant, Salisbury Plain is encircled by an awesome array of military hardware. Within the perimeter fence an empty, windswept landscape of chalk downland stretches away into the distance. Once the most extensive sheep pasture in southern England, the Plain is now the setting for massive troop movements that have left the flower-rich turf to degenerate into coarse grassland or be churned up by incessant tank manoeuvres. At one time the Plain was home to large flocks of the Great Bustard, the turkey-sized bird shot to extinction in the 19th century long before the appearance of the first artillery range. Without the army the sheep pastures would have been ploughed up long ago with the help of government grants but many argue that the destruction of archeological sites and the loss of public access is a high price to pay. In November 1935, while on a visit to Angus Wilson at Tidcombe, the writer **Mary Butts** was horrified to see how the landscape had been ravaged:

The plague of blood red huts was/is bad enough, patch of blood on the green land. But the accompaniments, the slum purlieus of each camp. Hoardings and vile villas and petrol stations, and that most beastly sight, the rotting bodies of cars .... Miles of barbed wire too over the green turf, and here and

The Great Bustard

49

there a farm or an ancient cottage in a hollow, as if stranded, cut-off, abandoned from what had once been its own.

I can give no idea of the pain it gave us - a septic wound on the earth's face and a scratch on our spirits that poisoned too.

Today as the the heavy metal scream of shells exploding among the burial mounds of Bronze Age chieftains shatters the silence of a landscape already scarred by battle, the blood axe pattern of revenge becomes clear. The Down Barn Destructor at Larkhill looks out towards the site of the gibbet at Shrewton and south to the hill fort at Old Sarum. The shape of man's insatiable lust for violence is etched across the face of the Plain, superimposed upon the sacred geometry of an earlier, more peaceful society. Within this triangle of retribution the monoliths of Hardy's 'Temple of the Winds', where the sun's first rays light up the figure of Tess Durbeyfield asleep on the sacrificial stone, stand on the horizon.

Stonehenge

Henry James concluded his tour of Wessex in 1872 with a visit to Salisbury and Stonehenge that, despite being *a rather hackneyed shrine of pilgrimage*, moved him to reflect:

... the mighty mystery of the place has not yet been stared out of countenance; ... It stands as lonely in history as it does on the great plain whose many-tinted green waves, as they roll away from it, seem to symbolise the ebb of the long centuries which have left it so portentously unexplained. You may put a hundred questions to these rough-hewn giants as they bend in grim contemplation of their fallen companions; but your curiosity falls dead in the vast sunny stillness that enshrouds them, and the strange monument, with all its unspoken memories, becomes simply a heart-stirring picture in a land of pictures .... At a distance you see it standing in a shallow dell of the plain, looking hardly larger than a group of ten-pins on a bowling-green. I can fancy sitting all a summer's day watching its shadows shorten and lengthen again, and drawing a delicious contrast between the world's duration and the feeble span of individual experience. There is something in Stonehenge almost reassuring to the nerves .... the immemorial gray pillars may serve to represent for you the pathless vaults beneath the house of history.

Three years later while staying with friends in the Avon valley below Salisbury, **Francis Kilvert** made his own pilgrimage to the monument. James, the urbane American traveller, was above all struck by the enigma of Stonehenge and might well have agreed with Virginia Woolf that its *singular and intoxicating charm .... is that no one in the world can tell you anything about it*, while to the country parson approaching the stones on foot across a plain that *heaved mournfully with great and solemn barrows,* this temple to an older god was an awesome spectacle:

It seemed to me as if they were ancient giants who suddenly became silent and stiffened into stone directly anyone approached, but who might at any moment become alive again, and at certain seasons .... might form a true 'Chorea Gigantum' and circle the Plain in a solemn and stately dance.

As I entered the charmed circle of the sombre Stones I instinctively uncovered my head. It was like entering a great Cathedral Church. A great silent service was going on and the stones inaudibly whispered to each other the grand secret .... one leaned forward towards the east, as if bowing to the rising sun. While some had fallen flat on their faces as if prostrate with adoration before the Lamp of Heaven, or as if like Dragen they had fallen across the threshold of the Temple before the advent of a purer faith, and in reluctant acknowledgement and worship of One Greater than They.

As we went down the southern slope .... we left the stones standing on the hill against the sky, seeming by turns to be the Enchanted Giants, the Silent Preachers, the Sleepless Watchers, the great Cathedral on the Plain.

Stonehenge, Francis Kilvert's
great Cathedral on the Plain.

Old Sarum

Brought up in Salisbury just after the war, the writer **Stevie Davies** used the city as the setting for her first novel ***Boy Blue*** (1987) in which her men are weak minor characters or are away at the war leaving women to prove their resilience and resourcefulness. By adopting the motif of the lost boy-twin in war time, Davies explores the terrible cost of man's alienation from the feminine principle, an essential truth symbolised for her by the city's most illustrious monuments. Old Sarum with its *concentricities of enclosure and protection, its entrance a birth passage, its focus the mound of breast or womb* was one of the many sacred sites dedicated to the earth goddess before its violation at the hands of a new warrior culture. Through successive waves of invasion, the new culture of aggression replenished itself:

remoulding the countryside in waves of change that would throw a military hillfort upon the breast-like mound of the Great Mother. The pygmy men came there all clad in mail to occupy the central womb of Sarum; and threw up fortifications; and words to them were chanted war cries let loose like shafts of arrows fortifying their utility of place. The ecclesiastics came and built their palace by the breast of the hill, and sang the glory of their king in rich and swaggering splendour beneath the stillness of the breast.

Old Sarum with remains of its Norman castle and cathedral within the ramparts of a much earlier hillfort.

Stevie Davies
(1946 -)

'Boy Blue' begins in December 1944; V2 bombs fall silently from the sky and the country is in the grip of winter. As aircrews stroll round the ramparts between bombing raids, the emblems of death connect the hillfort to its original purpose as a place of renewal. *Around the circumference of the outermost ring, the rose hips like globes of glowing blood fruited year by year, and behind them the redbreast perched upon the barbed-wire boughs of the hawthorn.* When Christina goes to work in a munitions factory she dreams of giving birth to a ten pound bomb *which slid out from between her legs in a trail of cold slime.* She has no desire to be part of the war machine and becomes terrified at the thought of giving birth to a boy. There is a flourishing black market in unwanted babies, and when Christina gives birth to twins she decides to keep the girl and arranges with a nurse for the boy to be taken away.

On receiving the news that her young husband is missing in action Christina questions the wisdom of a decision taken without his knowledge and makes her way to the cathedral in search of an answer. Sitting on a bench in the precincts she remembers how, as a child, the family bible had been her flower press and how, more recently, when she reopened the book to commit her secret to the written word, a bright red poppy had fallen from the Song of Solomon. Once inside *the great and beautiful mortuary where the stony warriors sleep*, she feels only anger and resentment. Between the crusader knights, recumbent in the certainty that their cause had been just, lie *the battalions of bishops, their faces crumbling in a grisly manner*, by whose authority men have for generations been sent to fight God's holy wars. Above them hang the shroud-like banners of the Wiltshire regiment, tattered remnants of a more recent carnage. Nothing had changed throughout the long history of the cathedral, God has no time to consider Christine's dilemma and as she leaves His house convinced that God owes <u>her</u> an explanation, she glances toward Old Sarum where years before she had gathered the scarlet poppies and where she will soon scatter her husband's ashes.

Regimental banners in the north aisle of Salisbury cathedral.

In a moving coda to the novel a young man nearing his 24th birthday arrives at Old Sarum at the end of a winter holiday exploring the archeological sites of Wessex. Having slept in his van by the roadside he rises early to be greeted by a landscape cloaked in dense mist. Drawn by the frosty silence through the entrance and out into the centre of the earthworks he feels like being in an egg *as a seed of conception.* He is utterly alone in the swirling white mist:

Then, like mercury, it ran away for a moment .... it drained away leaving him enveloped in a sac of light. Drops of dew were hanging from the joints of bramble sprays and hawthorn boughs. These airborne globes of water reflected the tree that held them, as if a tear should enclose an eyelash .... illuminating the old year clinging on barrenly round the sides of the hill in a thorny wilderness. It was like being behind a vast and shining bead curtain, strung with glassy, light-gathering pearls of moisture.

As he stands there the layers of history peel away to reveal a more obscure, forgotten past until he loses all sense of time and space or personal identity:

But the sun was breaking through in places, to disclose the bare boughs of bramble and thorn, the blood-red of rose hips round the chalky path, striking and poignant, like the sacrifice of one who has bled beads of life's blood .... When each particular had been truly seen, the mist rolled back in again and cancelled it. Beyond and around the plain went on for ever, pooled mist and sea of halcyon quiet .... The strangeness deepened; deepened further, deepened. He was on his knees on the frost. It was agony of cold, it was killing but it was homecoming. He cried, he was going mad ....

Boy Blue has reached the end of his journey and by his symbolic rebirth he is united with the spirit of the father he never knew. There in the centre of *the ancient mother sanctuary,* crowned with thorns and resplendent in a sparkling necklace of blood red rubies, the sins of gender are atoned.

Salisbury

Despite the claims of both Wells and Winchester, the city where Trollope conceived 'The Warden' in 1852 while *walking one midsummer evening round the purlieus of the cathedral,* will always be associated with the world of Dr Grantley, the devious Mr Slope and awful Mrs Proudie. **William Golding** once explained how he had leant over Harnham Bridge where, a century earlier, Trollope had paused near the medieval foundation that gave him the idea for Hiram's Hospital. Gazing into the water, Golding found it difficult to imagine how his predecessor had managed to write so much about the place without considering its most dramatic feature, the cathedral spire:

Low cloud, mist, fog, inflate the spire so that it loses definition and looms like the promise of mountain country. Dry heat and light bleach the stones to a bone white against blue sky, the immensity of which brings out the delicacy and fragility of the structure .... the midsummer madness of a shivering spire fevered by mirage; the floating spire when mist has severed it from the earth; the drab, factual spire of rain and cold and wind; the enchanted spire that was lit at sunset.

Datestone on Harnham bridge

St Nicholas' hospital that gave Trollope the idea for Hiram's Hospital in ***The Warden***.

Golding discovered that the author of the Barsetshire Chronicles had left *a corner of his job to fill in*, and when completed in 1964, the landmark ignored by Trollope had become the subject of his fifth novel. In ***The Spire*** Dean Jocelin looks out over the surrounding countryside and sees in a flash how the half-completed structure *lay a hand on the whole landscape, altering it, dominating it, enforcing a pattern wherever* (it) *could be seen, by sheer force of it being there .... The countryside was shrugging itself obediently into a new shape.* Situated near the confluence of five rivers, the city appears to nestle in the palm of a gigantic, outstretched hand with the spire, rising gracefully some 400 feet above the watermeadows. In John Constable's celebrated painting the cathedral is set against a tempestuous sky, matched only by the view upstream from Britford described by Francis Kilvert. As he strolled in the meadows:

The sun was setting in stormy splendour behind Salisbury and the marvellous aerial spire rose against the yellow glare like Ithuriel's spear, while the last gleams of the sunset flamed down the long lines of water carriages making them shine and glow like canals of molten gold.

This graceful and enduring symbol of Christianity has called the faithful for the last 750 years and today visitors still peer out of railway carriages hoping to catch a glimpse of the landmark that will announce their destination, unaware that logically it should never have been built. By the early 13th century, Old Sarum - *ventris, expositus, sterilis, aridus et desertus* - had become too bleak for the bishop. Disputes with the castle only added to his problems and in 1220 Richard Le Poore decided to abandon his Norman cathedral on the hill and build a larger, more magnificent structure in the valley where the springs ran *cristall clarior, caro purior, ambrosia dulcior*. Constructed in a frenzy of activity over the next forty years on an ambitious double cruciform plan with local stone from the Chilmark quarries, the cathedral became the most glorious example of Early English architecture.

Nearly a century later it was decided that the cathedral should have a spire, an audacious afterthought to impress the faithful and rival the older and more illustrious foundation at Winchester. In 1334 Richard of Farleigh was awarded the contract to heighten the tower and raise a spire upon it. He took the precaution of leaving the heavy timber scaffolding within the cone and a piece of the Virgin's robe in the capstone, inserted with due ceremony, but there was no provision to support the extra weight - 64,000 tons of stone and wood bearing down on four central piers not designed for the purpose. Two straining arches were built at the insistence of Bishop Beauchamp in the late 15th century and, despite some buckling of the Purbeck marble columns around each pier, the faith entrusted in the original builders has proved well founded.

The structural report submitted by Christopher Wren in 1668 concluded that in the event of further settlement buttresses would be required to support the walls as *the only cure, for when so great a Pyle is once overpoysed, all Bandage of Iron will be but as Pack thread.* William Lysle Bowles, the 19th century poet and clergyman who lived in the Close, would have been aware of this report. Convinced the spire would one day fall and kill him, he carefully

Salisbury cathedral rising from the banks of the Avon.

paced the equivalent distance from the base of the cathedral. It brought him to within a yard of his front door and, unconcerned about the danger posed by flying masonry, was able to sleep more easily in his bed.

In *The Spire* Jocelin's rise to the position of Dean had been swift and, as he later admits *I took a monstrous pride in this great house of mine*. One day the Dean had a vision in which the whole building appeared as an image of worship. At the crossways beneath the central tower he threw himself down on the stones and was *initiated into their secret language*. The body of the church became the figure of a man lying on his back, the only thing missing was the spire thrust upwards in the shape of two hands clasped in prayer. Jocelin had been called and set about his appointed task bathed in light:

It smashed through the rows of windows in the south aisle, so that they exploded with colour, it slanted before him from right to left in an exact formation, to hit the bottom yard of the pillars on the north side of the nave. Everywhere, fine dust gave these rods and trunks of light the importance of a dimension. He blinked at them again, seeing, near at hand, how the individual grains of dust turned over each other, or bounced all together, like mayfly in a breath of wind. He saw how further away they drifted cloudily, coiled, or hung in a moment of pause, becoming, in the most distant rods and trunks, nothing but colour, honey-colour slashed around the body of the cathedral.

Blinded by tears of joy, Jocelin is oblivious to the story of Abraham and Isaac depicted in glass and illuminated by a burst of sunlight. Without a firm foundation God's work will entail great sacrifice. Jocelin's monumental folly requires the destruction of those around him and ultimately he too will perish. Work is already disrupting the life of the cathedral; thick clouds of dust hang in the air, and *the rich fabric of constant praise* is broken by the sound of crude laughter from the heathen workforce. Jocelin is too busy giving thanks to attend to the needs of those around him. Father Adam appears so insignificant that the Dean decides to call him Father Anonymous and ignores the letter he brings from the cathedral's patroness. He becomes irritated by Pangall's fear of the workmen and as the lame man's tears fall at his feet, *the sunlight on the stone drew* (Jocelin's) *eye upwards*. The Dean is more concerned with his own immortality, finding time for the dumb man who obediently carves the head that will adorn one corner of the tower. Immortalised in stone Jocelin's wide eyes are blind. *At the moment of vision, the eyes see nothing.*

Disruption turns to chaos with the onset of winter and the Dean is reminded of his own mortality. A workman falls to his death leaving *a scream scored all the way down the air which was so thick it seemed to keep the scream as something mercilessly engraved there*. Water rises in the gaping hole dug at the crossways and seeps into the graves beneath the choir, filling the cathedral with the stench of death. Revelations of Pangall's impotence and his wife's adulterous affair with the master builder reawaken Jocelin's lust for Goody Pangall. But the Dean is disgusted by the act of procreation and it lies, like the filthy tide of mud in the pit, deep in his subconscious. As he crouches in prayer, fondling the model of the spire, his eyes alight on the floor tiles *each with two heraldic beasts, their clawed feet raised to strike, their snakey necks*

The decision, taken in the mid 14th century, to give the cathedral a spire, gave Golding the idea for Dean Jocelin's folly in ***The Spire***.

intertwined. That night in his dreams, crucified on his back in the marshes, Jocelin is visited by the devil *clad in nothing but blazing hair*, the red hair of Goody Pangall. The spire, his pride and joy, becomes a phallus erected in sin and deformed like those around him; a symbol of his own impotent faith.

As the rain clouds drift away and the floodwaters recede, Jocelin climbs above the confusion and into the purer air and blue sky on top of the tower but, with ravens circling overhead, the grotesque gargoyles *seemed diseased, as they yelled their soundless blasphemies and derisions into the wind, yet made no more noise than death in another country.* Obsessed with his mission, Jocelin continues to miss confession throughout Lent and refuses to heed the master builder's warning until one day the cathedral falls silent. Bracing himself for the crisis, the Dean joins the men gathered around the pit. The sides begin to collapse and as his eyes become more accustomed to the darkness he sees pebbles moving on the bottom *like the stirring of grubs.* The whole earth, the pagan earth, is about to erupt under the enormous pressure; the pillars begin to splinter and the air is pierced by a new sound, *the high ringing of unbearable, unbelievable tension.* Panic spreads through the crowd and Jocelin instinctively starts to pray with renewed intensity. *His will began to burn fiercely and he thrust it into the four pillars .... At last .... he knew that the whole weight of the building was resting on his back.* The stones stop singing and the crisis appears to have been averted.

Roger Mason is a practical man. He moves cautiously about the scaffolding with T square and plumbline monitoring the work. He knows the ringing noise has stopped because the building has settled, but he can no longer command the loyalty of his men and, without foundation, the work must be abandoned. The master builder is a man of little faith, his fear of heights does not extend to heaven and when Jocelin tries to explain how they have been chosen he is less convinced by the Dean's glowing compliments than by the news that Jocelin has thwarted his plan to move on to more securely based work at Malmsbury abbey. By turning a blind eye to Goody's adultery, Jocelin also knows that the master builder is tied to the woman just as surely as he is now bound to complete the spire.

While Jocelin contemplates victory his thoughts are interrupted by the sound of laughter coming from the crossways. The Dean, brushed aside by the mob tormenting Pangall, heard *the long wolf howl of the man's flight down the south aisle, heard the rising, the hunting noise of the pack that raced after him.* He sees only the dishevelled, half-naked figure of the man's wife pressed against a pillar and staring across the pit at her lover. Soon after, by the pit, Jocelin catches sight of a twig at his feet *with a rotting berry that clung obscenely to the leather.* He finds the image disturbing but only later, as he watches the midsummer bonfires burn on the hills around the city, does he realise the dreadful significance of Pangall's disappearance. The men who had suddenly stopped work, the men whom Jocelin had tried to befriend, were no better than devil worshippers. The Dean is now *impaled on his will* and the lame man lies buried in the pit *with a sliver of mistletoe between his ribs,* a sacrificial victim for whom Jocelin is equally guilty. Evil is not just out there *on the rim of the world* but down below where *the replaced paving stones were hot to his feet with all the fires of hell.*

The blood ritual becomes more elaborate as the depths to which Jocelin has sunk in pursuit of his lust are gradually revealed. Goody's arranged marriage to an impotent husband allows Jocelin to indulge his sexual fantasies but on discovering her pregnancy he arranges her removal to a nunnery and agrees to pay the dowry. Dressed in the black robes of his office the Dean hovers like a raven in the doorway of the woman's cottage clutching a bag of money. Terrified by the long shadow of her accuser, Goody cries out and the blood money of betrayal spills out over the floor to mingle with the blood of her aborted child. The words that express *the dreadful glow of his dedicated will* are from the Easter Carol - *This have I done for my true love* - and Jocelin is left to reflect on the appaling consequences of his sinful pride and destructive passion. The illusion that he was chosen for God's purpose is shattered by the arrival of his aunt, Lady Alison, and the disclosure that she had arranged his appointment for her own amusement while in the arms of her lover the King.

The spire begins to sway before impacting on the tower, the scaffolding comes crashing down and the pillars buckle like Jocelin's spine as he labours under the *great weight of glory*, exhausted by frequent visits from his angel. As the storm breaks, *Satan in the likeness of a cosmic wildcat leapt off all four feet on the north east horizon and came screaming down at Jocelin and his folly*. The cathedral is possessed by the devil howling through the deserted building, but by now the tempest is raging inside Jocelin's head where the scream and the laughter and the ringing in his ears are compounded by the roaring of the wind. With images of blood and red hair flashing before his eyes, Jocelin begins to ascend the spire as it lurches violently in the very teeth of the gale, knowing that only when the holy relic is driven into the pinnacle will the spire and the witch cease to haunt him. The spire survives but, like Jocelin's spine, is permanently deformed.

The vision, once so clear and so simple, has grown from the root of his lust into a luxuriant plant, *a riot of foliage and flowers and overripe, bursting fruit*, explicitly phallic and engulfing everyone. What remains of the *miracle of faith* finally crumbles when the dumb messenger shows Jocelin that the four pillars are built of rubble encased in stone. The shattered remains of those destroyed by his obsessive will - Pangall and Goody already dead, Roger Mason now a drunken wretch and Jocelin himself, brought low by the festering tumour in his back - provide the only foundation. As the broken man stumbles beneath the spire, alone in the ruins of his self-deception, he is flayed by the dark angel warming his back throughout his ordeal and filling his spine *with sick fire*. He writhes at the crossways at the foot of the Tree of Evil, racked with the pain of his tubercular growth and the agony of self-sacrifice.

On the surface Golding's story is about the human cost of building a spire but on another level the novel explores the nature of seeing as it moves from the blinding light of ecstatic vision to the clarity that follows the annihilation of self and the insight that comes with humility and atonement. Crippled with pain and overwhelmed with grief in the Deanery garden, Jocelin is struck by the sweet scent of apple blossom:

It was there beyond the wall, busting up with cloud and scatter, laying hold of the earth and the air, a fountain, a marvel, an appletree; .... Then, where the yard of the deanery came to the river and trees lay over the sliding water, he saw all the blue of the sky condensed to a winged sapphire, that flashed once.

The four central pillars with their Purbeck marble columns have bent under the enormous extra weight of the spire.

The fleeting glimpse of the kingfisher is sufficient, the *arrow shot once* carries no message, the experience is without meaning and in the moment Jocelin's sight is restored. On his deathbed, comforted by Father Adam, the man's face comes into focus. He is no longer Father Anonymous and the dying man is able to acknowledge; *It was just that what was written there, had been written small in a delicate calligraphy.* At the point of death his eyes fix upon the open window. *It was slim as a girl, translucent. It had grown from some seed of rose-coloured substance that glittered like a waterfall, an upward waterfall.* The apple blossom and the kingfisher become transformed into a cascading fountain. The spire that until now has been a diagram of prayer, an erect phallus and a dunce's cap, is revealed without ambiguity as an image of exultant beauty. As Jocelin drifts into unconsciousness there is no *gesture of assent* to his faith, only Golding's own validation: *In the tide, flying like a bluebird, struggling, shouting, screaming to leave behind the words of magic and incomprehension - It's like the appletree!*

Golding's final image is an emblem of purity and insight as complex and elliptical as the novel itself. Reaching up to heaven from the Garden with its fruit not yet formed, the apple tree stands as a symbol of Jocelin's innocence before the Fall, uncorrupted by the mistletoe that will transmute it into the Tree of Evil and implant the cankerous growth in his back. In the end, in his humility and his wisdom the apple tree is all that Jocelin sees but, like the playwright Dennis Potter dying of cancer, he sees *the blossomest blossom* with all the intensity of being.

Figsbury Ring

When, at the age of 14, E M Forster was packed off to school in Tonbridge, the move brought to an abrupt end years of happy childhood in rural Hertfordshire. There he had begun to develop the sense of place that was to become a central theme in several novels, notably **The Longest Journey** (1907) and 'Howards End' (1910). Years of unhappiness at public school were alleviated by visits to his mother's friend Maime Aylward in her *tall, sun-drenched house balanced high above Salisbury.* While there he developed the habit of long solitary walks and in the process the Wiltshire downs replaced the leafy Chilterns in the young writer's imagination. *It was almost as if the countryside was beginning to replace the father, the ancestral home, the children he would never have: the love of landscape was in some ways enough.* Forster's sense of the *bone structure* of Wessex, its topographical grain, can be traced to these walks with Figsbury Ring, a circular earthwork north east of Salisbury, his favourite destination. At the time Forster was nearing the completion of 'Where Angels Fear to Tread' (1905) and the idea for a story about illegitimacy and brotherhood was already beginning to emerge.

E M Forster
(1879 - 1970)

Years later he offered this insight into the creative process. His diary recalled *the emotional thrill which set my pen going .... I caught fire up on the Rings* and the experience *fructified my meagre conception of the half-brothers and gave Stephen Wonham, the bastard, his home. Figsbury Ring became Cadbury Rings, the valley of the Winterbourne below them turned into the Cad, a level crossing clanged and that part of The Longest Journey was born ....*

Stunted ash trees in Figsbury Ring where E M Forster *caught fire* and **The Longest Journey** began to take shape.

I received, I created, I restored, and for many years the Wiltshire landscape remained haunted by my fictional ghosts.

It was not the magic of the ancient site itself which set Forster on fire, but the chance meeting with a lame shepherd boy in the earthwork. The incident became charged with meaning for the young novelist, enabling him to transform the experience of place into a work of fiction. He was so struck by the boy's dignity and natural wisdom that he later wrote; *he was one of the most remarkable people I've ever met.* From that meeting Forster began to look clearly at the Wiltshire landscape until *it began to look back at me. A relation sprang up which will never cease.* In the novel the central character Rickie Elliot is portrayed as a *lonely and deformed boy*, the shepherd's lameness having provided Forster with a perfect symbol for his own sense of rejection and his homosexuality which, like Rickie's abnormality, was regarded by many as congenital. Stephen Wonham lives with Rickie's aunt at Cadover, a late Georgian house in the Cad Valley. Emily Failing has inherited Cadover but, unlike the Schlegels in 'Howards End' she has no affection for the house or the land that goes with it. Before Forster caught fire he too found the Wiltshire downs bare and dull and with an air of despondency Emily Failing considers that the view towards the Rings:

... though extensive, would not have been accepted by the Royal Academy. A valley, containing a stream, a road, a railway; over the valley fields of barley and wurzel, divided by no pretty hedges, and passing into a great and formless down - this was the outlook, desolate at all times and almost terrifying beneath a cloudy sky.

The Rings are the real spirit of the place and it is here, as the sound of church bells drift up from the valley, that Rickie recites the lines from Shelley that provided Forster with the title for the novel: *and so with one sad friend, perhaps a jealous foe / The dreariest and the longest journey go,* before his aunt reveals the true nature of his relationship to Stephen. Influenced by Wagner's Ring Cycle and his reading of Frazer's 'The Golden Bough', Forster's novel is endowed with symbolic structure in which the blood brothers become equated with the mystical twins Siegfried and Parsifal. At first Rickie refuses to acknowledge Stephen's real identity and then, on discovering him to be his mothers son rather than of the father Rickie so detested, Stephen becomes the symbol of a vanished past. Either way Rickie fails to accept the gift of life and is condemned to see things at second hand. Like Parsifal he allows the Holy Grail to slip from his grasp and the opportunity never comes again.

Forster's dedication for 'The Longest Journey' was Fratribus (to the brothers), a reference not only to blood brothers but the brotherhood of the Cambridge Apostles where, as the novel opens, Rickie and his circle of friends discuss the nature of reality. The structured quadrangular world of academic life is set against the *slowly modulating* Wiltshire downs with its barrows and circular earthworks where Stephen, athletic, hedonistic and archetypally heroic, is most at home. His room in the attic at Cadover is adorned with a picture of the earth goddess Demeter, its circular window a cyclopean eye keeping watch over the Rings. Near the end of the novel the two brothers pay a final visit to the monument where Rickie extracts a promise from Stephen to refrain from drink that he inevitably fails to keep, and Rickie is sacrificed while saving his fallen idol. For Forster the Rings become a symbol of renewal as Stephen, preparing to spend a night there with his young daughter, realises his purpose is to *govern the paths* between the generations. Published in 1907 to critical acclaim, Forster's complex novel is also his most personal and the one, despite its perceived shortcomings, that gave him the greatest pleasure:

The view from Figsbury Ring to where the *slowly modulating* Wiltshire downs gather around the spire of Salisbury cathedral.

The manor house in the village of Winterbourne Dauntsey used by Forster as the model for Cadover.

Stephen is the only character who exists for me outside his book, and restores to the world of experience more than he took from it. Now when I visit Figsbury, he lies behind it, as once it lay behind him.

Years later he returned to Figsbury Ring in the company of William Golding. They had been lamenting the destruction of the chalk grassland when a blue butterfly alighted at the entrance to the earthwork. As Forster admitted:

The butterfly was a moving glint, and I shall lie in Stephen's arms instead of his child. How I wish that book hadn't faults! But they do not destroy it, and the gleam, the greatness, the grass remain. I do not want any other coffin.

Wilton

Virginia Woolf
(1882 - 1941)

In September 1903 the Stephen family rented Netherhampton House in the Nadder valley near Wilton. **Virginia Stephen's** father was seriously ill and this was to be their last holiday together. She was just 21 and by then her journal was already revealing an idiosyncratic sense of place that was to distinguish the correspondence of later years. She was evidently pleased with her new surroundings; *a little gray stone house, too humble to be itself ornate, but evidently dating from an ornate period - & in its humble way an imitation of a genuine great house.* It had been built by the Pembrokes as a dower house and this accounts for the family coat of arms and its architectural pretensions. The following day Virginia set out with brother Adrian to explore the grounds and after eventually identifying the river, the pair made their way past the triumphal entrance to Wilton House and on into the little market town; a place where *the feudal spirit in England is not yet dead.* She found the mixture of subservience and smugness beyond the great house intensely irritating:

It has the look of a very faithful old family retainer - as I have no doubt those that live in its cottages are - pensioned off by the great people & unswervingly loyal to them. Its whole world is circled by the Park; its interest is concerned entirely with 'Her Ladyship' & the goings on at the Castle. In almost every street you can trace the influence of the Herbert family. The three inns are of course loyally christened after the various titles of the Pembrokes; their arms, slightly battered by weather, hang from all the signposts: they, in their turn, have scattered fountains & almshouses all around them, & generally keep the village so tidy & sweet that it makes the most respectable setting for Wilton.

Inn sign opposite the entrance to Wilton House.

The place may well have gone up in her estimation had Virginia been aware that in the late 16th century when Mary Herbert, Countess of Pembroke, extended her patronage to a group of young poets, Wilton House was an important centre of literary activity. The countess is thought to have given her brother Sir Phillip Sydney the idea for his prose romance 'The Arcadia', written at Wilton during a visit in 1580, and was herself the model for Urania in Edmund Spenser's 'Colin Clout' (1595). Her son William continued the family tradition and Shakespeare, who received considerable encouragement from the third Earl and his brother, dedicated his First Folio to *The Most Noble and Incomparable Pair of Brethren*. In 1603 the playwright was at Wilton to see his players perform 'As You Like It' in front of James I.

In 1906 the sculptor Henry Furse, from whom Virginia's father had rented Netherhampton House, invited his friend Henry Newbolt to share the place. The experiment proved so successful that the Newbolts remained until a few years before the poet's death in 1938. During this time the house became the centre for a wide circle of literary friends, including Walter de la Mare, who found the atmosphere so conducive that he returned for several weeks each winter. Ensconced in Newbolt's attic study, known affectionately as 'The Ark', the two men drew their inspiration from working together or gazing out across the fields to the chalk hills.

Wilton House from the south west

Netherhampton House painted by Rex Whistler on a visit in 1927.

The agricultural novelist **A G Street** was just a boy at Ditchingham Farm when the Stephen family arrived at Netherhampton. His literary aspirations ran no further than a regular column in the Farmer's Weekly until the appearance of Edith Olivier, a local author of formidable energy. Full of praise for Street's essay in the Salisbury Times on the pleasures of ploughing, she persuaded him to write his own account of life on the south Wiltshire farm. The result was ***Farmer's Glory*** (1932), praised at the time for its unpretentious style and honest, unsentimental portrait of rural life. Many other books followed in a writing career that spanned 40 years but this, his first published work, remains Street's most important contribution to the rural tradition. Brought together by their love of the countryside, the experience of growing up in Wilton had proved very different for these two Wiltshire writers and did much to shape the style and content of their work. Unlike his predecessor Richard Jefferies, Street was an energetic youth who learnt much from his farming apprenticeship, and was then only vaguely aware of the atmosphere of feudal authority that gripped Wilton at the turn of the century. Emanating from the gates of the great house it drifted through the town, becoming lodged most forcefully in the rectory where **Edith Olivier** spent the first half of her life.

As the youngest of 10 children Olivier grew up within the rigid confines of a respectable late Victorian family presided over by her autocratic father Canon Dacre Olivier. Confronted by such tyrannical devotion to duty, Edith and her over-protective sister Mildred took refuge in the kind of fantasy world recreated by Olivier in her first novel ***The Love Child*** (1927), published shortly after Mildred's death. *Evidently the story of the imaginary child, invented for company by a lonely woman, who can be seen and loved by others, but who must belong wholly to her creator, or she will disappear, arises directly out of her loss of her sister.* This at least was the critic Hermione

Lee's response to Olivier's disturbing picture of possessive love. Olivier had always cherished a secret desire to become an actress but as a spinster she never managed to escape the demands of her Wilton family. As Dean Chilvester, the canon is subjected to mild ridicule in 'The Seraphim Room' (1932), a study of life in a cathedral close based on Olivier's personal experience when the family moved to Salisbury in 1912, but Olivier gradually came to appreciate her father's staunch education and traditional values. On his death in 1919 she moved back to Wilton and to Daye House in the park where she divided her time between writing, local politics and the circle of Wiltshire aesthetes that included Siegfried Sassoon, Stephen Tennant, David Cecil and Rex Whistler who illustrated several of her countryside books.

Rex Whistler line drawing for Edith Olivier's novel *The Love Child*.

Martin

W H Hudson
(1841 - 1922)

Following the publication of *A Shepherd's Life* in 1910, **W H Hudson** refused to disclose the exact whereabouts of Winterbourne Bishop, the pseudonymous downland village that features prominently in the book. In response to persistent requests he did eventually confirm the existence of Bustard Down and since then his most celebrated work has always been associated with the village of Martin. The book was the culmination of several years spent gathering material from elderly residents in the villages of south Wiltshire, but the idea took root from a chance meeting with an old shepherd that reminded Hudson of his own self-imposed exile:

a disabled man who would never again follow the flock on the hills nor listen to the sounds he loved best to hear - the multitudinous tremulous bleating of the sheep, the tinkling of numerous bells, the crisp ringing bark of his dog. But his heart was there still, and the images of past scenes were more vivid to him than they can ever be in the minds of those who live in towns and read books.

Hudson had been brought up in South America but on arrival in England at the age of 33 he soon discovered that to become a writer meant living in London. This, for a man who detested city life, was a miserable prospect and to those who knew him, Hudson often appeared like one of the caged birds he campaigned so vigorously to liberate. He yearned for the outdoor life and went off on long walks whenever he could. A favourite destination was the abandoned town of Silchester and there in the summer of 1901 the author met James Lawes and his wife. The couple lived on the edge of a common at Aldermaston Soke where they let rooms to archaeologists excavating the Roman ruins. In addition to rheumatic fever brought on by long exposure to wind and rain, they discovered a mutual interest in wildlife and a common inheritance. Their conversations over the next few years led Hudson to explore the Wiltshire downs where Lawes had spent his working life. The result was 'A Shepherd's Life' in which Caleb and Isaac Bawcombe are taken directly from the life of the shepherd and his father William Lawes.

A downland shepherd.

Hudson has been struck by the old man's wonderfully clear *fawn-like* eyes that, from years of scanning the wide sheep pastures, seemed to stare right through him as though focused on some distant point. He recognised the expression immediately. His parents had emigrated to Argentina and as a child Hudson spent days in the saddle following his father's sheep. He never lost his love for the open horizons of the South American pampas and always seemed like *an old Gaucho, born on the plains, with the slow speech, and silent ways of the plainsman.* The unlimited freedom he enjoyed as a child explains Hudson's peculiar affinity with the bare chalk pastures of Salisbury Plain. It gave him a unique opportunity to observe wildlife that led to his pioneering work as a field naturalist and *an insight into the nature of wilderness itself and its relationship to the concepts of freedom and solitude* that shaped his belief in the interconnectedness of all living things.

The Lamb at Hindon where W H Hudson stayed in 1909 gathering material for *A Shepherd's Life*.

In Hudson's day Martin was one of the most exposed and isolated villages on the Plain; a few small farms and a straggle of thatch cottages along a winding street. Each autumn the chalk stream by which he renamed the village, would reappear mysteriously, flushing the roadside ditch with a tangled mass of luxuriant green watercress, mint and water crowfoot. The rest of the year the place was high and dry with little shade apart from an ancient yew in the churchyard and a few tall beech trees but, to Hudson, it came as a welcome relief from the picturesque villages hidden away in the Wylye valley.

As 'Afoot in England' (1909) and 'A Traveller in Little Things' (1921) suggest, Hudson preferred to keep on the move, but for some reason Martin exercised a peculiar fascination. He returned again and again, unable at first to explain its secret appeal beyond the memories of an old shepherd. He felt more alive here out on the empty downs; the air was purer, the colours more vivid and the birdsong more intense but there was something else. Above all wild animals he most admired the stag that still roamed through Cranborne Chase because *it moves us to a strange joy - an inherited memory and a vision of a savage, prehistoric land of which we are truer natives than we can ever be of this smooth, sophisticated England.* Hudson still yearned for the distant land of his youth and on one occasion, as he approached the outskirts of the village, he realised that what drew him back each time was *a sense of elation like that of coming home.* He was always most interested in men like James Lawes whose simple life brought them close to nature and here in this downland community the bones of early settlers, dislodged by burrowing rabbits and scattered about the fields, were a reminder of man's long and harmonious relationship with the natural world.

At the same time Hudson was painfully aware of the pressure for change exerted by vested interests and the demand for more food that was even then destroying the rich wildlife and archeological heritage of the Wiltshire downs. The desecration of so many earthworks by deep ploughing and the practice of grave robbing were disconcerting reminders of man's arrogant disregard for the past. On the Plain Hudson witnessed the transition from open sheep walk to military training area and elsewhere grazing land was being cut up into huge arable fields bereft of wildlife and enclosed by wire fences. As an ornithologist Hudson viewed with greatest concern the alarming decline of species once common on the chalk. The Great Bustard was already extinct and the Little Bustard, or stone curlew, frequented the uncultivated downs in diminishing numbers due to the activity of egg collectors, an evil trade that Hudson campaigned against all his life. When staying at Hindon he would often walk in Great Ridge woods between the Wylye and Nadder valleys, but apart from the occasional roe deer he was dismayed by the absence of wildlife. The larger birds of prey and other vermin had been driven out by zealous gamekeepers here and on other shooting estates. The raven that had nested in most Wiltshire woods until quite recently, was once plentiful around Martin when packs of deerhounds were fed on rotting horse flesh, but even this vulture of the sheep pastures had now disappeared.

Hudson's sense of injustice extended to the plight of the agricultural labourer and he sympathised with those driven by hunger to steal sheep despite the savage penalties handed down at Salisbury assizes. Above all he admired the wild spirit and animal cunning of the gypsies who were seldom caught. The introduction of the threshing machine in the 1830s threatened the lives of many labourers already forced to survive on a starvation wage of 7 shillings per week. Caleb Bawcombe's tale of the curse uttered by an innocent man sentenced to transportation led Hudson to investigate other tales of poverty and

Eentrance to the park at Fonthill Bishop near Hindon, an enduring symbol of feudal authority built in 1823 at a time when, according to Hudson, farm labourer's still lived in extreme poverty.

machine breaking that were to become known as the Captain Swing riots. One old lady at Fonthill Abbey (Bishop) remembered working as a girl for a tyrannical and sadistic master not unlike Hardy's Farmer Groby (see p101). Known as Devil Turner, he punished the slightest transgression by forcing the offender to stand on a chair in the yard for long periods, whatever the weather. The chapters entitled 'Old Wiltshire Days' include gruesome accounts of cruelty and grinding poverty; of men gnawing swedes to alleviate their hunger, children sent out stone picking in the cold and wet and women gathering firewood from the hedgerows to earn a little extra money.

The old shepherds not only knew a great deal about wildlife but were often skilled poachers not averse to taking the occasional rabbit or pheasant to supplement their own meagre diet. But Hudson is quick to disassociate them from the bloody encounters between organised gangs of deer poachers and the gamekeepers of Cranborne Chase, even though the law made no such distinction. Isaac Bawcombe killed a deer one bitterly cold winter that had escaped from a nearby herd but resolved not to be so reckless in future, a decision which brought its own reward. The gentlemen farmer who enjoyed his sport had noticed the abundance of wildlife on Isaac's patch of grazing. He was also a trustee of the village charity and when the shepherd reached 60, decided to recommend him for assistance that allowed Bawcombe to enjoy a prolonged and happy retirement. A commemorative tablet in the south chapel of Martin's parish church records the Talk Charity under which William Lawes had been a beneficiary.

Like Cobbett, Hudson loved best the independent, intelligent countryman and disliked intensely the servility engendered by the presence of a village squire. His affection for Martin stemmed partly from the absence of such an authoritarian figure although it did allow others to assume powerful positions in the community. One was Elijah Raven, a miserly eccentric, who rose to become secretary of the village benefit society and used his office to settle old scores. One one occasion he refused Caleb the sick money to which he was fully entitled and the dispute was eventually settled in Caleb's favour at Salisbury assizes. Raven was based on the real life character of Malachi Martin and Hudson later discovered to his astonishment that he had once stayed in the very same cottage in the main street where this reclusive old man had lived years before.

Unlike Gilbert White who subjected the wildlife of a single parish to detailed scrutiny over many years, Hudson was a great traveller. The sense of travelling was often more important than the destination. He seldom planned journeys in advance and rarely consulted the map or the guidebook for fear they might deprive him of the freedom to negotiate his own path. His most vivid and lasting impressions were often the result of chance encounters and his tendency to despair at the destruction of the countryside was offset by what Edward Garnett called his *intense zest for the living fact*. If Hudson's methods of collecting material appear arbitrary he knew that, unlike James Lawes who remembered clearly because *he had seen* (wild creatures) *emotionally*, his task as a field naturalist was to observe and record, and he never went anywhere without his binoculars or his notebook.

The headstone of William Lawes
d 1886
in Martin churchyard.

Yew trees in Martin churchyard are among the few remaining features in a village that has changed much since Hudson knew it. Sheep no longer frequent the downs, but the naturalist would have approved of the decision to graze them in the churchyard.

Hudson soon discovered that by encouraging Lawes to talk freely about his life he was likely to learn far more than by pursuing a particular line of enquiry, and the friendship that developed enabled him to build up a unique picture of rural life. The meandering course of James Lawes' anecdotes, like the author's journeys across southern England, is reflected in Hudson's conversational style. He often takes the reader into his confidence, explaining how he came to write the book or interrupting his description of a flock of starlings to relate an incident of men singing to their cattle in Cornwall. Meditations on the significance of what he has seen are scattered among accounts of wildlife behaviour to the extent that, as Edward Thomas remarked, *his writing reveals the author in the presence of birds as much as birds, visible or invisible, in the presence of the author.* Hudson's unifying vision of the natural world that included man is most evident in 'A Shepherd's Life' and it remains his greatest achievement, ensuring his place alongside Gilbert White and George Sturt, and his contemporaries Richard Jefferies and Edward Thomas, in the literature of the English countryside.

Cranborne Chase

In Hardy's ***Tess of the d'Urbervilles*** the exact location of Tantridge (Pentridge) is less important than its distance from Marlott (Marnhull see p98) in the Vale of Blackmore and its position on the edge of Cranborne Chase. Alighting on the highway at Tantridge Cross, Tess sets out to walk the last few miles to the seat of her d'Urberville 'ancestors' only to be confronted by a red brick mansion of recent construction and dubious taste. 'The Slopes', with its acres of glass houses, its manicured lawns and well-equipped stables screened by exotic evergreens, is more like a pleasure palace than the crumbling old manor house she had imagined. Even the hens Tess looks after are kept for the amusement of her employer in a ruined cottage that had once been home to generations of farm labourers. In this single image Hardy manages to convey his contempt for a world of conspicuous affluence that already threatens to overwhelm his beloved county. On moving south Mr Stoke had set about acquiring the lifestyle of a country gentleman with profits from the family business. But the respectability achieved by reviving the name of an old Dorset family is, for Hardy, as spurious as the nouveau riche mansion itself. Alec d'Urberville, the idle son who roams the countryside in a shiny new dog cart in search of young women, is the devilish playboy of romantic fiction. Tess immediately senses danger as her seducer stalks her across the lawn but is powerless to refuse the gifts he brings. Bright red roses and ripe strawberries that match her blushing cheeks also signal the loss of her innocence. In Hardy's day the Chase was:

Cranborne Manor and the church from a late 18c. engraving.

... a truly venerable tract of forest land, one of the few remaining woodlands in England of undoubted primaeval date, wherein Druidical mistletoe was still found on aged oaks, and where enormous yew trees, not planted by the hand of man, grew as they had grown when they were pollarded for bows.

Tess in the Chase *a maid no more*. *f*rom a woodcut by Vivien Gribble 1926.

The Chase was hunted over by Angevian Kings and remains of King John's lodge survive at Tollard Royal where a huge wych elm traditionally marked the spot around which his huntsmen gathered. The medieval Rights of Chase, administered by the Chase Court at Cranborne, imposed severe penalties on the local population, and until their revocation in the early 19th century, pitched battles between keepers and poachers were not uncommon, battles commemorated in names such as Bloody Coppice. Remodelled on a grand scale by the first Earl of Salisbury to accommodate James I when he chose to hunt in the Chase, the beautiful stone manor house at Cranborne incorporates the remains of another medieval hunting lodge. Contemporary with the original building is the 14th century wall painting in the parish church. It depicts 'The Misery of the Doomed' in which young naked women, one heavily pregnant, climb through the branches of the Tree of Deadly Sins in a vain attempt to escape their tormentors. The tree is growing from the head of a woman and ever since Eve first tempted Adam, women have been condemned by a religion that worships a male deity. Hardy could not have wished for a more graphic illustration of Tess's plight and it was here in the Chase against a background of feudal repression, religious persecution and ritual blood-letting that he chose to set the rape of his 'pure woman'.

3
Ripeness is All
The Vale
of Blackmore

It ever rolls away into shallow valley and low hill, with now and then a wooded height or the glittering track of a stream. The land is broken up into a thousand fields, fringed by luxuriant hedges. In every hedge are many trees; trees follow every buff-coloured road, and gather around every hamlet or cluster of farm buildings. It is a country of dairies. Everywhere are there cows, for the smell of cows is the incense of North Dorset.

From **Highways & Byeways of Dorset** by **Sir Frederick Treves**

Montacute

The village of Montacute has arranged itself comfortably at the foot of St Michael's hill, the wooded 'mons acutus' from which the place takes it name. Crowned since 1790 by a look-out tower, this noble landmark is part of the same geological outcrop that, in the neighbouring parish of Stoke Sub-Hamdon was once quarried for the sandstone that gives this part of Wessex its distinctive character. Ham stone has been used on almost every building in Montacute and the whole village appears to be bathed in perpetual sunshine. The novelist Sylvia Townsend Warner described the effect memorably in her 1949 guide to Somerset:

The quarry-men bicycling home at the end of their day go past like bumble bees, gilded with a stone pollen, and the village of Montacute .... is all the colours of a honey-comb. Montacute is an old place, with a great deal of pride and character. It calls the open space in the centre of the village "The Borough", and over shop windows the names of the proprietors are cut in the stone itself - a stately detail.

With the richly decorated tower of St Catherine's church and the gatehouse of its Cluniac priory, now part of Abbey Farm, the village is architecturally well-endowed, but its crowning glory is undoubtedly the great house. Safe in the hands of the National Trust since 1931, Montacute House remains for many the most beautiful of Elizabethan mansions. In the late 19th century when the novelist John Cowper Powys was a boy at the rectory, Montacute was still essentially a feudal village presided over by the Phelips family for whom the house was originally constructed in the 1590's. Brought up in the shadow of such a building A R (Bertie) Powys seemed destined to pursue a career in architectural conservation. The decision seemed fully justified years later when, as secretary of the Society for the Protection of Ancient Buildings, he was well placed to instigate the campaign to save Montacute House and supervise an extensive repair programme based on the principles laid down by the Society's founder, William Morris.

The Revd Charles Francis Powys came from a long line of west country clergymen and, having served as parish priest in Derbyshire for 14 years, he gladly accepted the Montacute appointment in 1886 and remained there until his retirement at the end of the Great War. Bound together by fierce tribal loyalties, his large and gifted family of 11 children drew its strength and independence from life at the rectory deep in the Somerset countryside and, in the case of the Powys boys, from the shared experience of public school. Littleton, the eldest and most orthodox brother who later became headmaster at the town's prep school, wrote enthusiastically of his time at Sherborne in 'The Joy of It', but John Cowper's most cherished memories were of those Sunday afternoons when, released from the rigors of boarding school, he and Littleton would arrive at the rectory in time for tea, having just run the 10 miles home round the Trent Lanes and the northern outskirts of Yeovil.

The east front of Montacute House from the garden.

Montacute rectory, home of the Powys family in the late 19c.

Bradford Abbas

John Cowper Powys had already painted an affectionate picture of Monacute in his first novel 'Wood and Stone' (1915) by the time he revisited the scenes of his childhood for the setting of **Wolf Solent** (1929). Written on trains and in hotel rooms across America towards the end of a debilitating series of lecture tours, this first and most cohesive of his four great Wessex novels was a remarkable achievement. As Powys later acknowledged, it was *a book of Nostalgia, written in a foreign country with the pen of a traveller and the ink-blood of his home.* Powys considered a sense of place sufficiently important to an appreciation of the novel to include a map of the area in the 1929 edition and although he still felt it necessary to divert the course of the Lunt (Yeo) and rearrange the rail network, his vision of the border country between Ramsgard (Sherborne) and Blacksod (Yeovil) is recognisably the same terrain negotiated with Littleton all those years before. Out of the lanes and meadows of his childhood Powys created the mental landscapes in which his characters operate, most memorably the subaqueous world of Wolf's mythology, the cultural geography of Gerda Torp's Dorset and the mystical realm of Christie Malakite's Somerset Levels.

Ramsgard, complete with its public school in the abbey precincts, its medieval almshouses and the great fan-vaulted church itself, has all the atmosphere of a small, carefully preserved cathedral city. Having decided to make a new start by accepting the post of private secretary to a local antiquarian, Wolf Solent leaves behind the alien world of the capital haunted by the face on the Waterloo steps, and returns to a place where his own personal history is bound up in the more illustrious annals of Ramsgard. Here among the unrivalled group of ancient buildings where Wolf's father once taught and now lies buried in the cemetery, Solent becomes reacquainted with

John Cowper Powys
(1872 - 1963)

his aunt, the gargoyle-faced Selina Gault. If Ramsgard, with its historic pageant and the bones of King Aethelwolf, has its roots firmly in the past, the thriving commercial town of Blacksod, full of small businesses and rows of artisan houses, holds the key to Wolf's future. Here he meets the two women through whom his precious mythology is firstly challenged and finally destroyed; Christie the ethereal daughter of an incestuous bookseller and the sensuous figure of Gerda whose provocative pose astride a headstone in her father's yard first excites Wolf's lust.

Sherborne Abbey framed by the town's medieval almshouses.

The old timber-framed house with its *crazily gabled porch* on the edge of The Green in Marlborough where William Golding grew up and where the snobbery endemic in provincial life gave him the idea for ***The Pyramid*** (1957).

Netherhampton House, *in its way an imitation of a genuine great house*, according to Virginia Woolf who stayed here in 1903. Walter de la Mare was a regular visitor between the wars as a guest of the poet Henry Newbolt.

At the end of ***Wolf Solent*** as John Cowper Powys' hero walks through a buttercup meadow in the evening light, the yellow pollen becomes *a super-substance, sunlight precipitated and petrified, the magnetic heart of the world rendered visible!*

The centre of Dorchester has changed little since Hardy wrote *The Mayor of Casterbridge* (1886) during his time at Max Gate. The scene was equally familiar to John Cowper Powys while working on *Maiden Castle* at 38 High St. in 1934.

The west front of Montacute House incorporating the 16c. porch from Clifton Maybank.

In the novel there appears to be no local precedent for the earthworks known as Poll's Camp but on the banks of the Lunt midway between the two market towns, King's Barton completes the settlement pattern in 'Wolf Solent', a village that approximates to Bradford Abbas beside the river Yeo where Powys' father had been curate. Powys would probably have been aware that less than a mile downstream Sir John Horsey (d.1564) had owned Clifton

Maybank House when he married a Phelips from Montacute, and that Clifton's beautiful Elizabethan porch had been re-erected as a dazzling centrepiece to the late 18th century west front at Montacute. Horsey lies buried in Sherborne Abbey, the resting place of Saxon kings, and the name chosen by Powys for his pseudonymous village may be a veiled reference to Wyke Farm in the parish of Bradford Abbas, once the abbey grange. The intricate network of historic association over which Powys stretched his own delicate web of illusion and damaged relationships radiates out from Bradford Abbas/King's Barton. Here in the course of his work on Squire Urquhart's bawdy chronicle of Dorset, his autobiographical hero stumbles upon what he thinks is a sinister pattern of sexual deviation and murderous conspiracy concerning his employer and the fate of his predecessor, Redfern.

Wolf has arrived back in Dorset with his mythology intact but never really tested. This *sinking into his soul* enables him to draw on some reserve of magnetic power that is like *the expanding of great vegetable leaves over a still pool*. He feels in some arrogant way that by this process he is *taking part in some occult cosmic struggle* between the forces of good and evil. Contemplating his new life he wonders whether the experience will shatter his protective mirror like a great stone dropped into the depths of his life-illusion. As Wolf first heads off to King's Barton on a late Spring evening, the setting sun is obscured by a thick band of cloud:

It was as if an enormous green tidal wave, composed of a substance more translucent than water, had flowed over the whole earth; or rather as if some diaphanous essence of all the greenness created by long days of rain had evaporated during this one noon, only to fall down, with the approach of twilight, in a cold dark emerald-coloured dew.

The watery green landscape of Wessex is a recurring theme throughout the novel. The enveloping film of vapourous mist works, like Wolf's mythology, to distort perspectives and enrich the view. On his journey Wolf becomes aware of travelling on the threshold of two landscapes, landscapes that become redolent with meaning when soon after, he finds himself caught between two powerful women. The watershed is in reality the ridge of higher ground running along the edge of Sherborne Park to Lillington Hill. One one side the far reaches of Blackmore Vale stretch away, a convoluted network of streams resolving itself into Caundle Brook before flowing on through the dialect poetry of William Barnes' river Stour and beneath Hardy's 'Stourcastle' footbridge (see p97). This is the secretive folk ballad country of Whitehart Vale and the Dorset hills inhabited by Gerda Torp, a landscape *whispering, so it seemed, some inexplicable prophetic greeting* to the returning native. On the other side the river Yeo, having extricated itself from the lake at Sherborne, flows more purposefully westward towards the expansive realm of Arthurian legend where *the immense Somersetshire plain .... lost itself in a pale, sad horizon, where, like a king's sepulchre, rose the hill-ruin of Glastonbury*. This is the spiritual home of Christie Malakite whose mother claimed descent from Merlin, but as Wolf gazes westward Powys is already looking forward to his next novel and then, from the top of the Tor, across the Bristol Channel to the land of his ancestors.

The Stour near Hammoon looking east to Hambledon hillfort, part of the ancient Dorset landscape associated with Gerda Torp in **Wolf Solent**.

The following day Wolf walks into Blacksod to check on the progress of Redfern's headstone and here he first sets eyes on Gerda Torp. He is so startled by her languorous beauty *that it seemed to destroy in a moment all ordinary human relations*. From the outset this ordinary country girl is transformed into a sexual object of virginal purity, draped in the tiresome cloak of classical allusion. *Her voluptuous throat resembled an arum lily before it has unsheathed its petals* and her dress emphasised *the delicate Artemis-like beauty of her young breasts*. After Wolf's visit to The Three Peewits her sweetness made *everything seem rich and mellow, as if it were seen through a diffused golden light, like that of the pictures of Claude Lorrain*. On their first walk together Wolf and Gerda climb the very real slopes of Babylon Hill on the eastern outskirts of Yeovil. Once at the summit Gerda plunges into the bushes that cover the slopes of Poll's Camp with all the agility of a young fawn. As Wolf awaits her return he becomes transfixed by the poignant song of a blackbird. *The delicious notes hovered through the wood - hovered over the scented turf where he lay - and went wavering down the hollow valley. It was like the voice of the very spirit of Poll's Camp.* And then he realised to his embarrassment that Gerda was the voice of *those green pastures and those blackthorn hedges*.

Down beside the river Gerda's naked limbs yield to the weedy embrace of the Lunt as she becomes absorbed in following the course of a water rat while Wolf is submerged in waves of indescribable liquid sensation, prompted by a clump of marsh marigolds beside the bank. These memories were still *more sacred to him than any living person. They were his friend, his gods, his secret religion. Like a mad botanist, like a crazed butterfly-collector, he hunted these filmy growths, these wild wanderers, and stored them up in his mind.* Wolf's mythology is still in good shape and even after his marriage to Gerda he remains immune to the needs of a woman with whom he has little in common. Neglected by her husband and weighed down by layers of literary reference, Gerda loses her blackbird song and escapes into the arms of her childhood sweetheart Bob Weevil. This at least is what Wolf first imagines and then actively encourages as he turns his attention to the wraith-like figure of Christie Malakite.

On first meeting Christie, Wolf had felt their minds connect *like two bodiless shadows in a flowing river.* He soon finds himself drawn to her on a much deeper level, the level of soul consciousness, that makes his love for Gerda seem *like playful lust, directed towards some beautiful statue.* While Wolf begins to feel increasingly trapped in his marriage, Christie remains a vague presence, *a pillar of mist* or *a column of smoke.* As this mysterious young woman sinks deeper into his being the struggle within Wolf becomes more intense until one evening, descending the slopes of Poll's Camp on one of his

Glastonbury Tor rising above the Somerset Levels, the spiritual home of Christie Malakite.

long, solitary walks, he feels freer and lighter, as though he had just left behind a great burden. The earthworks were now merely a place from which he gazed, searching the western sky, and as he does so he becomes aware of a new fragrance, the smell of distant peat-bogs, the aroma of the Somerset Levels. Wolf is conscious of *some deep race-memory* borne on these *frail essences* of vegetable life, as though they possessed *immortal souls*, and as he repeats the phrase the sound takes on the shape of Malakite's daughter.

Later, while on a picnic with Gerda at Poll's Camp, Wolf imagines himself flying away with Christie, *the child of that mystical plain down there, that 'chess-board of King Arthur'*, to the more chastened slopes of Glastonbury Tor, *the pollen-bearing pistol of the whole lotus-valley!* The Cretaceous hills of Dorset belong to a more remote geological past but Sedgemoor, emerging purified from some vast lake of more recent origin, now lay *like some immense, sad-coloured flower floating upon hidden water* that he found irresistible. As his young wife lies stretched out asleep on the ground, her head buried in the grass, Wolf conjures up *some legendary encounter between the body of Gerda and the crafty superhuman desire of some earth god.* He experiences an *obstinate hostility* towards the hillfort, a heathen place associated with the old gods that question his virility. Soon after, the image of Gerda becomes linked more explicitly to the *troubling symbol* of the Cerne Abbas giant when, sitting in his study, Wolf reflects on the distasteful nature of his work, his Faustian pact with Urquhart, and the rumours circulating about Redfern's untimely death.

The tract of countryside on the eastern slopes of the Yeo valley known to Powys as Trent Lanes, came to assume a special place in the author's imagination. As he recalled in his 'Autobiography', *the network of grassy lanes between high hedges ... possessed enchanted vistas.* Thinly disguised as Gwent Lanes, a name suggesting the Welsh ancestry of Christie's mother, and haunted by the solitary figure of Christie herself, this bewildering maze of country roads on the threshold of Somerset is where Wolf's personal transformation begins. Having walked for several miles across country from King's Barton he lies down beside the road and all his troubles with Gerda fade from his mind, absorbed into the primordial matter of vegetable flesh:

It was as though he had suddenly emerged, by some hidden doorway, into a world entirely composed of vast, cool, silent-growing vegetation, a world where no men, no beasts, no birds, broke the mossy stillness; a world of sap and moisture and drooping ferns ....

He was a leaf among leaves .... among large, cool, untroubled leaves .... He had fallen back into the womb of his real mother .... He was drenched through and through with darkness and with peace.

This extraordinary passage heralds the onset of autumn with its *sweet, rank, odours* and the protracted death of Wolf's mythology. This impediment to growing self-awareness must firstly rot away before he can be reborn into a world perceived in a more realistic light. The leaden grey skies and fibrous decay threaten to drag him down. *How heavily the heart's tongue ferns drooped earthwards under the scooped hollows of the wet clay banks! How heavily the cold raindrops fell - silence falling upon silence.* The alluvial soil of the Somerset Levels, washed clean each winter by the swollen waters of the Parrett and the Brue, is a lighter, more fertile deposit. Growth in this landscape of wide horizons and gentle hills is more rapid and more healthy but here, in a land of heavy clay that had already claimed Redfern and his father, the past is still close behind and, without Christie to guide him, there is as yet, no way out of the maze:

> *Each calamitous event that occurred during those deciduous months seemed to be brewed in the oozy vat of vegetation, as if the muddy lanes and the wet hazel-copses- yes! the very earth-mould of Dorset itself - were conspiring with human circumstances.*

Wolf had already begun to question his life-illusion before the occasion of his walk with Urquhart, whom he believes to be a necrophiliac, and Jason Otter, another homosexual. When they stop beside Lenty Pond to watch two local youths bathing, the mood is surprisingly harmless and Wolf feels the pressure of *a tide that was outside any 'dualism' - a tide that was threatening the banked-up discriminations of his whole life.* Lenty Pond, where Redfern had taken his evening walks, has long been the focal point of superstitions and all the mysterious rumours circulating in King's Barton, and when Wolf realises his mythology has been destroyed by his work for Urquhart he considers drowning himself in its dark waters. As a symbol of the good and evil at the heart of Wolf's life-illusion, Lenty Pond is powerfully ambiguous; the watery depths of his subconscious associated with the surfacing of the *great moonlight-coloured fish* of his sensations. The huge perch caught by Lob Torp is Wolf himself and it reminds him of the small fish that, as a child, he had been persuaded to return to the rock pool at Weymouth where his mythology had first taken shape.

Obliged by circumstances to accept Urquhart's cheque and resume work on his scandalous chronicle while anticipating the visit to Christie's house during her father's trip to Weymouth, Wolf prepares to face the double crisis that threatens his cherished life-illusion. On his way to Malakite's shop he considers that life stripped of his mythology will be little more than the kind of *stoical endurance* he is not yet willing to accept. Standing in the backyard his eyes alight on a stone in the wall covered in bright green moss, one of the many occasions throughout the novel when seemingly arbitrary natural objects assume a special, mandala-like significance. It reminds Wolf of the old pier supports at Weymouth covered in seaweed and he is once again immersed in the warm sensations of his mythology.

Standing in Christie's room with thoughts of seduction raging in his head, Wolf knows his happiness could so easily be destroyed. When, a few moments later, the opportunity does arise, the grey heron's feather that had slipped from Christie's book has the same disconcerting effect as the unselfconscious manner in which she shows him into her bedroom. The feather is such a potent symbol of a visionary world to which Christie has access that Wolf is caught between his desire for her body and *the unexplored regions in her soul.* The strange green glow from her lamp casts a spell over the room, so that her

The church at Bradford Abbas where the Powys father had been curate. Renamed King's Barton it occupies a central place in the geography of **Wolf Solent**. Here rumours circulate about the fate of Urqhart's assistant Redfern buried in the churchyard.

mother's mirror is lit up *as if by the swollen green bud of a luminous water-lily*. Mesmerised by the reflection Wolf fails to seize the moment and his habitual mentality reasserts itself. The image, so clear and full of promise, becomes lost in the murky waters of Lenty Pond and the face on the Waterloo steps with its reminder of all the misery Wolf has tried to escape. As his whole being begins to disintegrate, a will beyond his mythology rises out of the void *like a shining-scaled fish .... and leapt into the greenish-coloured vapour that filled the room!* But this fleeting image is too slippery to grasp and Christie is sacrificed for the sake of his selfish life-illusion. Stung by the rejection, she tries to make Wolf see that events take place outside the carefully arranged world of his imagination.

As the critic Carole Coates has suggested, the androgynous and amoral Christie represents the boy-girl figure in whose presence Powys felt possessed of a supernatural power he was always struggling to attain. Christie becomes the Grail Bearer but Wolf is unable to relinquish his old self, the opportunity is lost and the vision withdrawn, leaving his thoughts to circulate *like a dragonfly hovering over a stagnant pond* before his rehabilitation commences. In the weeks ahead the remains of his mythology seep away and, once resigned to the loss of Christie, he becomes more attentive to others. The evil rumours emanating from the tap room of The Farmer's Arms that once drifted over King's Barton are finally dispelled by the prosaic explanation offered by Urquhart's manservant for Redfern's reinterment. Most forms of sexual and physical abnormality exist in King's Barton but Powys treats them as expressions of human nature, arguing that the voyeurism they provoke is a more damaging social evil. Wolf's acceptance of abnormality is a necessary part of his redemption, sounding the note of stoicism on which the novel ends.

With the return of spring the final chapter, 'Ripeness is all', is full of references to the vitality and regenerative power of the natural world. The appearance of Lord Carfax brings a measure of resolution to the lives of several characters and, arriving home one evening, Wolf stops to listen to a blackbird before realising that, seated on his knee, Gerda's whistling has been restored. Turning away in his humiliation Wolf catches sight of a meadow full of buttercups through a gap in the hedge, *a floating sea of liquid, shining gold!* Telling himself that Carfax will soon be gone he feels himself irresistibly drawn to the field:

Back and forth he walked, while the sun, fallen almost horizontal, made what he walked upon seem unearthly. Buttercup-petals clung to his legs, clung to the sides of his stick; buttercup-dust covered his boots. The plenitude of gold that surrounded him began to invade his mind with strange, far-drawn associations .... It became a super-substance, sunlight precipitated and petrified, the magnetic heart of the world rendered visible!

Up and down he went, pacing that field. He felt as if he were an appointed emissary, guarding some fragment of Saturn's age flung into the midst of Blacksod!

Standing there covered in gold dust and bathed in a golden light, the king-cups by the Lunt and the yellow bracken on which he and Gerda had first made love seem now but the fools' gold of a false dawn. He felt the joy of being alive flow through him and longed to pour this liquid substance over all *the nameless little desolations* in the world; to anoint them and restore their beauty. He was aware of a subtle but important adjustment to his view of the world. His old mythology has gone and in the absence of Gerda and Christie the old dualistic landscape is replaced by a single unifying vision:

Then as he turned eastward, and the yellowness of the buttercups changed from Byzantine gold to Cimmerian gold, he visualised the whole earthly solidity of this fragment of the West Country, this segment of astronomical clay, stretching from Glastonbury to Melbury Bubb and from Ramsgard to Blacksod, as if it were itself one of the living personalities of his life.

On previous occasions Wolf's vision would soon have become clouded by his own life-illusion but now, standing by the pigsty on the edge of the meadow he is tethered to reality, aware that he has never before observed this familiar structure from behind. With this new perspective he realises that until now he had *visualised every single person of his life, in some treachery of meanness! How often had he caught them in some incredible posture of grotesque indecency! Oh, it was his own mind that was diseased .... not Nature.* Adopting the phrase *endure or escape* as his guiding principle he turns to face life with Gerda and the consolation of a cup of tea.

Blackmore Vale

On reaching the top of the downs the change is dramatic as the eye takes in the broad sweep of the vale. Behind is cornland; the fields are larger, the view more open, the old ridgeway tracks bleached and dry. Down below the scale is smaller and more delicate, a patchwork of intricate pastures broken at intervals by oak copses and larger blocks of woodland. The soil is heavy clay, the grass greener, the streams muddier and more prone to flooding. Arrow straight roads suddenly become irregular lanes sunk below ancient hedgerows, the atmosphere is moist and languid as the landscape resolves itself into a series of

Blackmore Vale, Thomas Hardy's *Vale of the Little Dairies.*

Hambledon Hill capped by one of the dramatic hillforts that encircle the Vale of Blackmore.

abundant vistas. The first impression of the vale layered in early morning mist is of a great inland lake encircled by towering cliffs. At dusk it becomes the open jaw of some Cretaceous monster, teeth capped by ancient earthworks, about to devour its prey. According to Hardy, the vale was once known as the Forest of Whitehart, an archaic landscape that took its name from medieval legend. Around its southern margins, in the shadow of the hillforts, places like Glanville Wootton, Hazelbury Bryan and Okeford Fitzpaine still echo to the sound of Norman barons and the forest through which they hunted. The d'Urbervilles may lie in Kingsbere church but their ghosts, like Tess herself, still haunt the vale.

Hardy grew to love the Vale of Blackmore and, apart from the 'Melstock' countryside of his youth, it forms the most significant part of his literary landscape. Tucked away in one corner of the vale, he used the estate village of

Medieval tile from the church at Glanville Wootton, now in the Dorchester museum.

Melbury Osmond, where both his mother and grandmother had been brought up, as the setting for 'The Woodlanders'. His choice of Marnhull, a few miles north of Sturminster, as the home of his 'pure woman' Tess Durbeyfield, is a tribute both to his love for this part of Dorset and a traditional lifestyle destroyed in a way that her violation most tragically symbolises. Hardy and his young wife Emma Gifford made their first home in Sturminster Newton and their brief period of happiness is celebrated in some of his best known verse. He took great pleasure in the knowledge that, walking along the banks of the River Stour he was following in the footsteps of his old friend and mentor William Barnes.

Sturminster Newton

The upper Stour will always be associated with **William Barnes** and the way of life celebrated in his dialect poems. He was born into a *down start* family just outside Sturminster Newton where his father earned a living as a hired labourer and by grazing cattle on Bagber common. Barnes spent much of his childhood along the banks of the *cloty Stour* and the river insinuates itself into so many of his poems:

William Barnes
(1800 - 85)

> *Be there any leaves to quiver*
> *On the aspen by the river?*
> *Doo he sheade the water still,*
> *Where the rushes be a-growen,*
> *Where the sullen Stour's a-flowen*
> *Drough the meades vrom mill to mill?*
> *Vor if a tree wer dear to me,*
> *Oh! twer thik aspen by the river.*

The mill at Sturminster Newton.

Barnes' gift for poetry was recognised by his mother and by the local vicar who encouraged the use of his library but the only formal education he received was at the church school in Sturminster until, at the age of 13, he became clerk to a firm of local solicitors. The death of his mother two years later was a severe blow and Barnes left home for Dorchester in 1818 to pursue a career in the legal profession. Here he met and courted Julia Miles and although Barnes seldom returned to Sturminster after their marriage in 1827, the purchase of two meadows in the parish, Creedmans and Moggs Mead, gave him particular pleasure.

Barnes wrote over 1000 poems throughout his long life and although some of his early eclogues, published anonymously, were concerned with the plight of the poor and the effects of enclosing the commons, he left the subject of rural deprivation to his friend Robert Young. Young, who was born and lived most of his life in Sturminster, was another dialect poet who wrote about the evils of drink, brutality and overcrowding under the pseudonym 'Rabin Hill'. Barnes' reputation has suffered because he chose to present what many regard as a biassed picture of rustic simplicity and stock rural characters, but the poems sprang directly from his own idyllic childhood lovingly recorded in the rich dialect of his native Dorset. The accusation that he provided Victorian townspeople with a nostalgic view of the countryside does not bear closer analysis. Whether writing about Shroton Fair, the church bells at Lydlinch or the mill at Fiddleford, Barnes has left a picture of rural life in the early 19th century as fresh and original as a Constable painting.

*   *   *   *   *

Following his marriage to Emma Gifford and, encouraged by the success of 'Far From the Madding Crowd', **Thomas Hardy** decided to abandon a career in architecture for novel writing. From London the young couple moved first to Swanage and then to Yeovil before settling in Sturminster Newton in the

Riverside Villa, Hardy's home from 1876 to '77 where he wrote *The Return of the Native*.

Thomas Hardy
(1840 - 1928)
as a young man

On Stourcastle Foot-bridge
(1877.)

Reticulations creep upon the slack stream's face
When the wind skims irritably past,
The current clucks smartly into each hollow place
That years of flood have scrabbled in the pier's sodden base;
The ~~water~~ floating lily leaves rot fast.

On a roof stand the swallows equidistantly in rows,
Till they arrow off & drop like stones
Among the eyot-withies at whose roots the river flows;
And beneath the roof is she who in the dark world shows
~~like a~~ as a lamp ~~...~~ light when midnight moans.

summer of 1876. Riverside Villa, their home for the next 18 months, stands at the end of a lane on a bluff overlooking the Stour where the river divides either side of a small island. As he gazed out of his study window even the clouds, *like a huge quill-pen,* were a reminder of his chosen profession Hardy's fascination with the macabre had grown out of his grandmother's tales of the supernatural but the gruesome stories recorded in his Sturminster notebook had a more specific purpose. The story of the doctor at Maiden Newton who accepted a woman's dead baby in lieu of payment and kept it pickled in a large jar on the mantleshelf, is reminiscent of the scene in 'The Woodlanders' when Dr Fitzpiers attempts to buy Grammer Oliver's brain. In another entry Hardy noted the crowds who gathered on Bagber bridge to buy toads' legs from an old wizard as a charm to cure scrofula. Sympathetic magic was still widely practiced in country districts when Hardy began 'The Return of the Native', and the episode in which Susan Nunsuch sticks needles into a wax effigy of Eustacia Vye (see p171), may well have its origins in the story of a local farmer who removed the heart from every dead calf, stuck them through with blackthorns and hung them in the chimney to ward off the disease.

On long summer evenings Hardy and Emma would walk along the banks of the Stour or row out on the river to gather water lilies. Later in the year after autumnal rains *great lumps of froth would float down like swans* and the evening sky appeared *like some vast foundry where new worlds are being cast.* Forty years later Hardy celebrated this, their happiest time together, in several poems that appeared in the collection ***Moments of Vision***.

The couple's inability to have children was already beginning to cast a shadow over their marriage when Hardy discovered that the servant girl caught in the house with her lover was now pregnant. He recorded the news with the rueful comment, *Yet never a sign of one is there for us.* And yet it was Hardy's decision to further his career by moving to London that brought to an end their *Sturminster Newton idyll.* Hardy had rather ominously just finished the first of his great tragic novels and married life was never so blissful again. In 'The Musical Box' Hardy acknowledged his failure to heed the tune's message, *O make the most of what is nigh,* and in 'Overlooking the River Stour' his vision of swallows skimming the water and a moorhen darting out from the bank and *planing up shavings of crystal spray,* is blurred by raindrops on the window. His happiness then was of a selfish kind and, as he admitted, he should have paid more attention to the woman behind his back and not let *These less things hold my gaze.*

The view from Hardy's garden with the footbridge hidden by trees and remains of the viaduct that carried the Bournemouth to Bristol railway.

Marnhull

Hardy's village of Marlott (Marnhull) lay in the north east corner of the vale, a straggle of thatch cottages with the Rolliver's Inn at one end and The Pure Drop at the other that had been home to generations of Durbeyfields. John Durbeyfield was in the haggling business and, like Hardy's own family, belonged to the small group of tradesmen that had once been the backbone of village life and was still the repository of its lingering beliefs. For Tess, who knew the contours of every hill and the twist of every lane around Marlott with an old familiarity, the town of Sharston (Shaftsbury) perched high above the vale, remained her furthest point of reference. With her National School education, Tess seemed remote from her mother's *fast-perishing lumber of superstitions*, but the soft Dorset dialect betrayed her simple country origins.

May Day was still celebrated in the district, but the Marlott Club is unusual in that all the participants dancing in the meadow are women and all are dressed in white except for the red ribbon that sets Tess apart from the rest of the company. The arrival of three strangers on a walking holiday attracts little attention but these educated young men include the desultory figure of Angel Clare. Triggered by the discovery that the family is descended from the ancient line of d'Urbervilles, Tess soon finds herself propelled into the harsh world that awaits her beyond the blue rim of hills. Blaming herself for the death of her father's horse on a journey to Casterbridge market he is too drunk to undertake, Tess reluctantly agrees to seek employment with a rich branch of the d'Urberville family on the edge of Cranborne Chase. Here, according to her mother's 'Compleat Fortune Teller' she will marry a nobleman.

Tess walks out through the vale in the early morning, accompanied by her mother and young sisters, *the group forming a picture of honest beauty flanked by innocence and backed by simple-souled vanity.* Waiting at the top of the hill for the dog cart that will take her to Tantridge, Tess is stranded between two worlds; *behind the green valley of her birth, before, a gray country of which she knew nothing.* Unprepared for the fate that awaits her at the hands of Alec d'Urberville she is in danger of becoming lost in a world of fairytale, the sacrificial victim lured into the dark forest by a wicked wolf. Blighted like one of the apples on her *stubbard tree* by a distant past, she finds herself

Marnhull, the Marlott of *Tess of the d'Urbervilles* with 'The Pure Drop' on the right.

trapped in the narrow confines of the folk ballad tradition in which her tormentor is finally stabbed to death in a seaside boarding house following her relentless pursuit across the Wessex countryside.

Four months later Tess returns to Marlott *a maiden no more*. The vale, bathed in early morning light, evokes painful memories of lost innocence for the young woman who now knows *that the serpent hisses where the sweet birds sing*. All is irredeemably changed and for the first time Tess feels alienated from the land of her childhood, a feeling that is to haunt her for the rest of her short, tragic life. Gazing out over the rich green pastures, the chequer pattern of small fields that once mapped her territory appears *like the meshes of a net* tightening around her. *It was in that vale that her sorrow had taken shape, and she did not love it as formerly. Beauty to her, as to all who have felt, lay not in the thing, but in what the thing symbolized.*

Forced by her situation to support herself and her family she returns to the fields, comforted by friends and determined to resume her old life. The timeless picture of rustic endeavour presented by the company of binders following behind the horse-drawn reaper seems far removed from the

The Vale of Blackmore from the top of Gold Hill, Shaftsbury.

nightmare world of Groby's threshing machine that awaits her at Flintcomb-Ash. But as the reaper bears down on the animals trapped in the last block of standing corn *unaware of the ephemeral nature of their refuge and of the doom that awaited them,* Hardy reminds us that Tess too is a creature of the fields. Death has re-entered the vale and she is left to bury her new-born child, *Sorrow the undesired,* in a corner of the churchyard reserved for suicides and the unbaptised.

By now Tess has acquired a maturity beyond her tender youth and with the arrival of spring she feels *the pulse of hopeful life warm within her.* Wishing above all to escape the painful reminders of her recent past she sets out once more on *a thyme-scented, bird-hatching morning* for the purer air and wider horizons of the Frome valley (see p173). At Talbothays dairy she finds brief happiness in the land of her d'Urberville ancestors, but her marriage to Angel Clare is soon shattered by revelations of her former life and she returns to Marlott humiliated, abandoned and with nowhere to hide. As the net closes in Tess is driven more frantically from one place to another in search of work to support her ailing family.

Flintcomb-Ash

Once Hardy's heroine reaches the bare, windswept downs between the vale of her birth and the valley of her love, she is at the mercy of the world. Events such as the death of Prince or the pheasants dying of gunshot wounds foretell her own violation and death at the hands of man. Wandering across this barren landscape in search of work and shelter, her journeys become more arduous, her movements more laboured, and Parson Tringham's remark to her father, *you don't live anywhere. You are extinct,* take on a painful reality. By the end of summer, work on the small dairy farm where Tess is employed, has dried up. Unwilling to return to Talbothays but in need of work through the winter months, she sets out to join Marian on an upland farm at Flintcomb-Ash, resigned to the worst kind of agricultural labour. Trudging along in an old field gown, her face tells its own sad tale of a woman brought low by *the cruelty of lust and the fragility of love.* As she approaches her destination, her identity lost in a landscape set to the key of winter, she appears as a figure of human suffering in a world grown cold and desolate.

Groby's *starve-acre* farm at Flintcomb-Ash is synonymous with the tyranny of modern agriculture and Hardy was careful to ensure it could not be mistaken for any real place but, within sight of Nettlecomb Tout, the remains of the village are traditionally associated with the hamlet of Plush. Situated in a slight depression to the south of Church Hill, Flintcomb-Ash is only just beyond the Vale of Blackmore. In the short distance between them the view changes dramatically from lush meadows and bosky hedges to a landscape of ruthless efficiency. Fifty years have elapsed since the days of 'Far From the Madding Crowd' and in that time pastures like those grazed by Gabriel Oak's sheep on Norcombe Down, have been transformed into huge arable fields by 'progressive' farmers in response to increased demand for grain and more intensive livestock production. This is now the picture at Flintcomb-Ash, a dreary prospect of root crops and fallow land:

Tess putting flowers on the grave of *Sorrow the Undesired,* from a woodcut by Vivien Gribble.

'Steam Threshing' by John Nash.

Here the air was dry and cold, and the long cart-roads were blown white within a few hours after rain. There were few trees, or none, those that would have grown in the hedges being mercilessly plashed down with the quickset by the tenant-farmers, the natural enemies of tree, bush and brake.

Tess and Marion are put to work hacking swedes in a remote field. As they crawl *like flies* across its huge, stony surface, forced to work on through rain that *raced along horizontally upon the yelling wind, sticking into them like glass splinters till they were wet through*, it would be difficult to imagine a more desolate spot. The rain is a foretaste of more severe weather and the onset of winter that *came in stealthy and measured glides like the moves of a chess-player* has an eerie beauty. Cold, moist air covering everything in white rind is followed by a period of dry frost *when strange birds from behind the North Pole began to arrive silently on the uplands of Flintcomb-Ash; gaunt spectral creatures with tragical eyes.*

The Cerne Abbas giant

Untroubled by their new companions and sustained by talk of happier days at Talbothays dairy, the two women work on through the most appaling conditions until the task of threshing last year's harvest brings with it a new, more brutal regime. The appearance of the steam traction engine had begun to revolutionise agricultural work in late 19th century Wessex, replacing the horse power and hand labour that had for centuries served the rural economy. This symbol of the industrial age was, like the railways, a powerful new force invading the countryside and Hardy reserved his most bitter condemnation for its alien master:

He was in the agricultural world, but not of it. He served fire and smoke; these denizens of the fields served vegetation, weather, frost and sun .... He spoke in a strange northern accent; his thoughts being turned inwards upon himself, his eye on his iron charge, hardly perceiving the scenes around him, and caring for them not at all: holding only strictly necessary intercourse with the natives, as if some ancient doom compelled him to wander here against his will in the service of his Plutonic master.

Throughout the novel images of a single colour circumscribe the fate of Hardy's *pure woman*, from the red ribbon to the bloodstain on the ceiling of a Sandbourne boarding house and from the redbrick mansion at Tantridge to the gaolhouse at Wintoncester. Red is the colour of lust and procreation, red is the house of death and there is blood on the tracks as Tess is hounded across the chalk uplands like a wounded animal. Cornered in the stackyard at Flintcomb-Ash, she is crucified on the *red tyrant* of progress by a sadistic taskmaster and a lecherous tormentor with blood oozing from a blow to the mouth that will flow more freely before Tess herself is dead. When all is ready Groby arrives *and by his orders Tess was placed upon the platform of the* (threshing) *machine* as though on some instrument of torture. Exhausted by the work she continues in a *stupefied reverie*, her movements by now entirely automatic, preferring the noise and relentless shaking of the contraption to the company of her old persecutor, and so she remains feeding the insatiable beast until the last sheaf has been devoured.

Cross-in-Hand

On the return leg of her abortive pilgrimage to the home of Clare's parents at Enminster (Beaminster) in Marshwood Vale, Tess is overtaken on the old ridgeway track by a reformed Alec d'Urberville at a place called Cross-in-Hand. *Of all spots on the bleached and desolate upland this was the most forlorn.* The origins of the stone monolith upon which was roughly carved a human hand, were a matter of speculation. According to d'Urberville, now an itinerant preacher, it was the base of a holy cross on which he makes Tess swear never to tempt him again, but in a landscape *bosomed with semi-globular tumuli* and strewn with phallic-shaped flints, Tess discovers that the stone is *a thing of ill-omen* erected to mark the grave of a thief. The unfortunate wretch had been nailed by his hand to a post on the spot before his execution. Below her in the Cerne valley the figure of Hercules asserts his virility on a hillside above the ruined abbey. The old gods still demand retribution and as d'Urberville leaves Tess to deliver a sermon in the shadow of the giant, his religious conversion is soon tested. *The President of the Immortals* has not yet *ended his sport with Tess.*

When news of her mother's illness reaches Tess at Flintcomb-Ash she trudges across the barren uplands towards Marlott for the last time to be greeted by a scene of despondency and dereliction in tune with her own forlorn state. Known locally as a slack-twisted fellow Sir John, like many in the village, spent more time in The Pure Drop than he ever did in church or on his allotment. His weakness for drink and idle chatter had of late been compounded by delusions of ancient lineage, but his decline from respectable tradesman to homeless peasant has more to do with the break up of life in the Wessex countryside than his own personal failings. Hardy had already written about the plight of the agricultural poor in his essay 'The Dorsetshire Labourer' (1883) but here rural depopulation and migratory labour are set in the context of personal tragedy. Tess Durbeyfield's reappearance in Marlott is seen by some as a threat to the moral welfare of the village and, on the death of her father, the cottage is soon let to a more deserving family. The next day is Lady Day and, banished from the vale, Tess and her mother join the general exodus of farm labourers in search of work. They head out over the downs for King's Bere to claim sanctuary in the land of their ancestors with the sound of the legendary d'Urberville coach still ringing in their ears.

The Turberville window in Bere Regis church (King's Bere) where, having left Marlott, Tess discovers the tombs of her ancestors.

Hermitage

Hardy began developing the story that became his favourite novel as early as 1874 but, following the success of 'Far From The Madding Crowd' (1874), he wished to avoid the reputation of Country Life novelist so early in his career and the idea was shelved until 1887 when it appeared as ***The Woodlanders***. As the title suggests, the novel is concerned with the life of an isolated rural community but unlike Egdon Heath, where the author was happy to provide readers with a map of the area, the topography of 'The Woodlanders' has proved more elusive to those for whom the identification of place is so important to the enjoyment of Hardy's fiction.

Beasts of the forest writhe on the Norman font at Melbury Bubb.

Little Hintock, the hamlet buried deep in the woods, lies at the foot of the hills that rise dramatically above the vale, but even Hermann Lea, indefatigable cartographer of Hardy's Wessex, was uncertain about its exact location. Hardy's mother had been brought up in Melbury Osmond and the novel was to have been set in the village with the hall as Hintock House, but Hardy decided to shift the whole estate several miles to the east below High Stoy for fear that the disreputable Felice Charmond might be mistaken for a member of the Ilchester family. By following the instructions given to Barber Percomb at the beginning of the novel, the reader comes eventually to the hamlet of Hermitage. The intervening woods are said to represent the landscape of the novel, but the setting remains unconvincing. Melbury Osmond is still the estate village of Little Hintock where Giles Winterborne is buried and the charcoal burner's hut where he dies is just beyond the estate at Delborough (Chelborough) in King's Hintock Wood. The surnames given to Grace Melbury and Felice Charmond (cf Osmond), confirm Hardy's preference for the original setting below Bubb Down although he was more concerned to create a forgotten world where a sense of the past is, for once, more important than geographic reality. In response to queries as to the precise whereabouts of Little Hintock Hardy confessed with some amusement; *to oblige readers I once spent several hours on a bicycle with a friend in a serious attempt to discover the exact spot; but the search ended in failure.*

Turnworth House (demolished), the model for Hintock House in ***The Woodlanders***.

For the timber merchant George Melbury or for those, like Marty South, who supply him with thatching spars, the woodland provides a livelihood and they negotiate its pathways with familiar assurance. But as the story unfolds, the author's 'confusion' soon spreads to those outsiders who intrude upon this secretive world - in this context the name Hermitage becomes appropriate - and find themselves entangled in the undergrowth. The barber from Sherton (Sherborne), lost in the lanes around Little Hintock, is followed by the stranger

The Dorset Oozer mask from the village of Melbury Osmond, home of Hardy's mother and the model for Little Hintock.

with the hat who loses a sense of both time and place in the woods and by Dr Fitzpiers, lured into its darkest recesses by Suke Damson. But this is Midsummer's Eve when the nymphs of Little Hintock hope to catch a glimpse of their future partners. The wood becomes populated by *weird shadows and ghostly nooks of indistinctness* when the *imagination could trace amid the trunks and boughs swarthy faces and funereal figures*. A year later, as Grace Melbury picks her way carefully through the trees in search of Giles, those same spectral shapes and *faint cloven tongues* are banished from her mind. Fear for the safety of her old sweetheart and a past she can no longer reclaim has a greater urgency.

Hardy is no longer content simply to celebrate rural life and there are only hints of the seasonal festivals that colour his earlier novels. References to legend and fairytale are used to highlight human frailty in a community forsaken by the world on the edge of a deserted highway. Too deeply rooted in the past to survive and too apathetic to withstand external forces, Little Hintock is overwhelmed by lethargy and decay. It is *one of those sequestered spots outside the gates of the world where may usually be found more meditation than action and more listlessness than meditation*. Until the appearance of Fitzpiers and Mrs Charmond, nothing much disturbs the place and news arrives *like the exhausted swell of a wave in some innermost creek*. The countryside around may be rich and productive but life in Little Hintock is draining away; it deserves its diminutive. Like the woods that were once part of a great medieval forest, the village has shrunk to a few cottages and farmsteads scattered around Melbury's old manor house and become enveloped in the Hintock estate.

'The Woodlanders' differs from all Hardy's novels in that there is no single protagonist and the voice of his rustic chorus, consigned to the timberyard and marginal to the life of the novel, is taken up by the greenwood sighing and grieving for the whole community. The mood is above all reflective, sustained by memory and association and a sense of time past. To Grace Melbury, sent away to be educated by an ambitious father, the place appears on her return as *dear old Hintock* and the familiar woodland colours are now like *an old painting restored*. Characters unable to express their feelings or consumed by restless energy are condemned to lives of isolation within the estranged world of Little Hintock. There is little real sense of community and love unrequited spreads throughout the social order like a disease. Giles Winterborne has a *marvellous power to make trees grow* but is unaware of the love growing within the young woman beside him. Until his death Marty South's silent discourse is with the young saplings they plant together:

Hardly anything could be more isolated or more self-contained than the lives of these two walking here in the lonely hour before day .... And yet their lonely courses formed no detached design at all, but were part of the pattern in the great web of human doings then weaving in both hemispheres from the White Sea to Cape Horn.

The dissatisfaction felt by outsiders who drift into Little Hintock and become entangled in the lives of its inhabitants, takes the form of amorous diversions and economic exploitation with disturbing consequences. Alone in a house she finds oppressive, Felice Charmond longs to escape the *miserable little hole* in

Old Beech trees with *vast arm-pits and great pocket-hole.*

Girl in a Dorset cottage c1890.

search of amusement and the wig, made from hair Marty South is forced to sell, makes her more desirable in the eyes of Fitzpiers. On the death of Marty's father the lease on a number of cottages reverts to the estate and Mrs Charmond's decision to have them demolished makes Giles homeless and less eligible as a husband for Grace. When, shortly after, her carriage overturns at the corner where Giles' cottage used to stand, Felice is thrown into the arms of Dr Fitzpiers and an uncertain future. Grace, finding herself suspended between *two storeys of society* experiences what Hardy called *the ache of modernism*. No longer comfortable in the company of the woodlanders and beyond the reach of her childhood sweetheart, she is finally resigned to an unhappy marriage in some Midland town with an unfaithful husband. Winterborne, with his homely virtues and country skills, represents all that is good in Little Hintock but his love for Grace cannot bridge the gulf between their two worlds. His death at the end of the novel signals the destruction of a way of life celebrated by Hardy in his early novels.

Although the woodlanders are industrious their movements appear cloaked in an atmosphere of drowsy intoxication that drifts through the novel. The air is heavy with wood smoke and the scent of cider apples rising from cottage doorways to mingle with the smell of rotting leaves. Things are seen through a smoky haze, dense fog or dappled sunlight that distort the picture. The emphasis on certain features and the omission of others to convey atmosphere was a technique developed by Hardy as a result of attending the new Impressionist exhibition in London while working on the novel. He was especially influenced by the *much decried, mad, late Turner* at a time when he became more interested in *the deeper reality underlying the scenic*. This new style is evident from the beginning of the novel when Barber Percomb finds Marty South's cottage *in an exceptional state of radiance, the flickering brightness from the inside shining up the chimney and making a luminous mist of the emerging smoke*. Drawing closer he sees *an impression-picture of extremest type, wherein the girl's hair alone, as the focus of observation, was depicted by intensity and distinctness*. Elsewhere the colour of scenes is enriched as though seen through a stained glass window or painted on a magic lantern slide. Hardy's picture of the vale bathed in autumnal light is painted more in the rich allegorical style of Samuel Palmer than the agricultural detail of a Constable landscape and he uses the effect to re-examine the relationship between Grace and her husband at a critical time. Accompanying Fitzpiers to the top of High Stoy she bids him farewell:

And so the infatuated surgeon went along through the gorgeous autumn landscape of White-Hart Vale, surrounded by orchards lustrous with the reds of apple-crops, berries, and foliage, the whole intensified by the gilding of the declining sun. The earth this year had been prodigally bountiful, and now was the supreme moment after bounty. In the poorest spots the hedges were bowed with haws and blackberries; acorns cracked underfoot, and the burst husks of chestnuts lay exposing their auburn contents.

Grace's pleasure in this abundance is tinged with regret at the sterility of her own predicament as she watches Fitzpiers ride forth, knowing the real purpose of his journey. Her husband's family from Oakebury Fitzpiers (Okeford Fitzpaine) is one of the oldest in the vale and a matter of some pride to Grace's father, but as Eldred plods off into the distance he becomes a parody of the chivalrous knight, reduced to a tragi-comical figure that is more Pelinor than Percival. 'Darling', the horse he rides, was given to his wife by Giles in the hope of winning her hand, and as he disappears over the hill reciting Shelley - *Towards the loadstar of my one desire / I flitted, like a dizzy moth, whose flight / Is as a dead leaf's in the owlet light*, - his mind is filled with thoughts of Felice Charmond awaiting him at Middleton Abbey (Milton Abbas). Giles Winterborne was in the apple trade and each year at this time he travels the district with his cider press. He emerges from the vale *impersonating chivalrous and undiluted manliness* just as Fitzpiers moves out of sight:

Itinerant workers pressing cider apples in a Dorset farmyard.

He looked and smelt like Autumn's very brother, his face being sunburnt to wheat-colour, his eyes blue as corn-flowers, his sleeves and leggings dyed with fruit-stains, his hands clammy with the sweet juice of apples, his hat sprinkled with pips, and everywhere about him that atmosphere of cider which .... has such an indescribable fascination for those who have been born and bred among the orchards. Her heart rose from its late sadness like a released bough; her senses revelled in the sudden lapse back to Nature unadorned.

As so often Grace is caught between the past and the present. While dismissing any heroic suggestions, her *passionate desire for primitive life* is momentarily aroused by the man standing before her and as they gaze out over the western sky their minds are free to journey together through the heavens. Later in the novel when she is recovering from illness, Giles rises *upon her memory as the fruit-god and the wood-god in alternation*, but only when Grace discovers him dying of fever does she see clearly *the purity of his nature, his freedom from the grosser passions, his scrupulous delicacy* that until then she had either ignored or dismissed as merely fanciful.

Characters refuse to be lured into a world of folk tale and romance suggested by the references to tree worship and the wildwood that echo throughout the novel. Images of innocence and honour are either evidence of lingering superstition or are quickly dispelled by Hardy's use of literary conventions to underline human weakness and Victorian morality. When Fitzpiers, wandering through the wood on a spring evening, is entertained by Melbury and his men with tales of adventure and witchcraft, he becomes captivated by the scene. Lingering before the dying fire, the air heavy with the smell of sap and the song of a nightingale, he falls to musing on his encounter with Grace and the idea of settling in this enchanted spot. Some days later his curiosity is aroused by the lithe movements of his beloved when he catches site of Grace, dressed

Green man with vine leaves depicted on a roof boss in the nave of Sherborne Abbey.

in white and *sylph-like,* in a clearing. For a moment she becomes a fairy princess and rare creature of the forest but the white hart, from which the vale takes its name, was once hunted by his ancestors and the knowledge that he has just come from the arms of Suke Damson leaves Grace with a bitter taste. Like Sergeant Troy and Alec d'Urberville, Fitzpiers is closer to the villain of Victorian melodrama than the knight of courtly love. The primaeval forest, reduced now to a working wood managed by an estate that until recently had employed the mantrap to dispense its own savage justice, has lost much of its mythical quality. Dazzled by the brilliance of Fitzpiers, Grace too becomes ensnared in a world of which she has little experience.

As E M Forster pointed out, trees rustle through the book. There are trees everywhere; in the park, in the hedgerows and in the woods, trees that are planted and cut down, shed limbs in winter, come into leaf each spring. The reader is invited to peer through a tangled mass of branches like some mischievous creature and observe the dramas being played out in the lanes and glades of Little Hintock. The great pollarded elms in the grounds of Hintock Hall and the huge twisted beech trees in more remote parts of the wood are, like the hamlet itself, remnants of a medieval landscape. These magnificent specimens, *the half-dead oak, hollow and disfigured with white tumours* or the *old beech, with vast arm-pits and great pocket-holes in its sides where branches have been removed* were, for Hardy, symbolic of the way in which rural life was being attacked by the disease of modernism. After the storm Grace looks out of the hut on a scene of dereliction; *dead boughs were scattered about like ichthyosauri in a museum* while, unbeknown to her, Giles lies outside in a hovel dying of fever:

all she could see were more trees, in jackets of lichen and stockings of moss. At their roots were stemless yellow fungi like lemons and apricots, and tall fungi with more stem than stool. Next were more trees close together, wrestling for existence, their branches disfigured with wounds resulting from their mutual rubbings and blows .... Beneath them were the rotting stumps of those of the group that had been vanquished long ago, rising from their mossy setting like black teeth from green gums.

The smell of death is everywhere. All vegetable matter is either diseased or parasitic and reflects Hardy's interest in the ideas of natural selection prevalent at the time; a view of nature unthinkable today in the context of bio-diversity. More ominous perhaps are the rows of alien young fir trees planted by Giles that even in Hardy's day were beginning to disfigure the Dorset landscape. Just as the novel opens with the solitary figure of Marty South in the firelight, so it ends with her graveside vigil. She alone *had approximated to Winterborne's level of intelligent intercourse with nature* and, following Grace's departure, she is finally free to claim his memory. Finding her voice for the first time, her soft Dorset dialect rising in the moonlight is a lament not just for the man she had loved but for the way of life they shared. Marty South, who has sworn to continue Giles' work, will survive, but the life of the Woodlanders is already fading as Hardy turns to contemplate the bleak prospect of Flintcomb-Ash.

Coppice woodland from a line drawing by Robin Tanner.

4

Precarious Pleasures
West
Dorset

the remarkable situation of the town, the principal street almost hurrying into the water, the walk to the Cobb, skirting round the pleasant little bay, which in the season is animated with bathing machines and company, the Cobb itself, its old wonders and new improvements, with the very beautiful line of cliffs stretching over to the east of the town, are what the stranger's eye will seek; and a very strange stranger it must be, who does not see charms in the immediate environs of Lyme .... The scenes in its neighbourhood, Charmouth, with its high grounds and extensive sweeps of country, and still more its sweet retired bay, backed by dark cliffs, where fragments of low rock among the sands make it the happiest spot .... for sitting in unwearied contemplation.

From *Persuasion* by **Jane Austen**

Lyme Regis

Arriving in Lyme in the summer of 1982, the American travel writer **Paul Theroux** became the latest in a long succession of visitors to marvel at the town's precarious foothold. *Delicately made and seeming to defy gravity,* (it) *seemed magnetised to its steep cliffs.* Spurred on by the thought of stumbling across a dead body, his walk from Charmouth soon turned into a dash for safety as he was forced up onto the sea wall by a swiftly rising tide. *But the wall was covered in sea-slime, and so it was very slippery. I crossed it on all fours and at Lyme I felt as if I had won a close race.* Obliged to slither over rocks, slip on muddy paths and tumble down steps in Lyme, fictional characters have been brought to their knees in much the same way for the last 200 years to the consternation of the reading public.

Jane Austen never concealed her dislike for Bath and family holidays at one of the more discreet south coast towns were anticipated with more than usual excitement by all the Austen children. The Devon resorts of Sidmouth and Dawlish were succeeded in an easterly progression by a visit to Lyme in November 1803. The family returned the following summer and Jane remained with her parents while brother and sister negotiated the more fashionable distractions of Weymouth. The town and its surroundings were much to her liking but she found Lyme society a little provincial. From her account of the weekly ball held in the Assembly Rooms, pulled down recently, according to

Jane Austen
(1775 - 1817)

113

John Fowles, *by a Town Council single-minded in its concern for the communal bladder*, the sea air had clearly revived her talent for caustic asides. The Barnwalls, related to an Irish viscount, were *queer-looking people just fit to be quality at Lyme* and Miss Armstrong was *very conversational in a common way; I do not perceive wit or genius but she has sense and some degree of taste, and her manners are very engaging. She seems to like people rather too easily.* But for many Lyme will always be associated with a singular dramatic incident in **Persuasion** (1818) in which the Musgrove family decide to make up a party and visit Lyme where Captain Wentworth's friend Captain Harville has settled in lodgings on Marine Parade. Before bidding farewell, the party decide to take one last walk along the great stone breakwater:

Lyme became something of a literary shrine in 1818 with the publication of **Persuasion** in which Louisa Musgrove takes her now celebrated tumble down the steps known as Granny's Teeth.

Thatch cottages on Marine Parade.

There was too much wind to make the high part of the new Cobb pleasant for the ladies, and they agreed to get down the steps to the lower, and all were contented to pass quietly and carefully down the steep flight, excepting Louisa; she must be jumped down them by Captain Wentworth .... The hardness of the pavement for her feet, made him less willing .... he did it, however; she was safely down, and instantly, to shew her enjoyment, ran up the steps to be jumped down again. He advised her against it, thought the jar too great; but no, he reasoned and talked in vain; she smiled and said, 'I am determined I will:' he put out his hands; she was too precipitate by half a second, she fell on the pavement on the Lower Cobb and was taken up lifeless!

The model for Captain Harville's lodgings where Louisa was taken to recuperate is thought by some to be the pink thatched house on Marine Parade. Others favour Bay Cottage, now a cafe, at the west end of the Parade but Lyme has changed much since Jane Austen's visit. Aware perhaps of its tourist potential, the uneven flight of steps known locally as Granny's Teeth is, by general agreement, the scene of Louisa's accident. According to his son, **Tennyson** set out along the cliff-top path from Bridport in 1867 intent on acquainting himself with the resort depicted in the novel. On arriving at the home of his friend Francis Palgrave, Tennyson refused offers of refreshment and demanded, *now take me to the Cobb, and show me the exact spot where Louisa Musgrove fell.*

Between the wars a succession of literary figures stayed at one of the town's two principal hotels.

The Poet Laureate's visit firmly established the town as a literary shrine and since then writers and the reading public have jostled each other to pay homage at the foot of Jane Austen's well-worn steps. As a result, few places of its size have such a fine literary pedigree; a heritage every bit as rich as its fossil-strewn foreshore. Kenneth Grahame stopped to inspect the Cobb on a trip to Cornwall in 1912, E M Forster was here in February 1921 and a few years later G K Chesterton, another admirer of Austen's work, signed in at the Three Cups on the first of several visits. J R R Tolkein, who as a boy had been brought here by his guardian Father Morgan, returned with his own family between the wars and Beatrix Potter, leafing through some early sketch books, decided to illustrate her last book, 'The Tale of Little Pig Robinson' (1930), with drawings made in 1904 on a childhood holiday in Lyme.

The poet **C Day Lewis** discovered the delights of sailing while on holiday in 1936 and two years later he decided to buy the thatch cottage at Musbury in the Axe valley that was to be his home for the next twelve years. Throughout his life he wrote a series of popular detective novels in the name of Nicholas Blake. One of the earliest and most successful, 'The Beast Must Die' (1938), begins and ends against a background of Lyme and the Dorset coast. In it the murderer dies adrift in his dinghy *fighting a clean enemy for a change - the wind and the sea*. He is, not surprisingly, a writer of detective stories and in his autobiography 'The Buried Day' (1960) the author recalled the sensation of sailing in Lyme Bay. *The sea puts me into a trance of pleasure, deepest on a blowy day when the waves sparkled and Golden Cap glowed in the sun .... I spent hours in a pure, timeless present, mind and body responding to each slant of wind, drenched with the salty sunshine.*

Another writer to evoke happy memories of Lyme was **Llewelyn Powys**. Towards the end of the last century the whole Powys family left Montacute for the first of several annual holidays on the Dorset coast. They often stayed in Ozone Terrace at the western extremity of the town, a splendid affirmation of the sea air's restorative quality. Here the secretive pleasures of the Undercliff were a more appealing alternative to the windswept reaches of the Cobb. *A hundred dells with secret silent lawns surrounded by rankest undergrowth* became their fairy glade. Powys' response to this magical atmosphere echoed that of Tennyson years earlier: *This exactly represents some of the romantic landscape before the mind's eye in the Idylls: little winding glades, closed all around with grassy mounds and wild shrubs, where one might fancy the sudden appearance of a knight riding, or a spell-bound damsel.* With the Undercliff covered in hawthorn blossom the scent was, for Powys, of a languorous promiscuity hanging in the air, *a rich smell, redolent of a careless happy sensuality*; and the tales recounted to his brother Willie were of late summer afternoons *spent with buxom nursemaids tumbling in the bracken*.

The view from Broad Street out across Lyme Bay to Golden Cap.

In the early 19c two momentous events occurred along the notoriously unstable cliff-line that shattered the genteel atmosphere of Lyme and reshaped its literary landscape more profoundly than Louisa Musgrove's reckless descent. The cliffs towards Charmouth are composed of Blue Lias, an outcrop of Jurassic shales crammed full of fossilised marine life. With each new rock fall the shoreline is littered with rich pickings for the amateur geologist. In 1811, while digging among the rocks at the foot of Black Venn cliff, Mary Anning unearthed the most complete Ichthyosaurus, or fish lizard, to have been found anywhere. It was a defining moment in British palaeontology and, encouraged by the importance of her discovery, her renewed efforts were rewarded by more exciting finds, notably the winged reptile Pterodactylus. As an enterprising young woman Mary earned a living selling specimens in Lyme but failed to receive the official recognition she deserved from scientists, many of whom used her discoveries to enhance their own reputations.

The old fossil shop where *can be purchased, at the same counter, fresh prawns or fossil ammonites, filleted soles or pieces of a saurian backbone.*

The Undercliff from the Cobb.

To the west of the town the geological confusion of densely wooded outcrops known as the Undercliff is one of the most remarkable lengths of coastline in Britain. For centuries the cliff-face has been slithering seaward, the result of rainwater seeping through layers of porous chalk and greensand to meet a thin band of impervious clay. Jane Austen described the scene above Pinhay Bay:

... with its green chasms between romantic rocks, where the scattered forest trees and orchards of luxuriant growth declare that many a generation must have passed away since the first partial falling of the cliff prepared the ground for such a state, where a scene so wonderful and so lovely is exhibited ....

The most spectacular landslip occurred on Christmas Eve in 1839 when, after months of heavy rain, great fissures began to appear in the cliff-top fields at Downlands Farm. Some 50 acres of farmland sheered away from the cliff-face taking with it several cottages and came to rest in the sea leaving a huge chasm nearly a mile long. In ***The French Lieutenant's Woman*** (1969) **John Fowles** provides an aerial sweep over this strangely beautiful wilderness: *The cultivated chequer of green and red-brown breaks, with a kind of joyous indiscipline, into a dark cascade of trees and undergrowth .... the terrain is very abrupt, cut by deep chasms and accented by strange bluffs and towers of chalk and flint, which loom over the lush foliage around them like the walls of ruined castles.*

The whole area is one great suntrap fed by countless streams, a lost world of dense primaeval forest, *its green Brazilian chasms choked with ivy and the liana of wild clematis.* In these humid ravines the flowers bloom earlier, the trees grow taller and the shrubs thicker than elsewhere. Stumbling along the coast path through a tangle of vegetation, the walker finds himself suspended between the sea, far below and out of sight, and the chalk cliff-face rearing up and disappearing into the mist, the peace disturbed only by the occasional roe deer crashing through the undergrowth or the cry of a buzzard wheeling overhead. Otherwise the place is shrouded in an eerie silence; *there are crevices and sudden falls that can bring disaster, and places where a man with a broken leg could shout all week and not be heard.*

The Cobb snakes out into the water like some petrified sea monster, a bifurcation of fossil-rich limestone protecting Lyme from the most ferocious southwesterly seas. The Dorset topographer Frederick Treves thought it had *the curve of a shepherd's crook, with an adventitious tentacle of masonry projecting from the summit of its bend. It wanders into the water in a hesitating manner which is quite in keeping with the uncertainty of the town.* Llewelyn Powys, sounding more like Kenneth Grahame, thought the extraordinary structure gave Lyme *its idiosyncratic character .... from the hills above, it takes on the appearance of a vole's flat tail left dangling in the water outside its slippery retreat.* For John Fowles, Lyme's most celebrated resident, the Cobb is quite simply *a superb fragment of folk-art. Primitive yet complex, elephantine but delicate; as full of subtle curves and volumes as a Henry Moore or a Michelangelo.*

Rebuilt with huge blocks of Portland stone after the great storm of 1826, the Cobb stands as a monument to nineteenth century engineering, and a dramatic stage on which Fowles introduces his enigmatic heroine. By her presence the *scarlet woman of Lyme* challenges the solid mass of prejudice embedded in the very structure on which she stands. Shrouded in black she gazes out to sea

John Fowles beside the Cobb.

The Cobb snaking out into the water with Black Venn and Golden Cap in the distance.

more like a figure from myth, than any fragment of the petty provincial day. As Charles Smithson approaches, the woman turns and he beholds a face, not conventionally pretty, but one that he can never forget. In this single encounter the memory of Louisa Musgrove and all the heroines of Victorian fiction is shattered by the French lieutenant's woman, a strange Pre-Raphaelite character forever associated with Meryl Streep in the 1981 screen adaptation.

Lyme has always seemed a treacherous place. Each year, with its gentility a little more tarnished, the town threatens to slip further downhill but, underpinned by a rigid social hierarchy, has always managed to defy the law of gravity. The Georgian houses, stacked one above the other up Broad Street or clinging like limpets to the wooded slopes, rival each other for the most impressive view of the bay. The more fashionable visitors have always taken their exercise on Marine Parade and the Cobb, unaware that from above they might be scrutinized by those with a particular interest in their movements. For Lyme, as Fowles makes clear, was *a town with sharp eyes* that bristled with gossip. With its grounds protected by mantraps, the elegant Regency property known as Marlborough House is a fortified eyrie to one of Lyme's most tyrannical and predatory residents. Mrs Poultenay was *like some plump vulture, endlessly circling in her endless leisure* and her prey was the French lieutenant's whore whose elevation to the status of companion had been achieved by the same sense of Christian duty that motivated all Mrs Poultenay's actions. Her rivalry with Lady Cotton for the dispensation of charity is like the *thunderous clash of two brontosauri* doomed to extinction as surely as the Great Bustard shot by Charles on his uncle's Wiltshire estate.

Regency villas on the slopes above Lyme peer out across the bay like Mrs Poultenay in her clifftop eyrie.

Ware Commons forms the most accessible part of the Undercliff frequented by poachers and gypsies and is, by general consent, a place for secret assignations. Here among the outcasts and sinners and away from prying eyes, Sarah Woodruff could be alone with her thoughts. Mrs Poultenay had no need to venture far in search of *poor Tragedy*. The housekeeper was her willing spy and, furnished with malicious reports of Miss Woodruff's movements and regular doses of laudanum, the lady of Marlborough House could well imagine the scenes of debauchery that, according to tradition, took place deep in the woods on Midsummer's night. Sarah was forbidden to go there again but, *she saw through the follies, the vulgar stained glass, the narrow literalness of the Victorian church.* She saw through Mrs Poultenay and by continuing to defy her employer, deliberately sealed her fate.

As Lymers are quick to point out, the woodland springs have made the Undercliff notoriously unstable, and when on a bright morning Charles stumbles up through the undergrowth from Pinhay Bay in search of fossils, he enters a world shaken out of its theological complacency by the appearance of Lyell's 'Principles of Geology' (1830-33) and undermined more dramatically by the recent publication of Darwin's 'The Origin of Species' (1859). Haunted by the tragic face of Sarah Woodruff, from which sorrow welled up *as purely, naturally and unstoppably as water out of a woodland spring,* he was quite unprepared for the repressed emotions about to overwhelm him in the timeless luxuriance of this Garden of Eden:

The ground about him was studded gold and pale yellow with celandines and primroses and banked by the bridal white of densely blossoming sloe; where jubilantly green-tipped elders shaded the mossy banks of the little brook he had drunk from were clusters of moschatel and woodsorrel, most delicate of English spring flowers. Higher up the slope he saw the white heads of anemones, and beyond them deep green drifts of bluebell leaves. A distant woodpecker drummed in the branches of some high tree, and bullfinches whistled quietly over his head; newly arrived chiffchaffs and willow-warblers sang in every bush and treetop. When he turned he saw the blue sea, now washing far below; and the whole extent of Lyme Bay reaching round, diminishing cliffs that dropped into the endless yellow sabre of the Chesil Bank, whose remote tip touched that strange English Gibraltar, Portland Bill, a thin grey shadow wedged between azures.

For Tennyson and Llewelyn Powys these alpine meadows were home to fabulous beasts and medieval knights, but Fowles preferred to see them as *the ground that Botticelli's figures walk on, the air that includes Ronsard's songs.* **The French Lieutenant's Woman** is a modern novel and the Renaissance, that *green end of one of civilization's hardest winters,* reminds us of all that the Victorians failed to achieve. The author guides his disorientated hero through a tangled mass of branches and out onto a grassy platform where below him lies the figure of a woman asleep, hair fallen loosely across her face. Charles finds the picture of innocence both tender and disturbingly erotic when, at that moment, Sarah awakens to return his gaze and *in those brief poised seconds above the waiting sea, in that luminous evening silence broken only by the waves' quiet wash, the whole Victorian Age was lost.*

In the days that follow Charles becomes increasingly obsessed with this mysterious creature of the Undercliff, a rare exotic bird driven off course by the wind of change blowing through *the century's stale metaphysical corridors.* She fell into no category of woman he had ever encountered, displayed none of the female deference of her age but *seemed almost to assume some sort of equality of intellect with him.* When Sarah slips on the muddy path and is helped to her feet by Charles, he still refuses to join with the rest of Lyme in believing she is truly a fallen woman. Only later, seizing the opportunity to throw herself on his mercy, Sarah 'confesses' that, unable to marry Vargennes, she had given herself to the French lieutenant and so *married shame.* In this way it is the startled creature with hair the colour of a vixen's coat who springs

The view of Lyme from the Cobb, *with the principal street almost hurrying into the water,* described by Jane Austen in **Persuasion**.

the trap, ensnaring Charles in her loneliness and vulnerability long before the explosive encounter in an Exeter hotel reveals the true nature of her relationship with the Frenchman.

Before their final meeting in the Undercliff, Charles is dispatched to his uncle's Wiltshire estate. As the coach turns into the ancestral park and the Palladian mansion comes into view he is filled with a reassuring sense of order and continuity evoked by the familiar landscape. The disturbing events of recent days begin to fade into the prospect of his rightful inheritance. Duty, he acknowledges, will always be both his mistress and his wife. Winsyatt is situated in rolling parkland between Chippenham and the downs where, three years later, a young lovesick curate wandered musing over the loss of his beloved Ettie Brown (see p17). In a novel illuminated by authorial asides and the contemporary voice of Victorian poets, Fowles is strangely silent about the position of Winsyatt in what has become 'Kilvert country', all the more curious because the curate's diary reveals a man who, in his honesty and passionate response to life, had more in common with Fowles' heroine than her conventional Victorian admirer. On his return to Lyme, Charles discovers that Miss Woodruff has been dismissed for continuing to frequent Ware Commons and that by his uncle's decision to marry he is effectively disinherited. The twin props of Duty and Respectability have finally been removed and Charles is cast adrift on a sea of doubt and self recrimination:

... there entered his mind a brief image of that ancient disaster he had found recorded in the blue lias and brought back to Ernestina - the ammonites caught in some recession of water, a micro-catastrophe of ninety million years ago. In a vivid insight, a flash of black lightning, he saw that all life was parallel: that evolution was not vertical, ascending to a perfection, but horizontal. Time was the great fallacy; existence was without history, was always now, was always this being caught in the same fiendish machine. All those painted screens erected by man to shut out reality - history, religion, duty, social position, all were illusions, mere opium fantasies.

A scribbled note from Sarah awaits him at the White Lion and the following morning as he slips out into the half light his despair is quickly dispelled by the sea air *as sharp as lemon juice.* Leaving the town behind his spirits rise to meet the day as though somehow prepared for the fate that awaits him:

It seemed strangely distinct, this undefiled dawn sun. It had almost a smell, as of warm stone, a sharp dust of photons streaming down through space. Each grass-blade was pearled with vapour .... above his path the trunks of the ashes and sycamores, a honey gold in the oblique sunlight, erected their dewy green vaults of young leaves; there was something mysteriously religious about them, but of a religion before religion; a druidic balm.

A fox crosses the path untroubled by Charles' presence and a little further on a roe-deer browsing the undergrowth looks up *with the same divine assumption of possession,* as though <u>he</u> was the intruder in a place unsullied by man and charged with unutterable grace. The air was alive with birdsong and Charles *felt himself walking through the pages of a bestiary*, filled by a sense of wondrous co-existence with all nature:

He stopped for a moment, so struck was he by this sense of an exquisitely particular universe, in which each was appointed, each unique. A tiny wren perched on top of a bramble not ten feet from him and trilled its violent song. He saw its glittering black eyes, the red and yellow of its song-gaped throat - a midget ball of feathers that yet managed to make itself the Announcing Angel of evolution .... The appalling ennui of human reality lay cleft to the core; and the heart of all life pulsed there in the wren's triumphant throat ....

There was a more immediate bitterness to this natural eucharist, since Charles felt in all ways excommunicated. He was shut out, all paradise lost. Again, he was like Sarah - he could stand here in Eden, but not enjoy it, and only envy the wren its ecstasy.

Underhill Farm. John Fowles lived here while writing **The French Lieutenant's Woman**.

With a sense of rising panic Charles makes his way to the thatched barn where Sarah has taken shelter. On awakening, *there was a wildness about her. Not the wildness of lunacy or hysteria - but that same wildness Charles had sensed in the wren's singing .... a wildness of innocence, almost an eagerness.* He had come to help her leave Lyme but found her passion irresistible and *the moment overcame the age.* But as Fowles argues, it is Smithson's inability to recognise the woman's feeling and imagination that represent his greatest defect and he remains trapped in the age he had come to epitomise.

The thatched barn was half ruinous when Fowles invented it, but just over the Devon border and half hidden by trees stands the abandoned shell of Underhill Farm where the novel was written. Even as Fowles sat there like some doomed Conrad character in his earthly paradise writing the story in which the most rigidly held beliefs of the Victorian era were effectively undermined, the house was itself slowly cracking and shifting on foundations just as questionable. With the help of royalties from the book's phenomenal success he was able to retreat to safer ground and a more substantial edifice, but for all its elegant assurance Belmont House, fancifully rebuilt in 1785 for Eleanor Coade and dressed with artificial stone from her factory, remains the kind of grand decorative illusion preferred by Georgian architects and appropriate to writers of fiction.

*   *   *   *   *

In recent years **Graham Swift** has returned to the theme of religious belief destroyed by scientific discovery that preoccupied the latter part of the 19th century. In his novel ***Ever After*** (1992) Swift ventures briefly into territory appropriated by Fowles, inspired by the momentous discovery that has since made Lyme a mecca for fossil-hunting tourists. As the novel opens a research fellow is sitting in the garden of his Cambridge college contemplating the collection of notebooks in which is recorded the growing dis-ease that afflicted a distant west country relative and helped redefine the ethical basis of Victorian society.

Graham Swift
(1949 -)

Matthew Pearce is a young Oxford graduate and surveyor who decides, in the summer of 1844, to combine some gentle geological investigation with *a little amorous exploration* among the eligible crop of young women who flocked to Lyme each season. His religious upbringing, by which all the *profounder questions of existence were settled*, allowed him to go out into a world of practical endeavour with an untroubled mind. He has probably seen Mary Anning's lchthyosaurus in the British Museum but, taking shelter at the base of Black Venn cliff where he watches her workmen split open a large piece of Blue Lias rock, he is suddenly confronted by the eye of a monster. *He stood face to face with the skull of a beast that must have lived .... unimaginably longer than even the most generous computations from Scripture allowed for the beginning of the world.* This awful realisation was, for Matthew, *the moment of my unbelief. The beginning of my make-belief.* The significance of the experience continues to gnaw away at his conscience until, years later, it erupts engulfing those closest to him and sends shock waves through succeeding generations that eventually resurface at the feet of the Cambridge don with devastating effect:

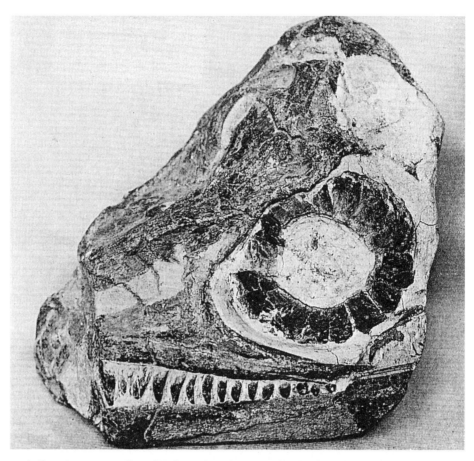

The eye of a monster now in the Dorchester museum.

A flapping tarpaulin. Sticky gobs of rain, a bruised, galvanic sky. The long, toothed jaw; the massive eye that stares through millions of years. He is the creature; the creature is him. He feels something open up inside him, so that he is vaster and emptier than he ever imagined, and feels himself starting to fall, and fall, through himself. He lurches onto the path, as if outward movement will stop this inward falling. He passes a startled young woman, who has fallen also, but less than her own length and on to solid ground. He blunders down another path .... which takes him to the beach - as if to stop himself falling he must get to sea level.

Later Matthew realises how different it might have been. He could have gone to help the woman, missed the discovery and fallen in love. His marriage to the daughter of a Devon parson provokes a series of increasingly hostile debates with his father-in-law that reveal Matthew's growing dissatisfaction with the historical accuracy of the Old Testament. The nagging implication of time, of Geological Time, posed by what the rector calls *the insuperable bone of our contention*, eventually leads Matthew to raise the question of extinction. He chooses a hot June day while his adversary is tending his hives. The rector points to the honey combs as a perfect example of God's creation, Matthew counters this with Darwinian arguments about the ability of species to adapt, declaring that Genesis is simply a poetic allegory.

Possessed of the notebooks, the Ellison scholar has the opportunity to piece together the life of his ancestor in much the same way as a palaeontologist will reconstruct a complete skeleton from assorted fragments. Matthew, forced to choose between his heretical beliefs and the God-fearing lie he is obliged to lead for the sake of his wife and family, had chosen freedom. Faced with a similar choice the Ellison scholar turns his back on the dry bones of academic research. Through the pages of the notebooks he too is confronted by the eye of a monster. Rather than die *in some embalming lagoon* he hands the documents to an ambitious rival and, given a second chance, embraces life; the life of a writer whose autobiographical novel reads like the notebooks of his Victorian ancestor.

The view inland to Marshwood Vale from Golden Cap.

Marshwood Vale

With its regular pastures and narrow sunken lanes Marshwood Vale is rich dairy country, a more introspective version of the Vale of Blackmore. From Lewesdon Hill and Pilsdon Pen the landscape is spread out below like a plumped-up quilt. In the heart of the vale, at a point where the river Char gathers itself to cut through to the sea, stands the village of Whitechurch Canonicorum. The name is surely a reference to its pale limestone church but

St Wite's shrine in the church at Whitechurch Canonicorum.

its dedication to St Candida, more probably Wite, an unknown Wessex saint of indeterminate gender, is unique. More remarkable is the rare survival of a complete stone shrine with authentic relics in the north transept. In 1900 the coffin was opened to reveal a leaden reliquary containing bones and the inscription, 'Here rest the remains of St Wite'. The Victorian enthusiasm for disturbing the dead continued well into this century and in 1916 a complete set of pagan Saxon grave goods was uncovered in a barrow on Hardown Hill.

Here in a single parish was enough material for an archaeological thriller when **Peter Ackroyd** began work on *First Light* (1989) set in the haunted landscape of Pilgrin Valley, a lost world littered with stones and derelict cottages on the Devon-Dorset border. Approached with some difficulty down a muddy track off the main Axminster to Bridport road, the dry valley grassland:

... is so bright that it seems to blaze and its line of flame to follow the curve of the chalk for many miles, sweeping across its ledges and plateaux, filling its shallows and depressions, rising with its dunes and hills. From the air it appears to be a huge river moving inland from the sea.

The curiously named village of Colcorum sounds deceptively like Whitechurch Canonicorum but a quick glance at the map is unlikely to reveal the secrets of Pilgrin Valley. The absence of signposts is a deliberate attempt to thwart the more inquisitive reader and avoid comparisons with the strange Mint family whose ancestors, as Mark Clare discovers, were buried in the valley long before the arrival of St Wite. Like characters in the novel, the reader can easily get lost in a landscape that, with its haunted tower and ancient wood, has grown out of the author's imagination and a more recent literary past.

While Hardy and his wife were living in Wimborne Minster awaiting the completion of Max Gate, he explored the locational possibilities of the surrounding countryside for his novel 'Two on a Tower' (1883). A few miles west of the town, rising above the wooded slopes of Charlborough Park, he discovered the tallest folly in Dorset. Struck by lightning in 1823 and rebuilt as a provocative gesture to the greater glory of the Erle family, this octagonal column became the Swithin observatory of Hardy's novel, a landmark on the Welland estate of Lady Constance. To avoid offending the owner of Charlborough House, Hardy decided to move his hollow tower to Weatherby Castle, an isolated conical hill just south of the main Blandford to Dorchester road. Renaming it Ring's Speer Hill, a reference to the encircling earthworks, Hardy replaced the small brick obelisk that crowns its fir-clad slopes with his own architectural hybrid.

Charlborough tower

Hardy's tragi-comedy was *the outcome of a wish to set the emotional history of two infinitesimal lives against the stupendous background of the stellar universe.* By taking Hardy's literary landmark, renaming it Swithin's Column and re-erecting it at the other end of the county, Ackroyd acknowledges his debt to the great Dorset writer, adapting the theme of 'Two on a Tower' to his own purpose in a novel of dazzling bravura that is *part archaeological detective story, part metaphysical extravaganza.* Ackroyd's description of his tower on top of an isolated hill planted with fir trees and ascended by means of a circular stone staircase, leaves the reader in little doubt as to its literary pedigree. Even the scrap of paper at the foot of the steps turns out to be a page from Hardy's novel.

In *First Light* Katherine Clare lives as a recluse above an antique shop in the centre of Lyme Regis with her husband and a dog called Jude. Crippled from birth she is destined to take a tumble down Granny's Teeth and continues to walk with great difficulty through the literary landscape of west Dorset. On one of their rare outings together Katherine and Mark wander into the enchanted world of Colcorum Wood, a vestige of the ancient oak forest that once covered much of Marshwood Vale and there, sensing her own mortality, she offers up a prayer for the dying of the light. At the edge of a clearing the couple come across an old vagrant perched on the branch of a fallen tree feeding bread to the pigeons. Known only as The Woodlander this latter-day Giles Winterborne (see p107) is an embodiment of the greenwood but, knowing that his death will come soon, he has prepared a detailed map of his leafy world and a list of all the creatures living in the wood to enable those who come after to continue his work.

Beyond the wood the couple next encounter the haunted tower. The place seems strangely familiar to Katherine but, as her husband suggests *perhaps you just read about it.* When Lady Constance first ascends her tower she discovers a handsome young astronomer but Ackroyd's characters find only an abandoned table and chair. Swithin has long since disappeared and the empty column becomes a reminder of their impotence. From the top the sea is clearly visible at Lud's Mouth away to the south where years earlier Katherine had first experienced the sense of loss and sadness, *the meaning of her time upon earth*, that had always threatened their life together.

Unlike Hardy, who rewrote the map of Dorset with thinly disguised place names of his own, Ackroyd's landscape is more elusive. He deliberately steers his characters away from the Undercliff where the imprint of Fowles' novel is still fresh on the ground and points them towards the cliffs east of the town. The name Lud, from the Old English 'Hlude' meaning 'the loud one', refers to one of the streams that break through to the sea at this point. Lud's mouth where Joey Hanover goes in search of ammonites is conceivably Charmouth, but further on the author's tracks become a little easier to follow. Here the cliff-line rises majestically to Golden Cap and below the summit lie the remains of Stanton church, dedicated to the archangel Gabriel.

Ackroyd's novel is a wonderful flight of fancy and the 'must fly' excuse offered by one of his lighter characters simply echoes an ancient desire to take to the air and soar like a bird. In the opening chapter the astronomer Damian Fall longs to be *drawn up into the immensity* and, walking on the downs, Mark Clare felt *that he needed only to run across the curve of this chalk and then he, too, would be able to rise into the sky, borne upwards by the serene light of these high places.* At one point Mark reminds his archaeological colleagues that in the sacred times men would project themselves into the sky from great ritual mounds. Situated near the highest point on the south coast, the ruins of St Gabriel's church provided Ackroyd with the perfect platform from which to launch into one of his tales.

According to tradition, in the days when evil spirits roamed the world, the children of St Gabriel's were lured from their beds while the village slept, but in their excitement they soon forgot what would happen if they ever set foot on earth again. As they speed through the night sky they become cold and frightened and beg to be taken home. Circling above the village the wicked creatures swoop low over the cliff, the children are tipped into the sea and turned to stone. In another version the circle of twelve stones on the shore marks the graves of those children who, convinced by a strange orphan called Old Barren that they could fly, had hurled themselves over the edge. As the archangel Gabriel and captain of the heavenly host, St Michael became the patron saint of churches built on high rocky peaks where, like St George, he would do battle with the fiery serpent. There is a Dragon's Hill just north of Lyme Regis and in the town the parish church is dedicated to the dragon-slaying saint. Dragons could also fly and the jagged rocks below Golden Cap may be the teeth of a monster vanquished in aerial combat, but that of course, is another story.

The ruins of St Gabriel's church at the base of Golden Cap looking west towards Lyme Regis.

Brought into sharp focus by her husband's growing absorption in his work, Katherine Clare's sense of dislocation is compounded by the news that, due to her disability, they cannot adopt a child. Retracing her steps through Colcorum Wood at the dead of night she makes her way back to the tower and climbs the stairs for the last time. Although her suicide demonstrates most graphically that earthly mortals are subject to the law of gravity, in the moment of decision, before flinging herself through the arched window, Katherine experienced an exquisite sense of freedom, a belief that she really could float above the trees. When Mark discovers her body he sees from her face that in the act of falling all the pain had left her; that fear had spread its wings at last. Walking along the cliff to St Gabriel's Point he peers down at the rocks far below and experiences that same freedom of choice. With the sound of bird song coming from the abandoned village, Mark steps back from the edge and makes his way down to the shore at Lud's mouth where years before, *in another time,* Katherine had stood alone. Now he was the one left behind:

Orange stone and blue air. The peacefulness here was a relic of lost time and, when he considered this, he realised also that his own life was simply borrowed from time, it was not his to throw away.

He waded out of the water and started walking towards the cliff-face. When he came up to it, he stretched out his arms and put his face and hands against the orange stone. It felt warm to his touch .... With his palms spread out against the stone, he seemed to sleep. And, as he slept, he took in the warmth of the landscape. The orange stone absorbed his salt tears.

Knowing that Katherine had wanted him to, Mark resolves to continue with his exploration of the burial mound in Pilgrin Valley. Since his first visit to Dorset he had studied its pre-history with a growing obsession until he felt:

... the pressure of its beneficence, its curves and folds cradling the life which seemed to have issued from it. It possessed an almost human presence, as if the generations of those who had dwelt upon its surface had left some faint echo .... When he lay upon the grass of Dorset it was as if he were being borne up by the hands of those who had come before him.

What puzzled Mark about the barrow built into the slope of the valley was how it appeared conspicuously off centre within a much larger circle of stones and how it came to resemble *a single eye staring up to heaven.* As he pondered its destruction his thoughts are disturbed by the sound of the wind sweeping down the valley and the movement of a shadowy figure among the trees. On reaching the mound he pressed his face against its grassy surface as though listening for signs of life. *He breathed in the dampness of the cold earth and, in his exhilaration, he believed he was reaching towards unimaginable passages of lost time.* As the excavation progresses, the evidence for some distant cult becomes more confusing and Mark begins to feel as if his own *protective layers were being stripped away.* Once inside the tomb the blind entrance inscribed with a map of the stars, the hanged man guarding the way through to the underworld and the coffin of 'Old Barren One', denote stages in Mark's own journey of discovery. The passage grave becomes a rite of passage for a man coming to terms with personal tragedy.

Charmouth Bay with Golden Cap, renamed Lud's Mouth and St Gabriel's Point in *First Light.*

Standing in the front room of a cottage in Pilgrin Valley, the old music hall artist Joey Hanover recognises the white plaster faces that had watched over him as a child. But when the real secrets of his past are finally revealed the trumpet blast of his guardian angels is replaced by the more familiar refrain of 'My Old Man's A Dustman'. And all the while the astronomer Damian Fall is losing his grip on reality as he tracks the movement of the great star Alderbaran in the observatory on Holblack Moor beside the Bridport road. The destiny of all three men seems inextricably linked to some pattern in the heavens, a pattern recreated by their ancestors on the face of the earth and one which, in the darkness, they struggle to understand:

Time. Another time .... We are so close to the beginning that we have dreams of origin and of the darkness from which we came. That is why we try to reach the light above our heads. He tells them of the sky. He raises his hands and tells them of the night. They are not fires above us but souls, the souls of those who came before us and light our way. They are the eyes of the dead, always watching. They are our hopes: that is why they are so distant and why there is darkness amongst them. They are the word for far. They are the word for dream. You must make your fires in the same pattern. Place your fires here, in the valley, in the pattern of the sky. And so make the stars your home.
.... In the valley of the seven stars. I have chosen this place. I have listened to the earth and chosen it. I have chosen the powerful green glowing upon the hilltop, and I have chosen the sacred avenue beneath the earth. Build here. Purify the ground with fire and walk out the circle. Measure the ground which brings on trance and prophesy. Build the house of stone within the circle. And bring me to this place when I am called away from you.

West Milton

When **Kenneth Allsop** moved into a disused watermill in this remote Dorset village he was already a seasoned environmental activist and well-known television presenter. Before long the muddy lanes around West Milton became disputed territory in a series of high profile campaigns attracting the attention of the national press, as the local community found itself caught up in an impassioned debate about the future of the English countryside. To those who sought to profit from its destruction or who stood by and watched it happen, Allsop could be an awesome opponent. For three years before his untimely death the slopes below Eggardon resounded to the clash with oil prospectors and forestry officials in a number of carefully stage-managed confrontations. Today, this corner of Dorset remains unscathed because Allsop and his small band of eco-warriors once shook it to its foundations.

Brought up in the dreary suburbs of West London, Allsop's close identity with the countryside arose from boyhood expeditions to Osterley Park and the gravel pits at Staines to watch birds. One day he discovered a copy of Henry Williamson's 'The Lone Swallow' and a whole new world opened up:

I experienced a confusion of excitement, wonder, disbelief and, almost fear. For the first time I had encountered someone who, it seemed, felt as I inarticulately and gropingly did about birds and the countryside.

Kenneth Allsop outside the mill house at West Milton.

He was soon devouring everything by Williamson he could lay his hands on and in later life the Devon writer became one of Allsop's closest friends. As John Fowles has pointed out, Allsop didn't just observe wildlife, he empathised with the natural world but soon realised that, in addition to pesticides and pollution, the greatest threat to birdlife was the destruction of habitat. He knew that the stone curlew and the nightjar would soon be extinct if remaining areas of lowland heath were not protected and that, once drained, the East Anglian marshes would no longer resound to the boom of the bittern.

Allsop's career as a journalist began just after the war on the Slough Observer but it was his discovery of the first recorded breeding pair of Little Ringed Plovers in Berkshire that gave him the idea for his first novel 'Adventure Lit Their Star' (1949). Throughout the '60s he launched a personal crusade to save the countryside through his Sunday Times column 'This Britain' and his television programme 'Down to Earth' long before ecology became fashionable, but he will be best remembered by the millions of readers who eagerly awaited his ***In the Country*** articles each week in the Daily Mail. A selection, under the same title, published the year before his death, was dedicated to his Wessex companions and founder members of the Defenders of West Dorset, Michael Hudson and the journalist Brian Jackman.

Having lost a leg during a training accident in the war, Allsop was often in great pain and moved about the mill with difficulty, but this did not stop him from climbing Eggardon Hill in all weather to gaze out over the ancient, rumpled landscape below him. He had a fine sense of topography and saw the great hillfort perched on top of a triumphant westward climax of chalk downland. Here on *this great limb, a dominion of wind, cloud and turf,* with rooks *blowing like charred scraps* over the fields, there was *a sense of pure form and power of rock formation* that he felt nowhere else. This was the home of the spider orchid and the kestrel, the harebell and the adonis blue butterfly, a lofty eyrie in the lea of the great ramparts where Allsop could be alone with his thoughts.

Looking down over the *tumbled anarchy of hills* he could make out the rooftops of his own village and the ring of farmsteads scattered along the spring line. Further round were *the deep pleats of old oak forest, washed around by a henna surf of dead bracken and mounting to rough dune-like wastelands* where a pair of rare montague harriers had nested the previous spring. Old green tracks, overhung by *wind-crippled* thorn bushes and arthritic oaks that seemed to move like Tolkien tree spirits, plunged deeply into a geological confusion of hills and *mysterious furzy coombes.* One of the many springs supplied Allsop's mill with drinking water, gushing from the hillside at a spot where *in April primroses cluster in an Arthur Rackham bower of meshed branches, mossy logs and cool fern fronds, a place which is dreary and a touch sinister.* Allsop's secret valley was even more sinister in November:

The last sweet sediment of the year's fruitfulness had been drained and gone, and it was a grey hollowness which was left. In the soggy chiaroscuro silence there seemed to be only one thing alive; a rather nasty fungus sprouting under the lime .... it had the corpse touch of a toad.

The mill had last ground corn over fifty years ago, but as Allsop liked to point out from a desk piled high with review copies, it was still a working mill and he felt enormously privileged to live in it. There had been a mill on the site since at least the Doomsday survey and its new owner was quick to appreciate how effectively the first Saxon settlers had diverted the chalk stream and harnessed its power inside a building from which the village had taken its name. The long history of continuous occupation was an almost palpable presence in the valley and Allsop felt part of this tradition as he worked to clear out the mill pond and restore the leat. Before long he began to discover an abundance of wildlife that exceeded his own high expectations. Dippers were nesting under the bridge, a pair of barn owls had colonised the ruined lime kiln downstream and buzzards circled on the thermals above Round Knoll. Allsop wrote in praise of the kingfisher, visible briefly through his study window like a pane of stained glass but, for a man who instinctively sided with the oppressed, he had little sympathy for the heron mugged by marauding seagulls after it had plundered the trout in his pond:

The heron is grey in spirit as well as in colouring, a melancholy character; it is a surly old tramp, and so it is picked upon by a crowd of rowdies and pelted and jeered out of town.

Eggardon Hill, with views out across Marshwood Vale, was a constant joy to Allsop during his time in Dorset.

He could always find some fresh and amusing way to describe the most prosaic species. The iridescent plumage of a starling perched on the gable end was like *a finial ornamented with rhinestones, a winged hippie with self-grown*

furbelow. Presented with food it immediately suffered a personality disorder, becoming aggressively punk with a voice that matched *the melodious euphony of a two stroke engine blowing a gasket*. The landing of a flock of house sparrows, *zipping like rubber bullets across the hedge and straight on target,* is reported with all the precision of a seasoned war correspondent. *They hit the ground like those puffs of dust when Tombstone's main street was being paved with hot lead.* This is the style that made Allsop's column so popular, conveying his passionate concern for nature in language that was both urgent and accessible.

In addition to the magnificent birds of prey that quartered the fields over Round Knoll, the spotted flycatcher was among his favourite birds. This *winged Nijinsky* that nested each year in the Virginia creeper entertained him throughout the summer with a performance of dazzling aerial dexterity. *Its vivacity, its trimness, its sprightliness - it is the very spirit of the light winds scented with May blossom and meadowsweet.* With its departure for Africa at the end of July Allsop always felt a melancholy pang, concerned that it might not evade the hawks that patrolled the wooded combs with ruthless precision.

Allsop was always alert to the pressures that threatened this enchanted corner of Dorset. He needed no reminding that the flycatcher's natural predator had recently been brought to the edge of extinction by pesticides, that the peregrine's hold on the Dorset cliffs was equally precarious and that man was the real predator. Dead trout in the stream and froth on the surface were a sign of detergents dumped upstream and he feared the dippers would not return. He pointed out how the conversion of barns and the removal of hollow trees contributed directly to the declining bat population and he loathed all blood sports. The persecution of the badger, was, he thought, the most barbaric and despicable activity and he had no qualms about exposing the workshop nearby that sold traps and tongs as *sporting appliances and sundries.*

The ugly steel frame barns that had begun to litter the hillsides were a clear reminder that Areas of Outstanding Natural Beauty and other prestigious designations mean very little in practice. Protection of the countryside could not be entrusted to the local council or self-appointed conservation bodies. Constant vigilance, individual responsibility and collective action were necessary to fight off multi-national corporations and state-owned monopolies. When a Texan oil company was given permission to sink trial bore holes on the top of Welcome Hill near West Milton, Allsop was ready with the Defenders of West Dorset. The usual arguments about 'benefits to the local economy' and 'what price beauty?' were aired in the local press but it was the mock funeral held on top of the hill in front of the cameras that drew the support of a much wider audience. Some while later Allsop was incensed to learn of the Forestry Commission's plan to clear fell 200 acres of primaeval oak forest on Powerstock Common and replant the area with conifers. The ferocity and persistence of Allsop's rant against official ignorance and blinkered indifference at all levels of the organisation finally shamed the Commission into a humiliating climb down. The forest was eventually handed over to the Dorset Wildlife Trust and remains one of its most beautiful and prestigious nature reserves.

Powerstock Common, Allsop's unofficial memorial, managed by the Dorset Wildlife Trust.

In May 1973 John Fowles and his wife were travelling through France. As they were crossing a bridge in the centre of La Rochefoucauld Fowles noticed a swift caught in the telegraph wires and thoughts of Ken Allsop flashed through his mind. A week later Fowles picked up an English newspaper and read of his friend's death from an overdose at approximately the same time as he had seen the dying bird. A few weeks earlier, listening to Brian Jackman's account of the stag's skeleton found on a remote Scottish hillside, Allsop had said *just stick my body on top of Round Knoll and let the crows and foxes pick my bones clean*. The decision to give him a Christian burial was never in doubt and he lies in Powerstock churchyard, but twenty five years later his spirit still hovers over Eggardon ready to pounce on anyone foolish enough to disturb the peace of this most precious valley.

In response to the great sense of loss that followed the announcement of his death, Allsop's family and close friends agreed to commemorate his life and work by establishing the Kenneth Allsop Memorial Trust to acquire a suitable wildlife reserve in Wessex. Eggardon Hill was the obvious choice on sentimental grounds but the Trust was unable to negotiate an acceptable price. As Fowles argued, Eggardon lacked the conservation challenge that Allsop thrived on; it was already a 'safe' ancient monument and was eventually secured by the National Trust. Powerstock Common was Allsop's unofficial local memorial and Fowles was more excited by the potential of a small rocky outcrop in the Bristol Channel.

Steep Holm is a carboniferous crag that appears to have broken away from Brean Down and anchored itself off the Somerset coast. It became a 'Stone Frigate' with gun emplacements in the 19th century and had reverted to luxuriant wilderness 50 years after being abandoned by the military. The island is the only British outpost of the Wild Peony which, like the Wild Leek, had been introduced by monks in the 12th century. It is also home to one of the largest breeding colonies of herring gulls and presented the kind of management problems Allsop would have enjoyed. The week before he died, Allsop and his wife had been birdwatching in Wales. His diary records the magical day when they saw kites, buzzards and a pair of peregrines. He would have been happy to know that this magnificent bird is now a regular visitor to the island purchased in his memory.

5

Secrets and Lies
The
Heart of Wessex

Rime Intrinsica, Fontmell Magna,
  Sturminster Newton and Melbury Bubb,
Whist upon whist upon whist drive in Institute,
  Legion and Social Club.
Horny hands that hold the aces
  which this morning held the plough -
While Tranter Reuben, T S Eliot,
H G Wells and Edith Sitwell lie
  in Mellstock churchyard now.
From ***Dorset*** by **John Betjeman**

Dorchester

Thomas Hardy
(1840 - 1928)

In the absence of any great architectural centrepiece the town's reputation rests largely on the literary achievements of **Thomas Hardy** whose legacy of Wessex novels and poems has transformed Dorchester into a place of pilgrimage. Step into the county museum, designed in 1881 by the architect Crickmay for whom Hardy once worked, and you become aware of a more distant past that in the late 19th century still hung about the town. Laid out on the south bank of the Frome, Durnovaria was once the capital of the Durotriges. *It announced old Rome in every street, alley, and precinct. It looked Roman, bespoke the art of Rome, concealed the dead men of Rome.* In the late 18th century the town's ramparts were levelled and laid out with tree-lined walkways at a time when Dorchester began to spread out across the large open areas that were still to be found within its walls. Much evidence has been destroyed but in a corner of Colliton Park are remains of the most complete Roman house in Britain. Among the mosaic fragments on display in the museum is one from Fordington depicting the head of Oceanus flanked by dolphins and fish, a reminder of the importance of water to Roman life. Several Roman cemeteries have been excavated outside the walls and it was the discovery of a burial site during the construction of Max Gate that prompted Hardy to consider a Roman novel set in Durnovaria. He later abandoned the idea in favour of ***The Mayor of Casterbridge*** (1886), the novel set in a more recent past with which Dorchester is more readily associated.

Hardy continued to spend time with Emma in London society but always felt more at home in Dorset and decided to pursue his ambition there drawing inspiration from the countryside of his youth. The move back to Dorchester in

1883 was not without its difficulties. He took a keen interest in the life of the town and became a JP soon after, but the return of the native was greeted with little enthusiasm in a place already uncomfortable with the moral tone of his work. Emma did not relish the prospect of living quite so close to her husband's family, especially the forceful presence of his mother Jemima. Dorchester had been a joint decision, but Hardy may well have sacrificed his marriage to follow destiny in the gloomy atmosphere of Max Gate.

Dorchester 1785. The tree-lined walkways planted on top of the Roman ramparts, the large areas of garden and meadows are still clearly visible.

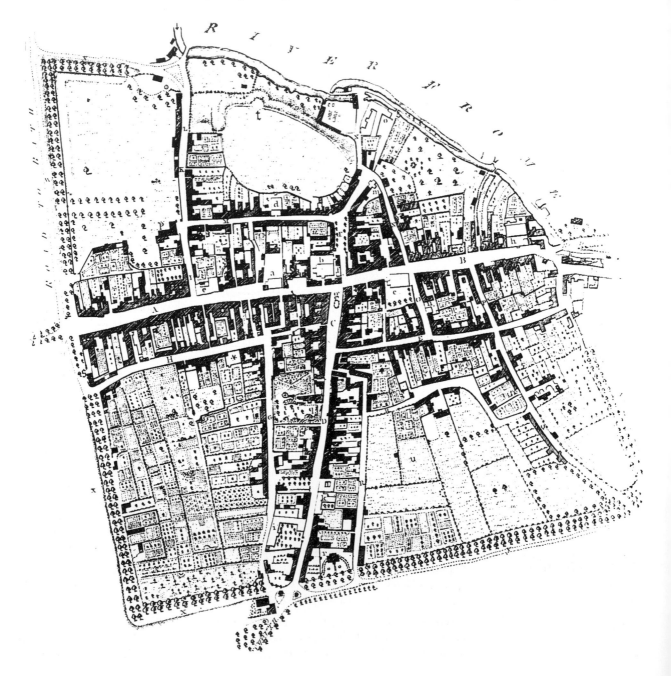

Max Gate the rather gloomy house designed by Hardy for himself and his wife Emma.

Situated on the furthest edge of Dorchester, the new house became as much a statement about his ambivalent relationship with the town as it was about his architectural taste. Max Gate looked out across open fields to the park at Winterbourne Came and a world still inhabited by William Barnes. The dialect poems of his old friend were, like the musicians' gallery in Stinsford church where Hardy's father played the violin, reminders of a way of life celebrated in 'Under the Greenwood Tree' (1872). Its destruction became an insistent theme in his later novels, including 'The Mayor of Casterbridge', where Henchard's weatherlore and reliance on verbal agreements are part of a time-honoured tradition threatened by Farfrae's more calculated methods, sound judgement and technical innovation. For a man with such a fine sense of craftsmanship and the beauty of local materials, Max Gate remains a contradiction. Hardy seems to have used the opportunity to declare himself part of the literary establishment by designing a rather dull late Victorian villa. Its harsh angular roofline, finished off with Welsh slate brought in on a rail network that threatens the Wessex of his novels, is far removed from the gentle thatch curves of the Bockhampton cottage built by his father. In the same way Hardy's plain and ponderous tomb in Stinsford churchyard, surrounded by the beautifully carved headstones to his parents' generation, is a final reminder of the great changes that took place in his lifetime and his elevation to the status of 'famous author'.

Although Hardy was laid to rest in Westminster Abbey his heart was brought back to Dorset and buried in Stinsford churchyard next to the grave of his parents.

History becomes an irresistible force in Hardy's Dorchester novel and he went to some trouble scouring the columns of the Dorset County Chronicle to verify the more bizarre incidents of wife-selling and the skimmity ride around which the plot revolves. Set in the 1840s against a background of uncertain harvests just before the repeal of the Corn Laws, the reckless indiscretions of a man for whom *character is fate* become a curse from which the mayor of

Maumbury Rings, the Roman amphitheatre, from a late 18c. engraving by William Barnes.

Casterbridge cannot escape. Maumbury Rings, the old Roman amphitheatre on the southern outskirts of the town, was once a place of human sacrifice and retribution where large crowds had, until quite recently, gathered to enjoy the macabre spectacle of the hanging fairs. It still retained a melancholy atmosphere conducive to secret assignations. Here Henchard is reunited with his wife and later, while the sun rests on the crest of the hill *like a drop of blood on an eyelid,* with a former lover who pleads for the return of letters that lead, indirectly, to her death.

The drunken lurch from responsibility that first seals Henchard's fate has taken place a generation earlier at a country fair in a remote part of north Wessex. On arrival the journeyman's first question, *Any trade doing here?* establishes a notion of commercial transaction and contractual obligation that runs throughout the novel. Unlike the swallow that flies into the refreshment tent there can be no freedom for the migrant labourer or the disillusioned husband. The seeds of Henchard's destruction are sown by his own headstrong temperament just a surely as the husked wheat in the furmity. Intoxicated by several bowls of the mixture laced with rum by a Macbeth-like hag who returns to haunt him, Henchard trades his wife at the hiring fair. Awakening from his drunken stupor the following morning, he gazes out upon a landscape *dotted with barrows and trenched with the remains of prehistoric forts.* The past is closing in but another 18 years elapse before his wife returns to find Weydon Prior has degenerated into little more than a fun fair. Market towns were slowly sucking the lifeblood from the countryside and she continues to search for Henchard on the road to Casterbridge.

The town had hardly grown beyond its medieval street plan. When Susan Henchard and her daughter arrive it appears to them *like a chessboard on a green tablecloth.* The countryside still came right into the heart of Casterbridge; butterflies danced through the streets and thistledown drifted in the mild autumn air. This was the Dorchester of Hardy's youth, an agricultural town and *nerve-knot of the surrounding country life.* The High Street was full of carriers' carts, farmers traded their livestock in the Market Place, sold their grain in the corn hall and the shops were stocked with every conceivable agricultural implement. Casterbridge was built on trade but as the county town it also possessed, in the shape of the shirehall and the gaol, the institutions of repression that enabled it to protect the interests of local landowners. Savage penalties were often handed down for poaching or sheep stealing, crimes committed by a half-starved workforce. Attempts by the Tolpuddle martyrs to establish a Trade Union in 1833 and oppose a reduction in the agricultural wage had been savagely stamped out at their trial in Dorchester. Hardy was well aware of this and although he never sanctioned the the Captain Swing riots, he drew attention to the evils of rural poverty during the agricultural depression in his essay 'The Dorchester Labourer', published two years before his Casterbridge novel.

Bowling Alley Walk along part of the southern ramparts.

Casterbridge was still *shut in by a square wall of trees, like a plot of garden ground by a box-edging*. To Elizabeth-Jane's perceptive eye it appeared old fashioned but the *sense of snugness and comfort* conveyed by the lamplight soon proved deceptive. On closer inspection tightly-packed timber buildings overhung the High Street in a state of disrepair. Most of the thatch had been replaced after the last fire, but *under the bargeboards old cobwebs waved in the breeze .... there were slate roofs patched with tiles, and tile roofs patched with slate*. The strangers stop in front of St Peter's *grizzled* church, with weeds growing from cracks in the tower. To some more familiar with the town it was *a old hoary place o' wickedness* and the complaint that *there's less good bread than good beer in Casterbridge now* sounds a warning as clearly as the tolling of the curfew bell.

Having taken the pledge after the sale of his wife, Henchard has transformed himself by hard work from migrant labourer to thriving corn merchant and mayor of the town, but with the reappearance of Susan the curse is sprung and he begins to pay off the debt incurred by his rashness. The seeds of discord are sown between Henchard and his business partner and in his decline, plotted by Hardy as a series of reversals and partial recoveries, Henchard is relentlessly stripped of his success and self-respect. Only through suffering can he undergo the change from a person of strong, often contradictory feelings, to a man able to acknowledge *my punishment is not greater than I can bear*. As he sinks lower in the world so he grows in stature until, bankrupt and homeless, he seeks love and reconciliation with Elizabeth-Jane. When his 'daughter' finally leaves to marry his old rival Farfrae, Henchard's acceptance becomes an act of redemption before his exile and lonely death.

In this, his Casterbridge tragedy, Hardy sets the psychological study of one man's downfall against the theatrical backdrop of Dorchester. Here the interplay between private and public spaces reflects the tension in Henchard's life. The name Henchard may have been derived from two old Dorchester families, Henning, and Trenchard whose mansion stood in the High Street until 1848. If true then Hardy managed to combine the name of a former mayor with that of a demolished building to give Henchard's tragic character a more convincing reality. Throughout the novel Henchard's fate is linked to some of the town's most prominent buildings. The mayor's banquet and his bankruptcy hearing, the zenith and nadir of his public life, take place in the King's Arms, the chief hotel in Casterbridge. More significantly the handsome Georgian facade of his house in the Cornhill, *faced with dull red-and-grey old brick,* suggests a mixture of dignity and passion, but the range of rough outbuildings in the backyard conceals a more disreputable past. High Place Hall is situated at the junction of Cornhill with the High Street where, from the first floor windows, the mayor's former lover Lucetta Templeman and her companion Elizabeth- Jane can follow the movements of Farfrae and eavesdrop the gossip that surrounds his dealings with Henchard. The side entrance suggests intrigue and above it a stone mask leers down like some vengeful Roman god. The building is modelled on Colliton House; restyled in the mid 18th century with smooth-faced ashlar, it provided Hardy with a suitably fashionable residence for Lucetta who shares a dark secret with the town's chief dignitary. The

The King's Arms

Henchard's house

Colliton House

St. Peter's Church

Dorchester Fair 1835, with the old town hall at the junction of the High Street and Cornhill.

market place, flanked by St Peter's church and the town hall, is the focal point of Casterbridge life and the scene of Henchard's humiliation during the visit of 'a Royal personage'. This high point in the civic life of the town is followed by the low life drama of the skimmity ride and its disastrous consequences.

The village of Durnover (Fordington) was still a separate rural community on the Wareham road presided over by Casterbridge council. This was where Farfrae chose to set up his corn merchant's business away from Henchard's own operation. *Here wheat-ricks overhung the old Roman street, and thrust their eaves against the church tower; green-thatched barns, with doorways as high as the gates of Solomon's temple, opened directly upon the main thoroughfare.* Durnover Hill was the centre of this activity, but below it alongside the river Frome was a rather less picturesque area of slum dwellings that had for generations provided a refuge for the shifting population of idle labourers, petty criminals and rebellious servants from the more remote villages. This was Mixen Lane (Mill Lane) that *stretched out like a spit into the moist and misty lowland* of Durnover Moor.

As a young man Hardy had been a close friend of Horace Moule whose father was the evangelical rector of Fordington. The Revd Henry Moule's concern for the moral welfare of his parishioners often made him unpopular among the residents of Cuckold's Row and Mill Lane until the outbreak of cholera in 1854. Incensed by the Duchy of Cornwall's refusal to alleviate the filthy, overcrowded conditions in which its tenants lived, Moule took his case straight to the Prince Consort where his report received a polite response but no action. The irony of Prince Albert's brief stop in Dorchester a few years earlier was not lost on Hardy who re-enacted the event outside the town hall in Casterbridge. Hardy was also clearly aware of the suffering and corruption that thrived in Fordington and his picture of Mixen Lane was no exaggeration:

Much that was sad, much that was low, some things that were baneful, could be seen in Mixen Lane. Vice ran freely in and out certain of the doors of the neighbourhood; recklessness dwelt under the roof with the crooked chimney, shame in some bow-windows; theft (in times of privation) in the thatched and mud-walled houses by the sallows. Even slaughter had not been altogether unknown here. In a block of cottages up an alley there might have been erected an altar to disease in years gone by.

The parish church at Durnover (Fordington) where Farfrae sets up his corn merchant's business.

Life revolved around Peter's Finger, the most notorious ale house in Durnover, where Jopp reads aloud Lucetta's old love letters to Henchard. The scandal spreads *like a miasmatic fog through Mixen Lane and thence up the back streets of Casterbridge* while in the tap room Nance Mockridge and Mother Cuxson plan the skimmity ride. By this form of rough justice effigies were paraded through the streets to the door of the guilty lovers accompanied by loud, raucous music. By the turn of the century a simplified version of this archaic custom was still occasionally practiced in rural England. The Wiltshire writer Ida Gandy recalled the occasion when a newly-wed couple were treated to 'rough music' in the village of Alton Priors when she was a child. Hardy uses the preparations to introduce Newson, the long-lost sailor and father of Elizabeth-Jane, who by donating a sovereign to the skimmity ride, unwittingly contributes to Lucetta's death.

If Mixen Lane is a necessary counterpoint to society gatherings in the King's Arms then the lower reaches of the river *embodied the mournful phases of Casterbridge life; as the south avenues embodied its cheerful moods.* Henchard's character has no firm foundation and the man's resolve to rebuild his life is repeatedly undermined by a combination of his own defects and circumstances beyond his control. With the news that Elizabeth-Jane is not his daughter, another prop is kicked away propelling him towards the waters of Frome. Superstitious by nature, Henchard is forced to conclude that this latest twist of fate is the result of *some sinister intelligence bent on punishing him.*

Mill Lane Fordington, the Mixen Lane of Hardy's novel, a notorious slum district in the 19c.

He wanders down by the river bank seeking consolation in a part of the town that most closely reflects his mood:

The whole way along here was sunless, even in the summer time; in spring, white frosts lingered here when other places were steaming with warmth; while in winter it was the seed-field of all aches, rheumatisms and torturing cramps of the year. The Casterbridge doctors must have pined away for want of sufficient nourishment but for the configuration of the landscape on the north-eastern side.

Henchard resembles a man drowning who manages to drag himself up onto the bank each time only to be pushed back down again. Standing in the meadow where the mob gather in the event of an execution, he looks up at the grim silhouette of the gaol rising above the hangman's cottage. The absence of a corpse on the scaffold suggests that Henchard is still blind to his fate and must continue to suffer before understanding the nature of his predicament. Having been declared bankrupt he goes to live by the river where the remains of the Franciscan friary reflect the extent of his own ruin and where the fragments of masonry built into Jopp's cottage are a reminder of a past he cannot reconstruct.

HANGMAN'S COTTAGE, DORCHESTER.

At the bottom of the High Street are two bridges where the more unfortunate outcasts congregate. Hardy makes another neat architectural distinction here between the *speaking countenances* of the two structures. The first, built of brick, is home to the most dissolute Durnovarians while the further stone bridge is the meeting place of a more respectable group down on their luck who spend much of their time staring blankly over the parapet. Unable to bear his shame Henchard forsakes the streets of his old town, arriving here by way of the riverside path to learn that Farfrae has not only acquired his business but has bought his house, most of his furniture, and is about to be elected mayor. He has, by now, resorted to drink again but the appearance of Newson and the prospect of losing Elizabeth-Jane, his one remaining hope, plunges Henchard into deep despair. His mind drifts uncontrollably downstream in the swirling waters of the Frome until, standing above the roar of Ten Hatches weir in the fading light, he is confronted by an image of himself provoked by the effigy from the skimmity ride floating on the surface. This symbolic death of self saves him from suicide and brings about a final reconciliation with Elizabeth-Jane before his death on Egdon Heath (see p172).

Grey's Bridge over the Frome where Henchard lingered with the more respectable Durnovarians.

Winterborne Came

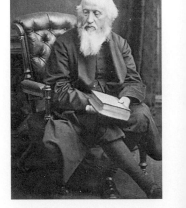

William Barnes
(1800 - 1886)

In 1837 the poet **William Barnes** enrolled as a 'ten year man' at St John's College, Cambridge to study for a part time degree in divinity. The success of his academy in South Street owed much to the energies of his devoted wife Julia and her sudden death in 1852 left him devastated. His eldest daughter took over the running of the school while Barnes turned his attention increasingly to poetry following the success of *Poems of Rural Life in the Dorset Dialect* (1844) and to his study of philology. Barnes' sympathies for the Dorset labourer and his interest in dialect did not endear him to the burghers of Dorchester, many of whom were high Tories. His application for the post of headmaster of the grammar school was predictably unsuccessful and the number of boarders in South Street declined. Fortunately, among the impressive list of former pupils, Capt Dawson-Damer was in a position to offer Barnes the living of Whitecombe and Winterborne Came in 1862.

South Street, Dorchester in 1860. Barnes' academy on the left was next door to the architectural practice of John Hicks.

William Barnes spent the last 25 years of his life at Came rectory in quiet seclusion surrounded by his books and members of his family. He would often walk the lanes to visit his son Willie who was rector in the neighbouring parish of Winterborne Monkton, resting on his return among the ruins of Farringdon church. Here on one occasion, while thinking of his beloved wife he wrote:

> *I seem to see the church's wall*
> *And some grey tomb beneath a yew,*
> *And hear the churchyard wicket fall*
> *Behind the people passing through.*
> *I seem to hear above my head*
> *The bell that in the tower was hung;*
> *But whither went its iron tongue*
> *That here bemoaned the long-lost dead?*

Barnes' reputation as a dialect poet continued to grow and the rectory became a place of pilgrimage for admirers including Tennyson whose own Lincolnshire dialect poems were later published and Gerard Manley Hopkins who considered Barnes *a perfect artist and of a most spontaneous inspiration; it is as if Dorset life and Dorset landscape had taken flesh and tongue in the man.* Hardy was a regular visitor, walking over the fields from Max Gate and in 1874 Francis Kilvert payed his respects to the *great idyllic Poet of England.* Kilvert thought the elderly Barnes *a very remarkable and a very remarkable-looking man, half hermit, half enchanter.*

The reconstructed remains of Winterborne Farringdon church.

Hardy first met Barnes while employed in John Hicks' architectural practice next door to the poet's boarding school in South Street. The young apprentice admired the older man enormously and the friendship that developed was probably the most influential of Hardy's life. The two men, separated by nearly forty years, had much in common. After some early schooling both were largely self-taught and shared a deep affection for the Dorset countryside. The traditional way of life celebrated in Barnes' dialect verse and Hardy's early novels was being eroded by a world epitomised by the use of standard English in school. This posed a dilemma that Barnes never properly resolved in his Dorchester academy. Hardy found his 'Grammar and Glossary of the Dorset Dialect' (1863) extremely useful but, unlike the philologist, his rustics used dialect words far more selectively. The fact that Hardy only ever reviewed one volume of poetry, Barnes' 'Poems of Rural Life', is a measure of his admiration for the man and his death in 1886 only increased Hardy's sense of isolation at Max Gate. His poem ***The Last Signal***, written after Barnes' funeral, is a moving tribute to his old friend and mentor:

> *Silently I footed by an uphill road*
> *That led from my abode to a spot yew-boughed;*
> *Yellowly the sun sloped low down to westward,*
> *And dark was the east with cloud.*
>
> *Then, amid the shadow of that livid sad east,*
> *Where the light was least, and a gate stood wide,*
> *Something flashed the fire of the sun that was facing it,*
> *Like a brief blaze on that side.*

Looking hard and harder I knew what it meant -
The sudden shine sent from the livid east scene;
It meant the west mirrored by the coffin of my friend there,
Turning to the road from his green,

To take his last journey forth - he who in his prime
Trudged so many a time from that gate athwart the land!
Thus a farewell to me he signalled on his grave-way,
As with a wave of his hand.

Barnes lies buried in the churchyard at Winterborne Came and, following an appeal launched by the Bishop of Salisbury, a statue was erected outside St Peter's in the old churchyard where his wife lies buried. As one former pupil observed, *the folk of Dorchester ignored him while he lived and only honoured him when he had passed beyond the sound of their applause.* In 1908 Hardy gladly agreed to edit the first selection of Barnes' poetry but, despite several more recent selections, his work remains neglected largely because he chose to write in dialect that enriches his verse but restricts its appeal. He is now best known for 'Linden Lea', the poem set to music by Vaughan Williams.

The rectory at Winterborne Came.

Maiden Castle

Even by his own standards, the years from 1929 to 1936 were a time of awesome literary achievement for **John Cowper Powys**. Three of his great Wessex novels were already in print when he returned from America in June 1934 with the idea for another Dorset novel. On arrival he went straight to East Chaldon to be near his ailing brother (see p224) and the novel began to take root in the surrounding countryside. Soon after he moved to Dorchester where, as a child, he had spent several happy years in South Walk while his

John Cowper Powys at Rat's Barn, Chaldon in 1934.

father was curate at St Peter's church. The decision may have been prompted by the discoveries unearthed at Maiden Castle during Mortimer Wheeler's excavations. Powys was certainly fascinated by the progress reports in the Dorset Echo and it was the significance of the earthworks compounded by a strong sense of the past that gave him the symbolic centrepiece for his novel.

Once in Dorchester Powys made a fresh start, abandoning his original idea for an historical novel in favour of a contemporary setting, but one in which his largely autobiographical hero Dud No-man is an historical novelist living, like the author, in rooms above 38 High Street East. *Maiden Castle* is in many ways a transitional work, a summation of the ideas explored in previous Wessex novels before Powys immersed himself in the mythological world of his Welsh histories. In view of the false starts and numerous interruptions, the completion of the novel was a considerable achievement, but the seemingly effortless style was only achieved by means of careful revision. Short of money, Powys reluctantly agreed to the publication of an abridged version, but was given little opportunity to approve the cuts made by his American publishers. His *poor ragged maiden* had been roughly handled and when it appeared in this country the original manuscript had been reduced by a fifth. It remained *the maimed product of an arbitrary editorial hand* for over 50 years until the University of Wales published the full authoritative version in 1990.

By reinstating some of the lengthier descriptive passages the unabridged edition has done much to restore a sense of place to the narrative, but unlike the earlier novels, full of beautiful evocations of the Wessex countryside written in exile, 'Maiden Castle' grew out of native soil. On his walks to inspect the excavations or by the banks of the Frome, the landscape of the novel was a constant presence and Powys felt less need to recreate it at length on the page. He had also become very wary of using real place names as a result of the costly libel case that followed the publication of 'A Glastonbury Romance' (1932). He felt safe enough in Dorchester or out on the earthworks but was careful to make clear that the Glymes cottages towards Stinsford, where important sections of the novel are set, had already been demolished.

The author's childhood years in South Walk had seen the publication of 'The Mayor of Casterbridge', and fifty years later this sense of a common heritage may have given Powys the confidence he needed to stray into territory already claimed by the great Dorset writer. The scene in which Dud No-man buys the young circus rider, Wizzie Ravelston, is a deliberate reversal of Henchard's wife-sale at the fair but, as the title suggests, his novel achieves distinction by an important shift of focus. Henchard continues to haunt the streets of Casterbridge in a way that No-man, alone in his room, can never do. On All Souls' morning as he gazes out over the roof tops, No-man's attention is caught by the gleaming waters of the Frome. It is, as he exclaims, a pastoral scene without personal association. Six months later the view is reversed when, walking through the watermeadows, he stops to consider the town's landmarks and how familiar they have become.

38 High East Street is on the left. John Cowper Powys wrote much of **Maiden Castle** while lodging here in 1935.

Roman mosaic from Fordington, now in the Dorchester museum, depicting the head of Oceanus flanked by dolphins.

Places often have a special significance for Powys, but visually Dorchester is seldom more substantial than the skyline of church steeples and factory chimneys visible from the Frome. As he walks back through the town he finds the sounds and smells more evocative but from beyond the familiar scents arose a *subtle perfume that was like the sweet dust of long buried generations.* The author is more interested in the layers of memory and meaning suggested by the town's past and their effect on his characters. The psychic atmosphere of Dorchester, or what Powys refers to as its aura, seems to have *a magical power over Dud's imagination,* enabling him to tap new levels of consciousness. He feels himself to be in touch with a collective past that promises *to bear him up,* a past beyond and beneath the surface history of Durnovaria. The waterways below the pavements of this Roman *camp on the waters* correspond to the *stream of human existence down the centuries that swept him out of himself.* Water is Dud's element and moisture its most delicate expression, and as he stands beside the river contemplating the secrets of the cuckoo-flower *soaked in the cold transparencies and wavering mists of the dawn,* his thoughts are interrupted by the appearance of Droit the Drowner whose job is to work the system of sluice gates that flood the meadows. With his enigmatic smile he reminds Dud of the Water Carrier and the dawning of a new Aquarian age.

Durnovaria's regular street plan, laid out with all the precision of Roman engineering, stands as a tribute to a highly organised and eminently rational civilisation. Facing it across a short stretch of open country languished the abandoned earthworks of Mai-Dun Castle, an impressive series of multiple ramparts that had survived as a monument to an earlier and very different culture. Walking towards it through a landscape devoid of trees, Dud No-man's imagination travels much further back in time as he struggles to comprehend the great *antediluvian monster* ahead of him:

It took the shape of an enormous seaweed-crusted shell, the shell of the fish called Kraken, whom some dim motion of monstrous mate-lust had drawn up from the primeval slime of the seabed ....

But above all as he surveyed that dark-green bulk rising at the end of the long, narrow road he was compelled to think of the mysterious nest of some gigantic jurassic-age bird-dragon ....

In the novel arguments concerning the origins and purpose of Maiden Castle reflect the bitterly contested theories about prehistoric sites current among archaeologists in the 1930s. The discovery of a Roman temple in the late 19th century by Edward Cunningham lead some, like Roger Cask, to assume the whole site could be assigned to a single period. Mortimer Wheeler's excavation finally confirmed the orthodox view that the site had been rebuilt on a massive scale during the Iron Age period as a defensive stronghold, but his findings were not published until a year after Powys' novel. Dud No-man's speculation that 10,000 years ago he might now *be gazing on the Cyclopean walls and towers and temples and parapets of a great, peaceful city of a far nobler civilisation than ours* was a view still expounded by the Diffusionist school, convinced that Maiden Castle was a Neolithic structure contemporary with Avebury and Stonehenge.

Maiden Castle, Cowper Powys' great *antediluvian monster*.

Intrigued by Cunningham's investigations, Hardy had used him as the model for his antiquarian in the short story 'A Tryst at an Ancient Earthworks' (1885) and thereby established a precedent Powys could not ignore. The earthworks, suggesting some great recumbent sea creature, anticipates Powys' monster and writers since have been awe-struck by the monument's size and by a distant ghostly spirit that seem to arise from within the ramparts. Hardy too was more than usually sensitive to its atmospheric vibrations and *strange articulations* and, as his story unfolds, a *gale race(s) in a straight line from the fort, as if breathed out of it hitherward.*

The storm whipped up by Hardy is transformed by Powys into the ghost wind of Glymes over which Uryen Quirm appears to have some strange control. Events, as in 'The Return of the Native', are measured over a twelve month period and, structured around the great fire festivals of the Celtic calendar, are used to reinforce the themes of sacrifice and sexuality at the heart of the novel. No-man is first introduced to the old man on All Souls' Day and is immediately struck by his dull, lifeless eyes and a sickly sweet smell that, like the day itself, reminds him of death and the onset of winter. The two meet again on Candlemas Day, the Christian equivalent of Imbolic. Uryen believes the old gods come alive again at Mai Dun and, having just returned from the earthworks, the wind begins to strengthen, producing an eerie noise in the roof. On days like this, according to Uryen, *there's a wind that blows out there* (Maiden Castle) *that's felt nowhere else - unless it takes into its head to follow you home.* Earlier on this *low pulsed* day while walking over to Glymes, No-man had felt *a sharp spasm of delight* on catching sight of the first celandine, a flower that so perfectly expressed *the tenuous image of this day of half-birth* And now, just as Uryen is about to return the missing head post from his mother's bed, something in the wind seems to threaten Dud No-man's carefully preserved anonymity.

Maiden Castle is above all an enclosed world heavily protected against the forces of reality and there, on a mild spring morning Uryen Quirm confirms what No-man already suspects; that he is the bastard son of this repulsive old *corpse god* squatting on the ground and pressing his forehead repeatedly against the turf. While No-man allows himself to be seduced by the almond-like fragrance of gorse bushes and *the amorous absorption of a pair of white butterflies,* he is obliged to listen to the old man's ramblings with a disconcerting mixture of anger and incredulity. Charged with a mystical power pulsing up through the ramparts, Uryen appears to his son like some ancient magician able to conjure up a whole world of mythical allusion in support of his claim for life after death. At its most dreadful the mental pain he suffers can, he believes, enable him to break through to a new level of reality by a process of *spiritual magic*:

And this kind only comes when the emotion of love-hate gathers to a point that's terrible. And you must know too that it only comes when the passion remains sterile. Any fulfilment dissipates its power. Nothing but unfulfilled love, love turned to hate, can beat hard enough upon the barrier of life, can beat hard enough upon what separates us from the secret, till it breaks through!

At this point No-man, normally so impassive in the face of female provocation, finally loses his temper. Clutching his stick, *more like the club of an ogre*, as though about to prove his contention that physical pain is infinitely more unbearable than mental pain, No-man sees them as *two prehistoric entities linked together by the invisible semen of paternity, but for that very reason destined to a struggle .... that could end only in the death of the one or the other*. No-man is rescued from tragedy by knowing the real identity of the man opposite him and by his own well-developed powers of restraint. As he struggles to come to terms with the other extraordinary revelation, that Uryen is the reincarnation on an old Mai-Dun god, the two men remain trapped in their own very different fantasy worlds. Throughout the novel No-man is seldom without his great oak walking stick, a necessary Powysian appendage and a cruel parody of the man's virility. On his way to the cemetery:

John Cowper Powys

He had been tapping the ground steadily with his great cudgel as he went along, and his awkward figure with its long arms, bony countenance, and close-cropped skull might have belonged to some necrophilistic Cerne Giant, intent on playing the werewolf in a civilised graveyard, rather than to an innocent antiquarian recluse.

This same man, we are told, had been *nervously incapable of consummating his marriage* and had, for the last ten years, been obsessed with *the naked form of his unravished maid* buried in the Dorchester cemetery alongside his mother. On discovering his illegitimacy he had adopted the pseudonym 'No-man' and 'Dud', a corruption of 'Dad' is a constant reminder of his own impotence. Unlike his father, No-man's belief in the power of sterile love is born of necessity but his *quiet cold-blooded lust* for Wizzie Ravelston gives him renewed energy to pursue his writing. Not surprisingly this young circus rider, bursting with a more natural vitality, soon tires of his peculiar sensations and fastidious bachelor habits. On a visit to the excavations, she experiences a rare sense of liberation climbing the ramparts and resolves to resume her circus life:

... something of the earth's most intimate sweat seemed to evaporate in the hot amorous air. She derived a curious sensual pleasure .... from contact with the sun-warmed grass .... as she bent down, she actually dug her nails into the thick-growing, honey sweet-turf.

From their first meeting a strong sexual chemistry has grown between Wizzie and Uryen Quirm and her passionate response to the earthworks is like making love to the old earth god himself. While others dispute the provenance of the latest archaeological finds, she alone realises what is happening to the man she loves. The recently unearthed *eyeless and earless beast-god* figure and the headless chalk torso have a disturbing effect on the assembled company, but it is Uryen's agreement to accept money for a series of articles on Welsh mythology that *blew (his) soul away like a dandelion seed.* The written word has triumphed as surely as the violation of Maiden Castle in the interests of scientific investigation.

The bronze figure of Tauros Trigaranus, a three-horned bull with human figures on its back, unearthed in the Romano-British temple at Maiden Castle in 1935.

The complex arrangement of ditch and rampart at the entrance to Maiden Castle.

Mortimer Wheeler's excavations provided Powys with the setting for one of the most important scenes in *Maiden Castle.*

On this the longest day, the Glymes menage gathers around the rim of a dried up dewpond some distance from the finds' tent, where No-man has managed to rekindle an abandoned picnic bonfire. The *blackened bowl of smouldering flame* is now, like No-man, bereft of desire and, offered up to the sun by the *great turf promontory*, is consumed by the insatiable fiery monster *sucking up, as if with a gigantic tongue, all the life .... from those dying flames*. Bound together by a web of neurotic energy and fragile relationships, this group of disillusioned, frustrated and introspective individuals struggle to contain their emotions in the heat of the day. With the disturbing images of ritual mutilation still fresh in their minds *none of them could shake off a vague impression of something momentous in the death of fire beneath the majesty of burning light.* For Thuella Wye nursing the pain of loneliness the flames, like poisoned blood, arouse her anger. Enraged by his reasoned response, she directs her outburst at No-man while Wizzie secretly wishes the others, *swept forward by some sudden psychic wave or irrational hostility*, would attack him. The suspense is broken by Uryen grabbing hold of the two women and dashing with them through the glowing embers in an act of purification:

... this blazing sun and this burning metallic sky had sucked all the devilry out of them .... and all the life-lust became spiritualized and etherealised, became like candle flames, those purest of all forms of fire, those guileless sisterhoods of fire.

Sacrifice and violation are themes central to 'Maiden Castle' but, if each male character except No-man is forced to surrender a part of himself in order to change, women are more often the victims. Mary Channing, the subject of No-man's novel, was burnt in front of a huge crowd at Maumbury Rings in the 18th century for murdering her sadistic husband in order to join her lover. Opposite the amphitheatre the circus ring with its freak shows is the scene of another spectacle. The rape of Wizzie by her lustful trainer old Funky and her rescue by No-man is a reworking of the Canning tragedy, but in addition to her child Lovie, the circus skills acquired from the old man ultimately hold the key to her freedom. Her feelings for him remain more alive and passionate that they could ever be for No-man.

The symbolic link between the two arenas leads inevitably back to the brooding presence of Maiden Castle which, as its name suggests and as Susan Rands has argued, is an enduring emblem of *womanhood for ever vulnerable and yet forever defended against the male assault*. Wizzie's cotton dress with its *romantic touch of rose colour at the bosom, like a wound from a spear,* is a reminder of her own violation at the hands of old Funky. At the end, left alone by his father's grave clinging doggedly to his sensations, No-man thrusts his stick into the ground, an equally forceful act of penetration in search of the passion buried beneath his feet that has eluded him all his life. The unwelcome and arbitrary editorial interference with Powys' 'Maiden' was simply the latest and in some ways the most damaging in a long series of violations endured by his earth goddess, from the first Roman attack to Mortimer Wheeler's more calculated dissection.

Egdon Heath

At Higher Bockhampton Hardy was brought up on the edge of two very different worlds. In front the land sloped away to rich water meadows. Behind, the gorse and heather of Puddleton Heath reached almost to the back door of his parents' cottage and, according to Llewellyn Powys, the *curious Druidical stone* that stood a short distance away in the bracken always fascinated the young Hardy. As a result the setting for **The Return of the Native** (1878) is more narrowly defined and more graphically portrayed than in any other Hardy novel. Egdon Heath is the name given to the large tract of waste that stretched in an almost unbroken arc from Dorchester to Poole. While the valleys of the Piddle and Frome along its borders are rich and fertile Egdon remains a barren wasteland, the haunt of wild ponies and a few furze cutters. The soil here is dry and sandy and nothing grows for long except the gorse and the heather.

Shunned by the outside world and traversed by ancient tracks, Egdon is the last vestige of a more primitive time and place *perfectly in accordance with man's nature .... but, like man, slighted and enduring*. The heath *had a lonely face, suggesting tragical possibilities*, and its stern appearance begins to assume a more malignant expression *arrived at during winter darkness, tempests, and mists. Then Egdon was aroused to reciprocity; for the storm was its lover, and the wind its friend*. Its face has the dignity of a prison facade, it is the natural realm of the ascetic and Hardy is already hinting darkly at the fate of those foolish enough to transgress the natural order. With an imagination fired by his grandmother's more lurid tales, the heath was a place to be avoided at night but the brooding presence of Egdon could only have

Egdon Heath, a place, *like man, slighted and enduring,* was bleak at all times to those not familiar with its moods.

been evoked by someone well acquainted with its moods. Dusk, we are told, is the best time to appreciate Egdon and as the light fades *the face of the heath by its mere complexion added half an hour to evening; it could in like manner retard the dawn, sadden noon, anticipate the frowning of storms scarcely generated, and intensify the opacity of a moonless midnight to a cause of shaking dread.* Each night at this time the great mass of Edgdon comes alive like the stirring of some hoary old giant about to meet his lover.

The sombre stretch of rounds and hollows seemed to rise and meet the evening gloom in pure sympathy, the heath exhaling darkness as rapidly as the heavens precipitated it. And so the obscurity in the air and the obscurity in the land closed together in a black fraternization towards which each advanced half-way.

The place became full of a watchful intentness now, for when other things sank brooding to sleep the heath appeared slowly to awake and listen. Every night its Titanic form seemed to await something; but it had waited thus, unmoved, during so many centuries .... that it could only be imagined to await one last crisis - the final overthrow.

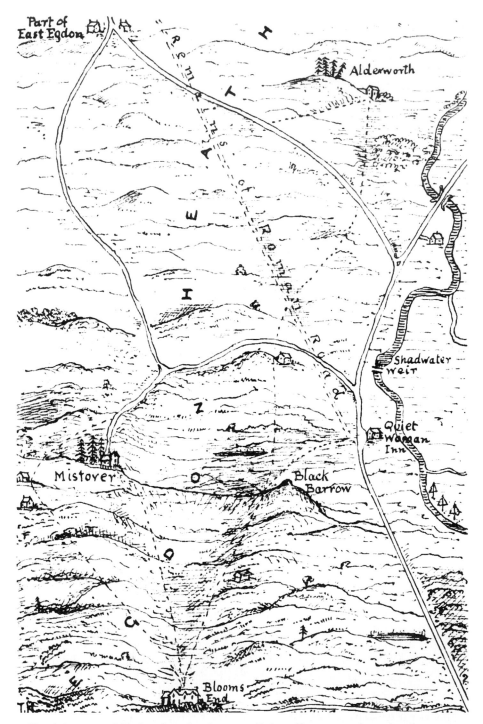

Hardy's map of Egdon Heath for *The Return of the Native*. Rainbarrow is renamed Black Barrow and the river Frome runs along the southern border.

Hardy's map of Egdon involved some slight adjustments in order to create a more coherent community within which the drama unfolds. The isolated cottages and hamlets that cling precariously to its margins disappeared long ago and, apart from the dusty tracks, the prehistoric burial mound known as

Rainbarrow is today one of the few recognisable features. Situated less than a mile from his birthplace, Hardy moved it to a more central position where *This bossy projection of earth above its natural level occupied the loftiest ground of the loneliest height that the heath contained .... It formed the pole and axis of this heathery world*, the focal point for strange nocturnal dramas, secret assignations and the stage on which the novel's central character makes her dramatic entrance. *There the form stood motionless as the hill beneath. Above the plain rose the hill, above the hill rose the barrow, and above the barrow rose the figure.*

For those who dwell on Egdon, Rainbarrow is not just a landmark but a place of pagan ritual and as the figure slips back into the darkness her place is taken by Hardy's rustic chorus gathering to honour the old gods and mark the onset of winter. This odd collection of peat-diggers, besom-makers and furze-cutters who earn a meagre living from the waste belong to the heath as surely as their more illustrious ancestors buried beneath the mound. They know its worst moods and have nothing to fear. Whirling and dancing through the flames they defy the darkness and their blaze, answered by other spots of light, becomes a celebration of life by the whole heathen community. The recurring cycle of festivals effectively controls both the pattern and timescale of the novel. Apart from the sentimental ending supplied by a reluctant author in response to editorial pressure, the story begins on November 5th 1842 and reaches its climax exactly a year later.

The brightest flames rose into the night sky from gorse fires scattered over the heath, while a little further off the more dazzling displays flared up from piles of straw and beanstalks raked from the fields. The one exception persisted a short distance from Rainbarrow at Mistover Knapp long after the others had died out. It burnt like a beacon, its steady flame suggesting split logs and a different purpose. Eustacia Vye's fire, clearly visible from the Quiet Woman Inn at the bottom of the valley, was meant as a signal to her lover Damon Wildeve. While listening for his approach, the young woman becomes aware of the wind booming and moaning over the heath and then, above it, *a dwindled voice* (that) *strove hard at a husky tune*. But this is no human voice, rather *the united product of infinitesimal vegetable causes*. What Hardy's musical ear detects is *the linguistic peculiarity of the heath*, the murmuring of innumerable dried heather bells:

Suddenly, on the barrow, there mingled with all this wild rhetoric of night a sound which modulated so naturally into the rest that its beginning and ending were hardly to be distinguished. The bluffs, and the bushes, and the heather-bells had broken silence; at last, so did the woman; and her articulation was but another phrase of the same discourse as theirs. Thrown out on the winds it became twined in with them, and with them it flew away.

The suggestion that Eustacia too is part of the heath and in tune with its moods is soon dispelled. The hourglass and the telescope she carries mark her as a person out of time and out of place on Egdon where such concepts are only vaguely understood. In the final version of the novel it is her adversary Susan Nunsuch who, by her skill in the black arts, precipitates Eustacia's death. But when we learn that Eustacia *had Pagan eyes, full of nocturnal mysteries* and that *Egdon was her Hades,* the suspicion of witchcraft persists. Although darkness is her cloak, the *Queen of Night* is portrayed without malice but as one for whom *the shady splendour of her beauty was the real surface of the sad and stifled warmth within her*. Ruled by the moon that lights her amorous assignations, *the pale, lunar touches which make beauties of hags lent divinity to this face, already beautiful*, and in the eyes of her creator she assumes the mantle of the moon goddess Artemis.

But Eustacia Vye is essentially another of those passionate, wilful and amoral female characters who inhabit Hardy's fiction. The daughter of a Corfu bandmaster raised in Budmouth (Weymouth) by her grandfather, she is cast in the role of outsider abandoned on the heath when the old sea captain retires to Egdon. Often bored, neurotic and incapable of appreciating the heath's subtle beauty, Eustacia craves the excitement of passionate love as her escape from the loneliness of a situation that compounds her gloomy disposition.

Fire, the novel's most powerful motif, is also Eustacia's most dangerous element, but the fire on Rainbarrow is not, for her, a celebration of life but rather a *blaze of love, and extinction*. Wildeve is her victim, another stranger to Egdon brought low by *the curse of inflammability*. Attracted by the fiery brand that is the emblem of Eustacia's passion, he is extinguished like the death's head moth that dashes itself against the candle during the lurid gambling scene on Rainbarrow. Eustacia's own death is predicted by the tongues of flame that curl around her waxen effigy just before Wildeve leaps into the *boiling cauldron* in a desperate attempt to save her.

But Wildeve is merely the agent of her destruction, a lingering sexual attraction revived once the glamour of a more alluring suitor begins to fade. Disillusioned with life as a diamond trader in Paris, Clym Yeobright returns home determined to set up a school near Egdon, but it is the prospect of escape to the glittering world of the French capital that excites in Eustacia a range of wildly fluctuating emotions. A dream foretells the nature of her tragedy and the circumstances of her death in which she dances with a man in silver armour. They dive into a pool on the heath and emerge into *an iridescent hollow arched with rainbows*. As the knight raises his vizor to kiss Eustacia there is a loud crack and his figure *falls into fragments like a pack of cards*. She awakes half in love with a vision and, ignoring the dream's message, sets out to meet her saviour. Returning home, having forgotten her promise to Wildeve, events begin to gather pace. *Eustacia once more lifted her deep stormy eyes to the moonlight, and, sighing that tragic sigh of hers which was so much like a shudder, entered the shadow of the roof*. The real tragedy arises from the inability of either Eustacia or Clym to acknowledge their fundamental differences. The single-minded pursuit of their separate desires is reflected most clearly in their attitudes to Egdon itself. Brought up on the heath Clym had been permeated with:

... its scenes, with its substance, and with its odours. He might be said to be its product .... Take all the varying hates felt by Eustacia Vye towards the heath, and translate them into loves, and you have the heart of Clym.

Hartland Moor to the north of Corfe Castle where the spirit of Hardy's waste lingers on the edge of extinction.

By agreeing to marry him, Eustacia is convinced she can realise her dream even though, as he reminds her, he *could live and die in a hermitage* on the heath. But out on Rainbarrow the lunar eclipse exerts a stronger pull, shining on his face *with a strange foreign colour, and shows its shape as if it were cut out in gold.* In the cottage at Alderworth they experience brief happiness *enclosed in a sort of luminous mist, which hid from them surroundings of any inharmonious colour, and gave to all things the character of light.* But their marriage has driven a wedge between Clym and his possessive mother. Blinded by love and trapped between the demands of two powerful women he throws himself into his studies, often working late into the night. Having failed to bring about a reconciliation between the two, Clym flings himself down and is reclaimed by the heath:

He was in a nest of vivid green. The ferny vegetation round him, though so abundant, was quite uniform; it was a grove of machine-made foliage, a world of green triangles with saw-edges, and not a single flower. The air was warm with vaporous warmth, and the stillness was unbroken. Lizards, grasshoppers, and ants were the only living things to behold. The scene seemed to belong to the ancient world of the carboniferous period .... amid which no bird sang.

As his sight deteriorates further Clym decides to earn his living as a furze-cutter and finds himself again inhabiting the natural world of the heath. In doing so he sinks even lower in his wife's estimation but, surrounded by snakes and insects, he finds satisfaction in the demands of hard, physical work unaware of the events that are widening the gulf between him and his mother. Having heard no word from her son, Mrs Yeobright eventually sets out in the heat of the day to walk the six miles to Alderworth. Pausing to rest near Clym's cottage on a knoll known as the Devil's Bellows, its pine trees, split and distorted by recent gales, seem to reflect her own exhausted state. Receiving no reply she turns away, *a broken-hearted woman cast off by her son,* ready to meet her fate on the blasted heath with the sun *like some merciless incendiary, brand in hand, waiting to consume her.* Resting on a bank of thyme she has a vision of freedom before her soul takes flight:

While she looked, a heron arose on that side of the sky and flew on with his face towards the sun. He had come dripping wet from some pool in the valleys, and as he flew the edges and lining of his wings, his thighs, and his breast were so caught by the bright sunbeams that he appeared as if formed of burnished silver. Up in the zenith where he was seemed a free and happy place, away from all contact with the earthly ball to which she was pinioned; and she wished that she could arise uncrushed from its surface and fly as he flew then.

Pine trees ravaged by recent gales.

Woodsford Weir on the Frome became Shadwater Weir in *The Return of the Native* where Eustacia and Wildeve are drowned.

Stumbling on his mother's body, Clym lays her on a bed of ferns in a mud hut and runs for help with bats whirling round his head. With a heath, a hovel and a blind fool, Hardy's version of Shakespeare's tragedy is almost complete. The immediate cause of death is a snake bite, but by not allowing her son to pursue his own life, Mrs Yeobright's fate is already sealed and the heath exacts its revenge.

Egdon is at its most malignant on the night Eustacia takes flight. Storm clouds gather and events move rapidly to their dreadful conclusion. *The gloom of the night was funereal; all nature seemed clothed in crape.* By the only light visible Susan Nunsuch prepares to summon up the powers of darkness as her victim leaves for Rainbarrow *occasionally stumbling over twisted furze-roots, tufts of rushes, or oozing lumps of fleshy fungi, which at this season lay scattered about the heath like the rotten liver and lungs of some colossal animal.* Crouching in the lea of the mound *as if she were drawn into the Barrow by a hand from beneath* Eustacia awaits the arrival of Wildeve, *her soul in an abyss of desolation.*

As D H Lawrence argued, the heath, *heaving with raw instinct*, is certainly the great tragic power of the novel. It gives birth to the characters who, by pursuing their own futile paths across its surface, rebel against the natural order and are crushed by impersonal forces. A prisoner of the heath, Eustacia plots her escape but prefers to drown in the Frome rather than return when her plans are thwarted. Only beyond the borders of Egdon can she find freedom, like the heron that flies out of the east but, appearing above Mrs Yeobright *as if formed of burnished silver,* the bird is a reminder that her freedom, like the holy grail, is beyond reach. Her son survives but as he prepares to deliver his 'Sermon on the Mount' from Rainbarrow his religious conversion, just like his plan to educate the people of Egdon out of their superstitious beliefs, is greeted with polite indifference. Clym's cousin Thomasin Yeobright is the only character to prosper. Asking nothing of her situation, her responses to the changing face of Egdon are eminently sensible:

To her there were not, as to Eustacia, demons in the air, and malice in every bush and bough. The drops that lashed her face were not scorpions, but prosy rain; Egdon in the mass was no monster whatever, but impersonal open ground. Her fears of the place were rational, her dislikes of its worst moods reasonable. At this time it was in her view a windy, wet place, in which a person might experience much discomfort, lose the path without care, and possibly catch cold.

Susan Nunsuch is not the only Hardy character with supernatural powers. The distinctly anti-religious theme of the novel is repeated in his macabre short story **The Withered Arm** (1888). Gertrude Lodge, the victim of a vengeful curse, is taken to see Conjuror Trendle deep in the heart of Egdon, a man well known for his healing powers. By the early 19th century white witches with their mixture of spells and herbal remedies were found only in those remote rural areas beyond the law and hardly touched by Christianity. Trendle is able to reveal the identity of Gertrude Lodge's enemy by divination but his powers are failing and more drastic action is required. She must lay her arm across the neck of a hanged man before the body goes cold. The shock of this gruesome ritual, still occasionally performed when Hardy was a young boy, was believed to turn the blood and change the constitution. On the day of the next Quarter Sessions Gertrude Lodge sets out across the heath towards Casterbridge gaol in search of the executioner.

Hardy would have been familiar with the story of Ina, the 7th century king of Wessex, retold in Camden's 'Britannica' (1586), and the likelihood that Shakespeare used it as the source for 'King Lear'. He liked to imagine that Lear's heath lay somewhere within the great expanse of Egdon, and at the end of **The Mayor of Casterbridge** (1886), he returned to the heroic theme of denial and banishment in a more literal version of Shakespeare's tragedy. Usurped by his rival Farfrae and rejected by the young woman who, until recently, he believed to be his only child, Henchard turns from Casterbridge, a broken man. Leaving the scene of his triumphs and his undoing, he skirts Egdon accompanied by Abel Whittle the labourer who, despite his harsh treatment at the hands of Henchard, takes pity on the man that had once been kind to his mother. By the time they approach the far side of the heath, Henchard is failing fast. Here they discover a ruined hovel, in which Whittle makes the dying man comfortable. Henchard's final rebuke - *and can ye really be such a poor fond fool as to care for such a wretch as I!* - has all the pathos of Shakespeare's own tragic figure. Arriving just too late, Elizabeth-Jane can do no more than respect his last wish to be buried in unconsecrated ground and without ceremony.

Egdon was an anachronism and, as such, it served Hardy's purpose but the wilderness he transformed into such a powerful literary landscape was already disappearing. He noticed the signs in 1895 when the first strips of cultivation and the first conifer belts began to appear on the slopes of the heath. The dry, sandy soil, for so long its salvation, was no obstacle to the combined forces of state forestry and modern agriculture. And so the *Titanic form* was soon buried beneath the plough and the plantation, its sad, stern face disfigured by gravel pits and blasted by endless tank manoeuvres A little further east on the shores of Poole harbour, Dorset is fortunate to possess some of the most important heathland reserves in the country. On the Arne peninsula and Studland Heath the spirit of Hardy's waste lives on. Here the smooth snake and the sand lizard, the nightjar and the Dartford warbler, those natural companions of Clym Yeobright, survive on the edge of extinction.

Hardy's *Valley of the Great Dairies*. Woodcut by Vivien Gribble for the 1926 illustrated edition of *Tess*.

The Frome Valley

On a fine spring morning, nearly three years after her ordeal (see p74), Tess Durbeyfield sets out from her native village intent on building a new life at the other end of the county. From Weatherbury (Puddletown) she walks the last few miles across Egdon Heath until the Valley of the Great Dairies appears spread out below her. Everything here is on a grander scale than the scenes of her childhood in the Vale of Blackmore; the farmsteads more extensive, the meadows more succulent, the dairy herds larger and more productive. From where she stands, uplifted by the warm breeze and the sound of birdsong, the waters of the Frome seem to flow *clear as the pure River of Life* and with joy in her heart Tess descends into the valley towards her destination.

Down among the water meadows the new perspective brings about a subtle change of mood. Tess appears *like a fly on a billiard-table .... and of no more consequence to the surroundings than that fly.* The valley is no longer what it seemed and, apart from a solitary heron, nature greets her arrival with drowsy indifference. Above Dorchester the Frome is a beautiful swift-flowing stream but here the valley widens out checking its pace until, *exhausted, aged, and attenuated* (it) *lay serpentining along through the midst of its former spoils.* While working on the novel Hardy wrote of Turner's watercolours that *each is a landscape, plus a man's soul* and once again he finds a metaphor to express the tragic current of Tess's life. Like the Frome she is no longer young and pure, and without clarity of purpose, becomes equally unsure of her direction.

At Talbothays Hardy presents a picture of Arcadia in an earthly paradise that required no precise location for its effect. The ancient barton consists of a group of cowsheds arranged around a central courtyard, the thatch encrusted with moss and the wooden posts *rubbed to a glossy smoothness by the flanks of infinite cows.* Dairyman Crick's yard is a scene of rustic simplicity filled with the sound of singing milkmaids as the narrative takes up the measured tones of the folk ballad tradition and the theme of love betrayed. Among the workforce is an apprentice farmer, the same young man who, some years before, had stopped at the May Day dance in Marlott (see p98). That same evening Tess is distracted by the notes from an old harp that *wandered in the still air with a stark quality like that of nudity.* Drawing closer through the garden her passion is aroused by the music and mingles with the rank, juicy vegetation in a scene of erotic intensity:

A Dorset milkmaid

She went stealthily as a cat through this profusion of growth, gathering cuckoo-spittle on her skirts, cracking snails that were underfoot, staining her hands with thistle-milk and slug-slime, and rubbing off upon her naked arms sticky blights which, though snow-white on the apple-tree trunks, made madder stains on her skin. Intoxicated by the notes *their harmonies passed like breezes through her, bringing tears into her eyes. The floating pollen seemed to be his notes made visible, and the dampness of the garden, the weeping of the garden's sensibility and the waves of colour mixed with the waves of sound.*

As summer lengthens, an atmosphere of sleepy contentment settles about Talbothays and all the while the two lovers are *converging, under an irresistible law, as surely as two streams in one vale* At first Tess, who has rarely been so happy, regards Clare with all his bookish learning as some illuminating presence, but as her love takes root in this fertile soil, so his infatuation begins to take hold:

Amid the oozing fatness and warm ferments of the Var (Frome) *Vale, at a season when the rush of juices could almost be heard below the hiss of fertilization, it was impossible that the most fanciful love should not grow passionate. The ready bosoms existing there were impregnated by their surroundings.*

The waters of the Frome flowing *clear as the pure River of Life.*

Standing in the meadows in the *spectral, half-compounded aqueous light* of early morning, the two felt utterly alone like Adam and Eve at the dawn of creation. As Clare watches, his beloved becomes transformed from earthly milkmaid into *a visionary essence of woman.* Above the mist Tess's face, catching the sun's first rays, glows with a strange phosphorescence, *she looked ghostly, as if she were a mere soul at large.* They wander on through layers of mist in this strange luminous landscape untroubled by the secrets that remain submerged. He calls her Artemis, goddess of chastity, unaware that the serpent has already entered the garden, unaware that she is more like Mary Magdalen. Nature, that had once seemed merely indifferent, now becomes a more sinister presence. As the couple walk along, they are observed by two herons *moving their heads round in a slow, horizontal, passionless wheel, like the turn of puppets by clockwork.* Where the fog thickens *the meadows lay like a white sea, out of which the scattered trees rose like dangerous rocks.* Drops of moisture hang like diamonds from her eyelashes, like pearls in her hair. The milkmaid becomes mermaid, becomes d'Urberville queen until, as the sun rises higher, the jewels disappear and Tess is the sensuous dairymaid once more, alone with her secret.

Love grows more passionate with each passing day. Inflamed by their first embrace Clare finds that *the aged and lichened brick gables* called to him, that *the creepers blushed confederacy*. References to the colour red reappear when Clare comes upon Tess unawares in all her feline beauty, her whole body bathed in early morning light. Her neck and naked arms, pulsating with passionate life, are pierced by shafts of sunlight and as she yawns Clare sees *the red interior of her mouth as if it had been a snake's*. Hardy's greatest tragic character grows in stature throughout the novel and as she stands on the redbrick floor of the farmhouse he seems unwilling or yet unable to destroy her. But all the while the past is close behind. In an image reminiscent of the gambling scene on Rainbarrow, *gloomy spectres* lurk *like wolves just outside the circumscribing light*; there is blood on the tracks, but for how much longer can Tess keep them at bay?

As Clare and Tess ride along in the fading light the dark mass of Egdon rears up ahead and the remains of an old manor house appear on the skyline. Their enchanted world, like the garlic-flavoured butter, is already turning sour, the air grows cold and it begins to rain. The object of their journey is a country station in time to meet the milk train. Unlike the Vale of Blackmore, the Frome valley has been connected to the capital, supplying it with milk like a wet nurse suckling some monstrous child. The main line railway snakes through a valley shrouded in mist, penetrating the meadows with a *fitful white streak of steam* that mingles with the steam rising from innumerable cattle in the early morning sun. As the engine hisses to a halt alongside the platform its wheels and pistons gleam in the light falling on the figure of Tess motionless beneath a holly tree. In this one moment Hardy offers us a glimpse of the old doomed Wessex with which Tess is always associated and the relentless power of the modern world that will crush her as surely as the steam threshing machine at Flintcomb-Ash.

The crudely restored Turberville portraits that once adorned the staircase at Woolbridge Manor.

Woolbridge Manor by the banks of the Frome.

At the dairy the couple take a last walk along the banks of the Frome through meadows radiant with pollen but summer is almost over, the cows begin to dry and Tess's short idyll at Talbothays is drawing to a close. Arrangements for the marriage begin in earnest and as Tess stands before the mirror in her wedding gown with words from the ballad of the mystic robe ringing in her ears, omens gather like storm clouds on the horizon. Her note to Clare containing the truth about her former life goes undiscovered, the carriage taking them to the church reminds him of the legend of the d'Urberville coach and as they leave the farm the thrice-time crowing of a cock signals more than a change in the weather.

A few miles downstream the joyous scenes at Talbothays are obliterated by the eerie atmosphere of a draughty, doom-laden old house once owned by the d'Urbervilles. Features displayed by the sinister portraits on the landing resemble those of the young bride and the past finally catches up with Tess. With the news of Retty Priddle's attempted suicide at the same spot where Eustacia Vye and Damon Wildeve meet their end in the waters of the Frome, the River of Life is transformed into the Valley of Death and Tess decides that she too must pay. The diamonds round her neck that wink in the firelight *like a toad's* are a mockery of her illustrious past and as her story ends *the fire looked impish*, the tender grins with the malevolence of her ancestral portraits and folk ballad tragedy becomes Gothic horror story.

Clare's rational intellect insists that Tess is no longer the woman he loved but the natural husband of Alec d'Urberville. *Within the remote depth of his constitution .... there lay hidden a hard, logical deposit, like a vein of metal in a soft loam.* His moral sanctity in the light of his own transgression reflects the prevailing attitude of society in which the woman, although more sinned against than sinning, is condemned, while the man's action is condoned. Clare can only really love Tess in his dream just as Hardy's love was only rekindled by the death of his first wife. Tess's acquiescence and Clare's disembodied state become reflected in the languid waters of the Frome as they glide, deflected and dividing through the meadows, before reuniting at the mill race. While sleepwalking Clare is able to negotiate a narrow footbridge above the foaming current as easily as he manages to suppress any hint of passion. The safe passage of Tess over turbulent water, her ritual death and resurrection, are but a parody of the spiritual journey. The enchanted world at Talbothays requires no identity but the dream sequence needs to be anchored in reality before it too drifts out of sight. Hardy chose Woolbridge Manor with its clumsily restored Turberville portraits, as the model for Wellbridge Manor. Having agreed to separate, the pair leave Wellbridge the following day, calling briefly at the dairy, but *the gold of the summer picture was now gray; the colours mean, the rich soil mud, and the river cold.* As Talbothays recedes into the distance the love that blossomed so briefly there in the Valley of the Great Dairies seems but a memory equally remote in time.

The grave at Binden Abbey in which Tess is laid to rest.

Woodcut by Vivien Gribble

6
Rock and Rollers
Portland
and Weymouth

Every aspect of the Weymouth coast sunk into my mind with such a transubstantiating magic that it might be said that when I think now of certain things I think with St John's spire and the Nothe, and the old Backwater, and the Harbour Bridge, and the stone groins, and the green pier-posts and the dead seaweed and the windrow-flotsam, and the stranded star fish! Yes, it is through the medium of these things that I envisage all the experiences of my life; and so it will be to the end.

From *Autobiography* by **John Cowper Powys**

Fleet

J M Falkner
(1858 - 1922)

Travel out of Weymouth on the main Bridport road, take the turning to East Fleet and before long you arrive at a sharp bend in the road. There, beyond a row of cottages, stands the restored chancel of the church made famous in **Moonfleet** (1898), **John Meade Falkner's** tale of smuggling on the Dorset coast. Brought up in Dorchester when his father was curate at Holy Trinity church, Falkner went on to Marlborough and then Oxford. A tutoring post in Co. Durham allowed him time to research the first of several historical novels and, following the modest success of 'The Lost Stradivarius' (1895), a mystery story set in 18th century Oxford, Falkner set to work on the book with which his name will always be associated. Drawing heavily on childhood memories of the coast and a boyish fascination with the tales of shipwreck and smuggling that still clung to it, 'Moonfleet' caught the imagination of a reading public alive to the stirring deeds of Robert Louis Stevenson's heroes. A century later the book remains one of the most thrilling children's stories ever written.

Falkner's most vivid recollections were of the old marble quarries gouged out of the cliff-face along the Purbeck coast. He first discovered the Tilly Whim caves while on holiday with his parents in Swanage and they reappear in 'Moonfleet' as Joseph's Pit where the injured John Trenchard takes refuge from the preventative officers. The cliffs here rise vertically out of the water and the crew of any ship dashed against the rock-face perished without trace. In heavy seas they were an awesome spectacle and:

... even with the slightest swell there is a dull and distant booming of the surge in those cavernous deeps; and when the wind blows fresh, each roller smites the cliff like a thunder clap till even the living rock trembles again.

179

Dancing Ledge on the Purbeck coast near Tilly Whim caves.

When the family moved to Weymouth Falkner soon discovered a tradition of smuggling still fresh in the mind of its fishing community. The Cutter Inn had, until quite recently, been a centre for the illicit trade and the pub at Osmington acted as a distribution point a few miles inland. At Wyke Regis, now a suburb of Weymouth, the graves of shipwrecked sailors washed up along Chesil Bank gave Falkner the idea for the beginning of 'Moonfleet'. As the novel opens the sexton is putting the finishing touches to a headstone for Elziver Block's son. His *little sea piece* depicting the encounter between a revenue cutter and a smuggling vessel in which the boy is killed, together with the inscription beneath it, bear a striking resemblance to William Lewis' gravestone in Wyke churchyard. Falkner continued to pay regular visits to Weymouth when, in 1881, his father was appointed curate in charge at Buckland Ripers only a mile or so from East Fleet. His knowledge of its history is evident from the novel's curious dedication:

A headstone in Wyke churchyard.

TO ALL MOHUNES
OF FLEET AND MOONFLEET
IN AGRO DORCESTRENSI
LIVING OR DEAD

The Mohuns had once been a powerful family; they were lords of Dunster Castle in the 14th century and built up substantial land holdings in the west country. The family could trace its origins back to the conquest and the name of one William de Moion is enshrined in the Blackmore village of Hammoon. The manor of Fleet had been in the possession of the Mohuns since 1567; they built the manor house early in the 17th century and various members of the family are commemorated in the chancel of Fleet's medieval church. By the time of Falkner's novel, set in the middle years of the next century, the

Hammoon Manor in the Vale of Blackmore.

Mohunes are no longer landed aristocrats and magistrate Maskew lives in one surviving wing of the old house. Its rebuilding as a stately home at the end of the novel, following John Trenchard's marriage to Grace Maskew, is consistent with extensive alterations carried out in the late 18th century by new owners. The building known today as the Moonfleet Hotel retains its Georgian portico and remnants of the original Jacobean manor on the shore of the long narrow lagoon from which the village takes its name.

Falkner clearly believed in the moral authority and charitable dispensations of the great family. Moonfleet, a corruption of 'Mohune-fleet' had been a feudal village; the Mohune Arms was known locally as the Why Not Inn, a pun on the black Y or crosspall on the family crest displayed in the church and on the almshouses. But in John Trenchard's day an air of neglect hung over the village and *everything that bore* (the image) *was stamped also with the superscription of decay*. According to legend a certain Col John Mohune, known as Blackbeard, had brought bad luck to the family and will not rest in the family vault until the treasure given him by Charles I is found and distributed among the poor. Meanwhile the almshouses stand deserted and dilapidated cottages are simply pulled down leaving *toothless gaps in the street and overgrown gardens with broken-down walls*. Maskew, who cares nothing for the welfare of Moonfleet, was concerned only to stamp out the smuggling that had spread like a disease since the demise of the Mohunes. The magistrate had been responsible for shooting Elzevir Block's son during a raid on a ketch carrying contraband goods and was now reviled throughout the district.

Fleet Manor, extensively rebuilt in the late 18c, from a contemporary engraving.

The restored chancel of Fleet's medieval church.

There is little direct evidence to link Fleet with smuggling but in the early 19th century men from most of the nearby villages appeared before Dorchester magistrates charged with running illicit shipments or receiving stolen goods. The men of Fleet may have been more content to await the next shipwreck on Chesil Bank, one of the most notorious stretches of coastline along the Channel. Here there were pickings rich enough for the more patient bounty hunter; kegs of rum and bales of tobacco, and when in 1748 'The Hope of Amsterdam' ran ashore in gale force winds with a considerable cargo of gold and jewels, the beach was swarming with looters for days after. The tradition of a secret tunnel leading to the Mohun vault where smuggled goods were stored was transformed by Falkner into one of the most chilling episodes in 'Moonfleet'. The flood that results in John Trenchard stumbling upon the tunnel entrance in the churchyard and discovering the coded message in Blackbeard's coffin is also based on well documented evidence. In 1824 the sea, whipped up by strong westerlies and a high tide, broke over Chesil Bank and swept away most of the cottages leaving a trail of devastation and dead bodies for miles along the beach.

John Trenchard's close encounter with Blackbeard is followed by Maskew's eviction of Elzevir from the Why Not. The young boy and the innkeeper are forced to leave Moonfleet and together they embark on a series of breath-taking adventures. Their skirmish with the militia further along the coast at White Nose, their daring escape up the tortuous cliff path, the discovery of Blackbeard's diamond and their exploits in Holland, are all told with a narrative vigour that culminates in their shipwreck on Chesil Beach ten years later in a prison ship bound for the East Indies. Elzevir Block is drowned saving the life of his adopted son; the old lander has brought ashore his last and most precious cargo.

Trenchard returns to discover himself a wealthy young man and is now, through marriage, lord of the manor and in a position to fulfil Blackbeard's deathbed wish. He embarks on a mission to renew the village and make it a law-abiding place once more. The almshouses are rebuilt as a haven for *worn-out sailors* and renamed the Mohune Hospital. Blackbeard's ghost is walled up in the family vault and with it all reminders of Moonfleet's turbulent past. The lavish rebuilding of the church is reminiscent of the Revd Gould's decision to finance the construction of Holy Trinity church on higher ground following the great storm of 1824. Falkner lived just long enough to learn with some amusement that a passage had been uncovered leading to the Mohun vault, but Trenchard's endeavours seem finally to have placated the ghost of his infamous forebear.

Wall tablet to a member of the Mohun family.

Portland basking offshore from Ringstead Bay.

Rocks and installations near Portland Bill.

Portland

To most people Portland is no more than some obscure reference point on the south coast, part of the strange litany of place names - Dover, Wight, Portland, Plymouth - that constitutes the shipping forecast. In many a northern city people walk past their town hall unaware that the cool white face of authority has been fashioned from the island's limestone quarries. Visitors in search of the picturesque seldom bother to explore this bare, windswept outpost and writers have seemed more intrigued by its eccentric shape than its sombre beauty. Rising abruptly to 500 feet, the island tilts gently southward to Portland Bill where the cliffs struggle to assert themselves. From Lyme Bay Portland appeared *indistinct and blubberlike* to Paul Theroux and might have been *a whale that had blundered against the Dorset coast to die*. The surreal landscape of abandoned quarries and rocky outcrops appealed to the painter Paul Nash who considered Pulpit Rock near the lighthouse to be *an impressive obelisk reminiscent of early cubist sculpture*, but Aubrey de Selincourt's response was decidedly unenthusiastic. Obliged to visit Portland in 1947 for his Dorset volume of the 'Vision of England' series, he acknowledged that *a pretty cottage on Portland would be indecent, like lipstick on a fish wife* but as so often the statement says more about the writer than the place. Relieved to be back in the ample bosom of the Dorset downs, de Selincourt stopped to savour the more familiar delights of Athelhampton House, secure in the knowledge that he had just thwarted disaster. *Portland is an island of bad dreams. To see this house was like waking up again to summer sunshine.*

Although Portland is more nearly an island than Purbeck, the scrawny neck of shingle connecting it to the mainland continues to deprive Hardy's *Isle of Slingers* of any true claim to offshore status. When the sea, breaking over Chesil Beach, threatens to assert its old authority and cast Portland adrift once

185

more, the short journey along the causeway is still a hazardous undertaking. In **Thomas Hardy's** novel ***The Well-Beloved*** (1892) Jocelyn Pierston fails to notice the gathering storm as he overtakes Marcia Bencomb on her way back to Budmouth (Weymouth) until *the drops, which had at first hit their left cheeks like the pellets of a popgun, soon assumed the character of a raking fusillade.* Having taken shelter under an upturned boat the two strangers resume their journey; *nothing but the frail bank of pebbles divided them from the raging gulf without, and at every bang of the tide against it the ground shook, the shingle clashed, the spray rose vertically.* The angle formed by the junction of Chesil Beach with the island becomes Deadman's Bay, a reminder of the countless souls lost in this most exposed and treacherous embrace. Even on a calm day there arose at regular intervals *a deep, hollow stroke like the single beat of a drum, the intervals being filled with a long-drawn rattling, as of bones between huge canine jaws.*

Pulpit Rock, *reminiscent of early Cubist sculpture* according to the painter Paul Nash.

19c. headstones in the churchyard at St George Reforne.

Since Inigo Jones first appreciated the sculptural qualities of Oolitic Limestone, soft enough to shape but remarkably durable, the surface of the island has become pitted with quarries. As Victor Hugo observed in his novel 'The Laughing Man' (1869), *to the magnificent ravages of the ocean have succeeded the measured strokes of men.* To the outsider or 'kimberlin', as he is known on Portland, the transition from Weymouth's pleasure beach to this lofty outcrop is both swift and dramatic. The castle ruins, the Verne Citadel barrracks-cum-prison and H M Borstal, clinging like limpets to the rockface, are grim reminders that kimberlins have seldom come to Portland out of choice. In the preface to his novel Hardy stresses the separate identity of this fiercely independent island race:

> *The peninsula carved by Time out of a single stone .... has been for centuries immemorial the home of a curious and well-nigh distinct people, cherishing strange beliefs and singular customs, now for the most part obsolescent.*

Hardy's choice of Portland for the setting of his penultimate novel not only enabled him to re-examine the effects of isolation and environment that had shaped his earlier novels, but more importantly it gave him the opportunity to explore the idea of romantic love in a close-knit community where the island's rocky consistency is evident in all aspects of its personality. Virtually the whole work force was engaged in quarrying and stone was everywhere from the dust in their clothes to the cottages they came home to each evening. Avis

187

The model for Avice's cottage in the village of Easton is now the island's folk museum.

Caro's place was much like the rest; *all of stone, not only in walls but in window-frames, roof, chimneys, fence, stile, pigsty and stable.* The stone trade is in the hands of a few island families and Hardy could have chosen to portray Pierston's feelings for Marcia Bencomb as love triumphant over blood loyalties, but he was more interested in the pursuit of beauty and the form it could take through successive generations of a third island family. Hardy's central character returns from London as a successful sculptor:

> *While the son had been modelling and chipping his ephemeral fancies into perennial shapes, the father had been persistently chiselling for half a century at the crude original matter of these shapes, the stern, isolated rock in the Channel.*

As Hardy insists, the harsh terrain was a breeding ground for romantic fancies especially among those, like Pierston, not directly engaged in the struggle for life. In this gentle satire on the *migratory, elusive idealisation he called his love*, Pierston's infatuation with three generations of Avice Caro becomes Shelley's *one shape of many names.* The striking resemblance between all three women is *the outcome of the immemorial island customs of intermarriage and of pre-nuptial union.* The Caros, like other local families, still bear features suggestive of the Romans who first colonized the island. According to tradition, a temple to Venus once stood at the top of the Roman road leading up to the island, and the ruins of Hope church where Pierston steals his first kiss from Avice *seemed to say that in this last stronghold of the Pagan divinities .... Christianity had established itself precariously at best.* But Pierston soon finds himself caught between the outsider he cannot love for long because she lacks the necessary *groundwork of character*, and the island woman without the *desired refinement.*

During his architectural apprenticeship in Blomfield's London office, Hardy liked to watch with some satisfaction the shipments of Portland stone being unloaded by the dockside, but comparisons between Pierston and his creator are more than circumstantial. For much of his life Hardy was in love with a succession of women and at least one critic has suggested that, prompted by the death of his cousin Emma Sparks in 1884 and her sister Rebecca the following year, he may have been drawing on fond memories of Tryphena and her elder sisters in his portrayal of the three versions of Avice Caro. Pierston displays little insight into the nature of his obsessive affliction and eventually

The ruins of Hope church on the eastern slopes of the island.

escapes it only through disillusionment. With the death of his well-beloved he turns his attention to the practical needs of the community but, by rebuilding a row of *old moss-grown, mullioned Elizabethan cottages* Pierston is shown to be a philistine. Fortunately the cottage in Easton that served as the model for Avice Caro's homestead was saved from dereliction by the birth control pioneer Dr Marie Stopes and is now the island's folklife museum. More significantly, by replacing the old natural springs with piped water, Pierston denies the deep source of his creativity. When discussing what he called *the stone mason's geometry* of Hardy's fiction Marcel Proust, whose 'A la Recherche du Temps Perdu' owes something to the structure of 'The Well-Beloved', suggested that the Dorset novels could be *laid upon one another like the vertically piled houses upon the rocky soil of the island*. The layered sequence of geological time has produced a substance more durable than the author's well-beloved; unlike the stone, the ephemeral nature of romantic love is eventually worked out.

Terraced houses at Fortuneswell stacked up at the foot of the island.

Weymouth

The town first acquired its reputation as a watering place when the curative effects of sea bathing were discovered in the late 18th century. The Duke of Gloucester arrived in 1780 and nine years later his brother George III's much publicised dip in the ocean transformed the place into a fashionable resort. As Queen Charlotte's attendant, Fanny Burney was present to record the occasion in her diary. *He had no sooner popped his head underwater, than a band of musicians concealed in a neighbouring machine, struck up God Save Great George Our King.* Hardy re-enacted the scene to comic effect in 'The Trumpet Major' (1880) when, having been *drawn out into the waves in the king's rear, 'the musical surprise' was possibly in the watery circumstances tolerated*

One of the many elegant Regency terraces that adorn Weymouth's famous esplanade.

rather than desired by that dripping monarch. Eager to repeat the experience the King returned to Weymouth each summer until 1805, staying at his brother's lodge on the sea front, and shortly after elegant Regency terraces with names like Charlotte Row, Augusta Place and Brunswick Terrace began to spread along the esplanade.

Virginia Woolf hardly fits into the category of travel writer, but few novelists display a more idiosyncratic sense of place. In 1936 she wrote to her sister; *I rather think Weymouth is the most beautiful seaside town in Europe, combining the grace of Naples with the sobriety of George the Third.* But as John Betjeman argued a decade later, every sheltered bay with a resort is compared to Naples. *The test is, is Naples called the Weymouth of Italy?* His answer was emphatically 'No' but his enthusiasm for the town remained undiminished. The Georgian terraces were, he thought, less grand than their Brighton counterparts but Weymouth *still looks civilised* and he concluded with a plea to save the town's greatest asset, its famous esplanade. The diminutive statue of George III had recently been painted in colours that *clash ridiculously with the noble Portland stone plinth.* The monarch still looks faintly absurd in full regalia on an enormous pedestal inscribed, according to Nicholas Pevsner, *in letters that seem intended for reading at the far end of the esplanade.* Walking along the front in the early '70s the architectural historian summed up the feelings of many when he asked *has any town a more spectacular seafront than Weymouth?*

A decade later the town was applauded by America's most acerbic travel writer, Paul Theroux, who *liked Weymouth immediately. It was grand without being pompous. It had a real harbour .... All its architecture was intact.* Weymouth was a place he felt he could live in. Another ten years elapsed before that other American anglophile Bill Bryson trudged into town in a debilitating drizzle. Relieved to have reached his destination he found that he liked the place rather more than he expected but the recent closure of the Gloucester Hotel where George III had stayed when it was still a private house, prompted the slightly jaundiced conclusion: *Today the town tries to maintain an air of Georgian elegance and generally nearly succeeds, though like most seaside resorts it has about it a whiff of terminal decline.*

George III's statue at the western end of the esplanade.

One of several Victorian shelters placed at intervals along the front.

One of the most remarkable features of **John Cowper Powys'** literary career is that, apart from 'Maiden Castle' (see p156), his other great Wessex novels were all written in America. In February 1932, having just read 'The Well-Beloved', Powys sat down with his brother's guidebooks to Weymouth and Portland and began his next Dorset novel. The work assumed a greater urgency following the disappointing sales of 'A Glastonbury Romance' and the completion of *Weymouth Sands* within two years, during which time he also managed to produce 'A Philosophy of Solitude', is a measure of the author's prodigious achievement. The novel first appeared in this country under the title of 'Jobber Skald' (1934), bereft of all references to Weymouth and its hinterland at the insistence of publishers who feared another libel suit of the kind provoked by his Somerset novel. Central to the original text was the sense of place so effectively removed from the English version leaving it *almost as free from any identity as a remote Norwegian fiord.* For the next 30 years the availability of this disfigured edition did much to prolong the neglect of Powys' work until in 1962 the publication of the original American text restored 'Weymouth Sands' to its rightful position.

Weymouth was where Powys had been most happy as a child, taking regular holidays with his grandparents in Brunswick Terrace, and here the geographic confines of his boyhood imagination began to take on a special significance. Exploring the bird-haunted marshes of Lodmoor or the ammonite cliffs in the company of his elder brother Littleton, he soon became aware of the remarkable geological features that marked his territory. Between the chalk cliffs to the east, the massive limestone slab of Portland to the south and the line of downs to the north, Weymouth spread itself gently around the edge of the bay. For Powys, the town had come to rest *in an enchanted mist of exciting memories*, memories that had attached themselves to the town's more prominent landmarks. The author's decision to set the novel in Weymouth came as no surprise to readers of 'Wolf Solent' (see p79) where Christie Malakite finally escapes the attentions of her incestuous father. Taking her young half-sister she leaves Blacksod (Yeovil) for the protective embrace and innocent pleasures of Weymouth's golden sand. 'Weymouth Sands' became both an act of devotion and an acknowledgement, years later, of the town's residual magnetism, lodged like a fossil deep in Powys' subconscious. It remained one of the author's favourite books partly because it enabled him to project aspects of his own personality through two of its main characters and, more importantly, because the delicious pleasure he had derived from *digging with a wooden spade in the wet sand near the sea's edge*, gave Powys the motif for a novel set on the margins of the sea between the urbane and the elemental, between sanity and madness.

Weymouth sands at the height of the season, circa.1900.

In 'A Glastonbury Romance' and 'Maiden Castle' Powys selected settings that enabled him to draw on an ancient mythological past, but the choice of Weymouth gave him the opportunity to explore the relationship between human behaviour and environment in a town of more recent origin. In this context the physical reality of Weymouth - the network of streets and terraces, the esplanade and the harbour - provides the framework within which the very different mental landscapes of Powys' characters are allowed to evolve. The town is surrounded by water, from Radipole Lake and Lodmoor marshes to the open sea, and the sounds and smells of these watery margins are carried on the evening air through the streets. Drifting in through open windows to mingle with the *beautiful smell of old fragrant carved wood*, they invade and unite the separate worlds of the novel's many lonely characters. While Magnus Muir undresses in Brunswick Terrace:

... the familiar smell of dead seaweed kept entering his room; and a strange phantasmal Weymouth, a mystical town made of a solemn sadness, gathered itself about him, a town built out of the smell of dead seaweed, a town whose very walls and roofs were composed of flying spindrift and tossing rain. Lying in bed in the faint glimmer from the grate he could hear the waves on the beach, and a great flood of sadness swept over him.

As a child John Cowper Powys often stayed with his grandparents in Penn House, a Victorian afterthought at the far end of Brunswick's bow-fronted terrace.

Throughout the novel the seafront is presented as a series of linear spaces that, like the characters themselves, rarely interconnect. From the ripple of bow-fronted terraces to the advancing waves, each narrow strip is part of a sequence of human activity. Distinguished by the statues of mad King George at one end and Queen Victoria at the other, the esplanade is the town's most dignified space from which the religious mystic Sylvanus Cobbold is evicted, consigned firstly to the beach and then eventually to a lunatic asylum for a series of public order offenses. Midway between the two royal edifices stands the Jubilee clock, the focus of so many gatherings and assignations at a point where the pebble beach gives way to an expanse of pure, golden sand. Immediately below the sea wall the area of dry sand is the preserve of adults who pass their time sleeping, reading or, deep in thought, struggling to relive childhoods when they too played in that ambiguous territory between the tides:

... the wet sands of Weymouth were imprinted by the printless feet, light, immortal, bare of what might easily have been the purer spirits of an eternal, classical childhood, happy and free, in some divine limbo of unassailable playtime.

The Revd C F Powys encouraged all his children to take a keen interest in the natural world and it comes as no surprise to discover that the Powys-like Latin tutor, Magnus Muir, is constrained by memories of his shell-collecting father or that several male characters gather objects from the beach in a rather touching, child-like manner. A deranged Captain Poxwell spends his days searching for cowrie shells among the rocks at the foot of Sandsfoot Castle and, in one of the most poignant encounters in the novel, the mad boy Larry Zed shows Perdita Wane his collection of pressed seaweed. The scrap-book, in which specimens carefully arranged on one side leaving an imprint on the blank page opposite, is a metaphor for a novel that draws heavily on the author's impressions of childhood and where only the dead, the senile or the insane are free from the pain and sense of futility that threatens to overwhelm most of the characters.

The Jubilee clock tower.

When the Jubilee clock strikes four the children abandon their sand sculptures and gather on the beach to await the Punch and Judy man. The puppeteer, operating beneath his *coffin-shaped stage*, becomes a caricature of the Marquis de Sade who held a particular fascination for Powys, and his daily re-enactment of this gratuitously violent ritual casts a shadow over the gleaming sand. For Powys the most pervasive influence in 'Weymouth Sands' is the restless ocean:

The sea lost nothing of the swallowing identity of its great outer mass of waters in the emphatic, individual character of each particular wave. Each wave, as it rolled in upon the high-pebbled beach, was an epitome of the whole body of the sea, and carried with it all the vast mysterious quality of the earth's ancient antagonist.

As the critic Glen Cavaliero reminds us, an odd assortment of tortured souls drift helplessly on these turbulent waters before being cast up on the shore where they are greeted by the piercing voice of Mr Punch *like a savage chorus of age-old mockery.* The adult world with its dark preoccupations moves relentlessly forward obliterating the make-believe land of crusader castles and labyrinthine water courses. The approaching tide carries a more disturbing message; that innocence, once lost, can never be reclaimed.

Several of the main characters are, from the outset, associated with the sea. The orphan Perdita Wane is borne across the water like her namesake in 'A Winter's Tale'. Arriving from the Channel Islands to take up her post as companion to Mrs Cobbold, she is met on the quayside by the ferryman Jobber Skald, a classless individual who lodges down by the harbour, *his nostrils quivering like a gigantic sea horse, snuffing his natural element.* That night when Perdita tries to recall what he looked like, the man's identity evades her grasp. Like an eel it slithers back into *the sound of breaking waves, the smell of tossed-up sea-drift, the rocking reflections of ships' lanterns.* While walking along the esplanade the Jobber stops to pick up a small seaweed-wrapped pebble and hurls it in a great arc out over the water. As the stone drops to the bottom so the moment sinks into Perdita's sub-conscious and by this single, powerful gesture the fate of two strangers becomes inextricably linked. Perdita imagines herself to be like the seaweed even though, as she acknowledges, she has *no stone to cling to.*

Weymouth harbour, home of the mysterious ferryman Jobber Skald in John Cowper Powys' novel **Weymouth Sands**.

When the Jobber shows Perdita the island where he was born, they journey to the southernmost tip, to Portland Bill. *Here they found themselves standing side by side upon what resembled some dancing floor of the sea-nymphs, so smooth it was, or the level tombstone of some ancient sea-god.* The waters swirl below this great wave-cut platform and the Jobber becomes aware of a large gaping fissure in the rock face out of which *jets of the original chaos kept bubbling up.* The power of this incident, like the stone in his pocket, seems to grow from a strong erotic urge and, returning by the cliff-top path he shows Perdita the Clipping Stone, a great natural sculpture in the likeness of two entwined torsos. Resting within this contorted shape they eat leaves of the sea holly plant once prepared on the island as an infusion and drunk by young brides, presumably as an aphrodisiac. It is perhaps significant that Powys felt it necessary for the couple to digest the plant in a ritual that seals their love before its consummation that night under the roof of The Sea Serpent's Head. It remains one of the few instances of sexual fulfilment in the whole Powys canon, all the more remarkable because their love placates the Jobber's hatred for Dog Cattistock. But at this point Perdita is still unaware of the bitter feud between the two men provoked by Cattistock's plan to close the largest quarry on the island. After drinking down by the docks, the Jobber gazes at the rising tide where the lights from the ships moored nearby are:

... blood red, like the Dog's skull, when he'd cracked it with his great stone! What big fish there must be now, floating so easily, so calmly with great languid nocturnal fins and twitching tails under that black blood-stained water .... The night-tide - aye! how many a wet evening had he watched it! Swirling, rolling, mounting, brimming up, against the slippery, green slime of this wharf-wall, it had always stirred him to the depths.

Sea holly and conch - John Nash.

Radipole Lake, like Lodmoor, is now an RSPB reserve.

Drained by the river Wey, the tidal mudflats known as the Backwater had once stretched inland as far as Radipole until the town council decided to build a dam and transform it into one large, ornamental lake. When the Jobber realises the swollen sea water *had nowhere to go* it sent a shiver through his huge frame, but the lonely figure of Peg Frampton felt this loss most acutely. Brought up in a house overlooking the estuary she had spent many childhood hours down by the water's edge *imbibing the sour tidal smells,* a threshold full of hope and happiness. She never fully recovered from this public violation of her private world and it left *an unsatisfied craving in her nature.* Raised by an indifferent father this sad, motherless child now sought refuge in a series of promiscuous relationships, an addictive pattern of behaviour that seemed destined to go on repeating itself.

J S Rodman has drawn attention to the way in which the distorted pulse of *a blighted landscape* resonates throughout the book. Cut off from the mainstream, characters spend their time in the stagnant waters of a plot where very little happens. Viewed from the margins, the meandering pace of the novel set in a town devoted to leisure seems inevitable. Inertia or a failure of will grips most of the characters in a way that frustrates the reader. Jobber Skald's murderous plan comes to nothing, Cattistock's much-publicised marriage is called off without explanation and Dr Bush's animal experiments provoke nothing more serious than an outburst of impotent rage from Magnus Muir. Threatening at times to break into action, the novel resolves itself into a serious of Powysian meditations, sensations and 'essences' like an approaching wave that dies away on reaching the shore. But beneath the surface the emotional turmoil of characters caught in what Cavaliero has called *the web of attraction and repulsion* drives them to seek pleasure in a series of brief liaisons. The undercurrent of instability translates itself into the domestic insecurity of characters who change partners or who, by their lifestyle, offend conventional morality.

One sequence of displacement is triggered by the removal of Sylvanus Cobbold to Hell's Museum and the eviction of Gypsy May from her hovel on the edge of Lodmoor where she lives with her adopted son Larry Zed. Hounded by a zealous council official, these most marginal and rootless characters find themselves caught between the marsh, the sea and the town with nowhere to go. In the first of several memorable passages Powys asserts the mad boy's rightful claim to this isolated spot. Larry Zed is the spirit of wild Lodmoor:

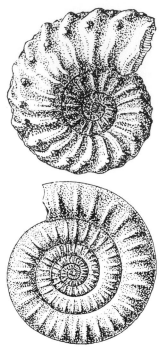

Ammonites from the Blue Lias cliffs to the east of Weymouth.

... presently young Zed pushed aside the great wooden fastener of the cowshed ... With his entrance a breath of the wet dawn came into the shed, together with a strange, almost mystical fragrance from the wide-stretching salt-marsh mud, as if in the night the silent daughters of the Old Man of the Sea had been sleeping upon it ... And yet with the cold, whitish light about him, with the curious dawn-smell entering with him, with the unique chilliness amid the vapours which suggested the slippery motions of great cold-bodied eels in the wet mud, with the sense in every direction of thousands of inert wintry marsh-plants invisible in the mist, Larry's figure had an almost mythical remoteness.

As the boy crosses the road and climbs the sea wall the early morning mist begins to clear. Stripped of his own majesty he stands transfixed by the terrible beauty of the rising sun: *But scarcely had these vapour-ghosts vanished from before him than a deep, narrow, crimson streak - as if it had been a bloody scar in an ashen-grey forehead - appeared just above the horizon.* And then again as he stares out to sea the red streak slowly turns crimson and *a galaxy of small feathery clouds ... caught this glory and bloomed over the water like a towering cascade of gigantic rose petals.* As the day unfolds Perdita Wane and Richard Gaul arrive and become involved in Gypsy May's dispute with the council. While Gaul studies the eviction order, Larry takes Perdita by the hand and leads her outside where, for once, the minds of these two characters are set free from all the distracting emotions and conflicting desires that beset them:

For standing there with its back to them on a tussock of grass, with one long leg curled beneath its wing, and its immense beak suspended above a glittering pool of water, stood a great, motionless, grey heron. Breath after breath of incredible pleasure did Perdita draw. She had never seen such a thing in all her days! It was not merely the heron that created the spell that held her. It was the melancholy waste of those dark brackish marshes behind it. It was the pallid cheek and blood-red hair of the lad, across whose profile she gazed at the huge bird, and whose fingers she was pressing against her side .... when the heron, catching the sound, one might almost have thought, of the beating of those two young hearts, spread its enormous wings and flapped away over the ditches, there surged up within her, with a dark delicious trembling, a particular feeling she sometimes had when she thought of death - its release, its finality, its great escape.

Liberation for Magnus Muir, brought up in Penn House by an overbearing father, proves a more painful experience. Having moved to the other end of Brunswick Terrace where he continues to be weighed down by the spirit of his dead parent, Muir provides the novel with a semblance of stability. Towards the end, when all around are on the move, the preoccupying image of Curly Wix, lodged in his heart like *a very ancient stone, shaped like an Ammonite*, suggests a deeper, more resilient bed-rock. In his 'Autobiography' Powys recalls the occasion when, as a boy, he staggered back to Brunswick Terrace with a huge ammonite hacked from the cliffs beyond the coastguard station, and by assigning his character to lodgings in Lias House, the author ties Muir

Upwey wishing well circa 1900.

even more firmly to his own past. Curly Wix, the seductive water sprite from Upwey is a rather reluctant guardian of the wishing well where, in the calcareous spring that gushes out at the base of the downs, the process of petrification begins. The improbable liaison with Muir in which the naive young tutor spends most of his time in anticipation of sensual pleasures while, unbeknown to him, Curly continues her affair with Sippy Ballard, is brought to an abrupt end by the news that she has run off with Dog Cattistock. Reeling from the impact, Muir strikes out along Chesil Beach towards the rocks at the foot of Portland's cliff until:

... feeling exhausted, he sank down on a rough limestone slab, overgrown with sharp indented rock-shells and gazed down into a rock-pool. Here living seaweeds, their lovely, light-floating filaments expanding in the swaying tide, revealed, as they stirred, all manner of rich, strange shells lying at the pool's bottom. Most of these as he gazed down, he could name, for the elder Muir had 'collected' such sea-treasures ....

Here, in this enchanted fissure, he could see purple and amber-coloured sea-anemones, their living, waving antennae-like tendrils swaying gently, as the tide swell took them. And tiny, greenish fish with sharply extended dorsal fins darted to and fro across the waving petals of those plants that were more than plants! But it was at the motionless shells at the bottom that he now gazed with his strongest sense of the past ....

Suddenly he forgot his father's interest in these things, for against his will the shell-like radiance of his lost girl's flesh and blood, that incredible transparency her face used sometimes to assume, shot through his senses like an arrow, an arrow of sea-pearl!

The tantalizing prospect of Curly Wix is in the end no more potent than the wishing well over which she presides, but here at the sea's edge the rock pool becomes a place of revelation where the two opposing forces in Muir's past life lie exposed and clearly visible. The awful realisation that he has lost his girl liberates Muir from what Rodman calls *the disabling spirit* of his father. Jerked into action by the stabbing pain he stumbles back along the shingle to where the waters of the Fleet have *a strange metallic look, a livid forlornness*. Turning from this cursed scene with a rising sense of panic, Muir finds himself stranded near the ferry bridge in a wasteland of broken stone walls and derelict sheds. By connecting Muir indirectly to the one person in Weymouth with whom he has any real affinity through the medium of the marine life in the rock pool, Powys has already suggested a way forward for Muir once the salt water has healed his wounds. Earlier in the novel Ruth Loder experienced the same *mysterious, inscrutable, sense of satisfaction that she lived where there were greenish-coloured fish and where greenish-coloured fish could go out on the tide.* Here at the very point where the two irreconcilable landscapes of Weymouth and Portland are joined by a tenuous strip of shingle, Muir is rescued from his despair by the rejuvenated figure of Perdita Wane. The woman he failed to meet from the Channel steamer almost a year before has returned to reclaim her old Viking sea-god Jobber Skald.

7
Powysland
Chaldon &
the Coast

Here in the green scooped valley I walk to and fro.
In all my journeyings I have not seen
A place so tranquil, so green;
And yet I think I have seen it long ago,
The grassy slopes, and the cart-track winding, so.

From ***The Green Valley*** by **Sylvia Townsend Warner**

East Chaldon

Trapped in a fold of the hills between the great seaward expanse of cliffs from White Nose to Swyre Head and the chalk ridge to the north, Chaldon has always been on a road to nowhere. Past the cluster of thatched cottages on the green and beyond the church, the road curves round the base of High Chaldon before sweeping northward over the ridge to rejoin the main road. To the south a series of dusty tracks snake uphill over Chaldon Down to meet the old ridgeway path along the top of The Warren. Here in this deserted landscape Chaldon reveals itself with a quiet modesty. Round barrows litter the ground and remains of extensive Celtic field systems tumble over the clifftop. The skeletal outline of Holworth, a village abandoned during the plague years, is still clearly visible near the solitary farm that bears its name and West Chaldon was once a separate manor with its own church. But this complex palimpsest of human endeavour is deceptive. The ridge line is broken by a row of barrows known as the Five Maries. The word 'Mary' is from the Anglo Saxon 'mere', or boundary, that once separated East Chaldon from the adjoining parish, a late incursion into the waste of Winfrith Heath commemorated by the aptly named West Fossil Farm. Place names, however, seldom admit to literal translation. Chaldon Herring, alias East Chaldon, incorporates the name of the first Norman lords of the manor and is not, as the village pub The Sailor's Rest suggests, a reference to the nearby sea.

Llewelyn Powys' claim that Chaldon was *very possibly the most hidden village in Dorset* may sound a little exaggerated but in 1904, when his brother **T F Powys** arrived from Studland (see p241) looking for somewhere to live *in surroundings harmonious to the grave temper of his mind*, the village seemed to fulfil his modest requirements. Out on the chalk hills he soon felt at home. *I like this long, white, downland grass .... nothing ever eats it, and it's like the curious grey hairs of some old woman. It never gets wet. In summer I often*

T F Powys
(1875 - 1953)

The Chaldon hills by C C Webb.

roll in it. Chaldon remained Theodore's home for many years, inspiring a remarkable collection of stories that have earned him a unique place in English literature. Between the wars the village became home to a growing circle of writers attracted to a life of rural simplicity by the presence of this bookish recluse. As Valentine Ackland recalled; *it was an extraordinary place: extraordinary things happened there and extraordinary people were to be found there*. Friends took lodgings in the village, trade at The Sailor's Return was never so brisk and the Post Office acquired a van to distribute the influx of correspondence. Ironically it was Chaldon's fame as a literary colony together with the threat of stray German bombs that eventually drove Theodore further inland to Mappowder where he remained in obscurity for the rest of his life.

Having decided to make Chaldon his home Theodore moved into one of the thatch cottages on the green and the following year married Violet Dodds, a village girl and solicitor's daughter. Three years later they purchased a plain redbrick house on the road to West Chaldon reputedly designed by Thomas Hardy and built by his brother. Theodore called the place Beth Car not, as the name might suggest, in deference to his Welsh ancestry but from the Hebrew for 'house in the pasture'. His friend Sylvia Townsend Warner always considered the harsh lines of Beth Car were made worse because *it was not tethered to the ground by any scheme of gardening*. Initial attempts to cultivate the half acre patch were soon abandoned, although according to his wife, Theodore planted onions beneath the weeping ash tree *to give it something to weep for.*

Theodore was a man of habit who rose early each day, read the Bible for half an hour and spent the rest of the morning at his desk. From the bay window he would gaze out across the shallow valley to the rounded slopes of High Chaldon and keep an eye out for unwanted visitors. He wrote slowly, no more than a page or two each day, copying out his rough draft in a beautiful copperplate hand. For years his books *grew like stalactites and stalagmites. He deposited them secretively and methodically* in cupboard drawers until the arrival of Stephen Tomlin (see p218). Theodore's marriage to Violet was, according to friends, the result partly of his desire to write about a world from which his fear of direct contact with village people and his own bookish inclination precluded him. Like his Parson Hayhoe who goes onto the clifftop to compose sermons, Theodore's stories took shape on his daily walks but, apart from the Dorset Echo, it was the local gossip salted away by Violet and served up at home that provided him with the most nourishing material. Warner maintained that had Violet not *drawn his attention to humanity* he would have continued exploring the philosophical landscape mapped out in 'Soliloquies of a Hermit' (1916). Of the three brothers T F Powys was by common consent the finest craftsman and the most ingenious writer, his work distinguished by a visionary intensity and a simple allegorical style. His preoccupations with good and evil, death and God, sprang directly from a contemplative life and his peculiar literary tastes. According to brother John:

In our family we have long known him as the formidable and most original among us .... Bunyan, the Bible, William Blake, the Old Protestant Mystics, and something that recalls the tone of the ancient mystery plays may be perhaps .... influences in his attitude to life.

Beth Car, still with its weeping ash, was the home of T F Powys for many years.

Farming and the changing seasons provide a constant backdrop against which most of his rural dramas are played out using a large cast of recognisable characters and a range of images of farm and field, many of them inspired by his early agricultural experiment in Suffolk. Reviewing his qualifications for writing 'Mr Tasker's Gods' in 1916 Theodore said *I knew the ways of the land, village customs and the right time to plant and sow, and I knew my Bible*. Together they enabled him to create a world that is both unique and universal. He began to populate a landscape of biblical austerity with a succession of greedy and brutal farmers, lustful sons and innocent maidens, malicious old women, negligent parsons and mysterious strangers gathered around the central landmark of High Chaldon. All this time he was, as Llewelyn said, hunting God:

During the twenty years my brother has walked over these downs, never once, not for a day, has he forgotten his quest. With grey, haunted eyes he has scanned the denuded, immemorial outlines of the hills. With ears pricked up like a cat's in a kitchen, he has listened to the village priest and the village pauper. Like a melancholy-eyed beagle moving in and out of the bracken, he has smelt God and will not be called off.

The village green at East Chaldon. Before moving into Beth Car Theodore Powys took lodgings in one of the cottages on the right.

Although Theodore knew Hardy and admired his work, his style is much closer to the fable and fairy tale than the literary conventions of the late Victorian novel. Ronald Blythe's assessment of the poet Clare applies equally well to Theodore: *his essential requirements in landscape were minimal and frugal, like those of certain plants which do best in a narrow plot of unchanged soil.* His knowledge of the countryside had been acquired by working the land and to this he added the perspective of long solitary walks and a familiarity with rural life acquired through years spent in the village. As Glen Cavaliero argues, this enabled him to create landscapes that are *not so much described as implied; the details are the barest, and yet for all the lack of scene painting they make the reader feel that he is there in a particular locality.* Folly Down, Madder or Dodderdown - the names immediately establish Theodore's ironic view of mankind - are all East Chaldon in which his fiction took shape, but by reinventing the few topographical elements the mood and moral weight of his fiction constantly change, like the shadow of clouds moving across the surface of High Chaldon. By employing a range of characters who recur throughout his work, he managed to create a coherent pattern of reference and stretch it over the distorted face of his native parish.

Illustration by Reynolds Stone for the T F Powys' short story ***Tadnol***.

The absolute limits of Powysland are easily distinguished. Characters seldom stray beyond the confines of Chaldon and Tadnol, an isolated farm at the northern end of the parish, becomes Silas Dottery's domain in ***Kindness in a Corner*** (1930). Unlike Theodore's fictional place names, Tadnol rarely appears elsewhere in his work, a fact that emphasises its lonely position on the edge of Hardy's wasteland. The novel also stands apart in the way he chose this area of sandy soil as the setting for his most light-hearted work. Silas Dottery's rectory is the 'Corner' of Tadnol, a refuge from the forces of evil lurking under cover of darkness on the heath in the form of Canon Dibben.

One of the few significant locations outside the parish occurs in ***Mockery Gap*** (1925). With Mrs Mogg's shop on the green, a church, manor and rectory Mockery has all the elements of a traditional English village. There is an ancient tumulus on the hill to the north, *a country of stone walls* to the east, and the place already begins to sound like Chaldon again. But, as Theodore is quick to make clear in his own fanciful way, Mockery is very near the sea and the hill is an old cliff-line. *Mockery cliff must have found the noise of the waves tiresome in past years, and so moved itself complacently backwards little by little, allowing the pretty meadows to be formed, proud of their cowslips.* West of the village lies Mockery Wood and deep inside the wood is a ruined church. The reader has been led gently to the spot that Llewelyn Powys and Gamel Woolsey were soon to find so enchanting (see p226). This is Ringstead Wood and Osmington Mills, perched nearby in a narrow cleft where a stream runs into the sea, is the most likely location for Mockery Gap.

East Chaldon churchyard, resting place of the many characters who reappear in T F Powys' stories of village life.

Sensing perhaps that the landscape was about to be populated by grazing unicorns, Theodore provided his novel with its own distinctive mythology. From the gold earrings, said to lie beneath the tumulus about which *the spirit of an ancient and buried king still hovered*, he moves to a world of fabulous beasts. By consulting an ancient map drawn *when the earth was excitingly alive with monsters and devils* that had escaped from people's imagination, Mr Gulliver fears that a firedrake will trouble his cattle while others await the arrival of a strange albatross known as the Nellie-bird. With all the power once ascribed to the devil, Theodore continued to rearrange the local topography by moving Blind Cow Rock - the real name was too good to change - several miles westward from the vicinity of Durdle Door to Mockery Bay where it exerts a sinister power over the inhabitants. Once the daytime visitors have left, on this occasion fossil-hunting members of the Dorset Field Club, and the sun begins to set:

The blind cow rock, that alone of all natural objects had never been beguiled by the sunbeams into looking pretty, now took upon it .... the blackness of despair .... Shadows, born of the shadow of the blind cow, began to creep here and there like monstrous toads and thick vipers .... And now the sea, more than any other emanation of eternal truth, changed its face .... while the tumulus on the cliff watched as if glad that the evening was come.

Woodcut by Ray Garnett for Theodore Powys' short story *The Key of the Field.* (1931).

Its presence, like a great whale, disturbs the vicar in his sleep; ships are dashed to pieces and there at low tide a fisherman sits weeping over the bodies of those washed up in his net. It soon becomes clear that this mysterious young man, with the power to satisfy all the desires of Mockery, is a close forerunner of Mr Weston. His arrival is eagerly awaited but the people of Mockery fail to recognise their saviour; a blind cow wanders into the sea and is turned to stone, a blind lane leads no further than a cottage by a pond and before long the reader is back in Chaldon following a curiously familiar group of characters. Anticipating the 'Fables' of his later work where inanimate objects are blessed with the power of speech, Theodore offers a warning in 'Mr Tasker's Gods' to the unsuspecting visitor:

Frontispiece by Gilbert Spencer to
T F Powys' *Fables* (1938).

The low thatched cow sheds, the big barn, the rickyard wall all denote rustic peace and security and gentle labours in Arcadia. The visitor, if he be wise, will keep, however pleasant the outlook, at a little distance from these abodes of joyful labour .... The old barn might speak, the rough local stones .... might tell tales. And even the oak posts with their heavy feet rotting in the dung have a way of whispering of fair things sullied and deflowered by the two in one, beast and man.

Theodore moves quickly from bucolic illusion to the stark reality of village life where children are savaged by dogs, pigs are fed human flesh and young women are violated by men or gored to death by bulls. But his purpose is not simply to expose the ugly side of human nature. Things happen with a speed and resonance seldom experienced in the outside world and by his vision Chaldon, like Stanley Spencer's Cookham, is transformed.

There is darkness, often literally, and chaos and divine retribution as the forces of good and evil struggle for the souls of men in a landscape of allegorical simplicity. As Theodore admitted he loved *the language of these hills*, a language of cross-reference by which the central feature of High Chaldon is elevated to the *delectable mountain* of Bunyan's range or an Old Testament peak. With the biblical invocation *Lift up thine eyes unto the hills* ringing in his ears, Theodore leaves the village *curled up below his feet, like a sleeping cat* and climbs to the summit where, like Hardy, he goes in search of solitude and inspiration. For the people of Madder, Dodder and Folly Down the hill is a more complex symbol, a means of ascension into heaven or a great burial mound and gateway to the underworld. Tinker Jar recalls with godly overtones, *while on the hills I was hidden by a cloud of mist,* and Mrs Crocker believes she has seen God *clothed in burning gold* on Madder Hill. The large black cormorant that terrifies the rapacious landlord to death in 'Innocent Birds' (1926) is the devil himself flown out of a thorn bush that had once burst into flames. For others the rounded hills resemble a woman's breasts and for Mr Billy in 'The Left Leg' (1923) Minnie Cuddy has been transformed into *one of the little Madder hills, green and thyme-covered .... her daisied limbs were there to be embraced by all men.*

The point at which Mr Weston pauses on top of the hill following his successful mission to Folly Down represents the pinnacle of Theodore's literary achievement. He went on to write numerous short stories including 'Fables' (1927), his most original and allegorical collection, together with the novel 'Unclay' (1931), before falling silent, but **Mr Weston's Good Wine** (1927) remains his undisputed masterpiece. The whimsicality and bitterness of his earlier novels give way to the measured authority and seamless progression of a writer at ease with his material. The title, from Jane Austen's 'Emma', suggests a world equally restricted in its extent and ironic in its perspective.

At the beginning of the novel an *almost death-like* stillness hangs over Maidenbridge (Dorchester) on a late November afternoon and the reader begins to suspect that Mr Weston, who *made a gesture with his hand as if he pulled the wires that set all these people in motion*, is no ordinary wine merchant. We are told that his young assistant Michael *had risen to high distinction in the*

High Chaldon, central landmark of T F Powys' allegorical world.

firm having suppressed an uprising in the bottling department and that, although Mr Weston drove very fast towards Folly Down, *the car never seemed to be, even when it turned the sharpest corners, in the least danger of overturning.* Above the village, with the wind in his white hair, the wine merchant *climbed a tumulus in the gathering darkness and regarded all the earth with lonely pity.* Before making his descent Mr Weston is acquainted with all the secret desires then being pursued in the lanes around Folly Down so that by choosing either the light wine of love or the dark, strong wine of death he may ensure the complete satisfaction of all his customers. His arrival has already begun to cast a spell over the lives of those below when the Mumby brothers' attempt to ravish Jenny Bunce is thwarted by the sight of 'Mr Weston's Good Wine' lighting up the night sky on top of the trader's van. There is an air of anticipation in Folly Down and when Mr Weston makes his entrance at the Angel Inn, time stands still and the fire burns more brightly in the hearth. As he goes on his round a strong intoxicating smell follows him along the country lanes. His appearance is regarded as perfectly normal by everyone and to some his genial face has an old familiarity.

Luke Bird, who only ever drinks water from his well and preaches to Squire Mumby's prize bull, is sad because of his unrequited love for Jenny Bunce. Knowing that if he can only fill his well with wine he will be allowed to marry the landlord's daughter, Luke returns home to await the arrival of Mr Weston and finds an owl has flown in through the open door. As the candle burns lower; *the soft sweet earthly wind crept in again to his room, bringing with it the scent of damp woods, the heavy scent of rottenness intermingled with the sweet freshness of the cool earth. The wind filled the cottage and caressed Luke.* Mr Weston was coming, with Jenny Bunce asleep in the seat of his car.

Ten Hatches weir on the river Frome where, in ***The Mayor of Casterbridge***, Henchard is confronted by an image of his own death provoked by the effigy floating in the water.

The remains of Rufus Castle above Hope Cove on the east side of the Isle of Portland where, as a boy in *The Well-Beloved*, the hero Pierston had carved the names Jocelyn and Avice on the rocks below.

The figure of George III cut in the chalk on Osmington Hill in 1815 to commemorate the king's patronage of Weymouth. Hardy used the hills and surrounding villages as the setting for *The Trumpet Major*.

The Dorset coast looking east to Durdle Door from Swyre Head, part of the *gull-haunted* cliff-line celebrated by Llewelyn Powys in some of his finest prose, notably **Earth Memories** (1934) and **Dorset Essays** (1935).

Throughout his life Theodore was preoccupied with death. He saw it as a joyful release from the vanity of immortality and many of his characters embrace the grave like a long-awaited friend. The Revd Nicholas Grobe, a rather bookish recluse partial to the poetry of William Cowper, had lost his faith in God on the death of his pretty young wife. Mr Weston, who admits to never having been to church, has a certain sympathy for this Powys-like unbeliever and decides that his dark red wine is the perfect remedy for Mr Grobe's complaint. If the rector and Luke Bird are essentially benign but unfortunate and deserve better, then Mrs Vosper, who *lived upon the mountain called Lust,* is the most loathsome creature in Folly Down. While procuring young maidens for the Mumby brothers, Jenny Bruce is led from the rectory *as if she were moving into the jaws of a huge snake that lies at the end of the lane.* Mrs Vosper's crime is the destruction of innocence and the vicarious pleasure it affords her, a crime so heinous that Mr Weston's wine is deemed too good a punishment. Retribution is swift, damnation for her requires no intoxication.

For the Mumby brothers there is scarcely a barn or a lane that has not at some time been the scene of a conquest but the great oak tree on the green, once a place of pagan sacrifice, remains a venerated bed of lust in Folly Down. Since falling in love with the angel's face that adorns the pub sign, Tamar Grobe had believed that one evening she would meet an angel under the oak tree. The time has arrived and Tamar, who had often dreamt of *perishing utterly in a vast flame of love*, follows Mr Weston's directions dressed in her

Luke Bird's cottage in Folly Down. One of George Charlton's illustrations for the First edition of **Mr Weston's Good Wine** (1927).

mother's wedding frock. The wind moans in the branches and Michael steps forward to greet her with outstretched arms and a bottle of dark red wine. After what seems like an eternity Mr Grunter stops on the green and, looking up, curses the tree where Ada Kiddle had been raped and for which he had been unjustly accused. His curse is followed by an almighty flash and the oak tree splits asunder to reveal Tamar, struck by lightning, still lying on her mossy marriage bed. Gathering her up in his arms Michael rises into the sky. Shortly after, the hands of Mr Bunce's grandfather clock begin to move again and a Ford van is seen driving through the village and over the hill.

When Elizabeth Muntz suggested fashioning his head from a block of local Purbeck stone, Theodore's reply was typically modest. *To be carved out of the heart of one of the noble, ancient hills, older than time itself, that is a great honour.* For a writer whose entire literary landscape had been shaped from within that same leonine head, the finished article in the Dorchester museum is not only beautiful but entirely appropriate.

* * * * *

In 1921 **Sylvia Townsend Warner** spent Easter at the Weld Arms in East Lulworth. Among the party was Stephen Tomlin, a charming young sculptor with Bloomsbury connections. When the others returned to London he wandered on over the downs looking for somewhere to set up a studio. Arriving at East Chaldon he stumbled upon T F Powys in a house full of unpublished stories. Tomlin was soon writing to Sylvia *there is a most remarkable man living just beyond the village. He is a sort of hermit, and he has a very fine head. He reads Dostoievsky ...* (and) *I believe he writes*. Impressed by the originality of Theodore's work, Tomlin persuaded him to send Sylvia a copy of 'Mr Tasker's Gods' and the foundation of a highly influential friendship was laid. Sylvia immediately recognized the manuscript to be the product of genius, a genius that enthralled and disturbed her, but undaunted she set out to meet the author. Her reputation for intelligent and witty conversation had already reached Beth Car and she was greeted courteously by Theodore who was notoriously wary of visitors. Like most people Sylvia was impressed by his appearance; *his beauty was of a pagan and classical kind*. She liked Violet immediately and warmed to Theodore's morbid sense of humour but soon realised that his cautious manner was based on real fear. The visit was a great success; both were on the threshold of distinguished literary careers and in the train back to Waterloo Sylvia was already planning the move to Chaldon that would change her life.

Determined to find an outlet for Theodore's fiction, Sylvia showed his most recent short story to her friend David Garnett. Garnett then approached his publisher, Chatto and Windus, where Charles Prentice agreed to distribute it with two other stories under the title 'The Left Leg' (1923). This was followed by 'Black Bryony', written several years earlier, and very soon the name of T F Powys became known to a growing circle of literary admirers. Augustus John called and T E Lawrence rode over from Clouds Hill on his motorbike only to be mistaken by Theodore for a tax inspector. Having failed to entice him to Oxfordshire, Ottoline Morrell descended on Chaldon but, satisfied that Beth Car was unlikely to challenge the reputation of Garsington Manor, she did not return. At this point in her career Sylvia's work on the hugely ambitious Tudor Church Music project was nearing completion and her visits to Chaldon became more frequent. Once there she was soon up at the Five Maries or sitting in a chalk pit with Theodore talking about death. Not surprisingly, several decidedly Powysian characters appear in her first collection of verse, 'The Espalier' (1925), notably in 'Farmer Maw', 'Mrs Summerbee Grown Old' and 'Peeping Tom', dedicated to Theodore. Other poems such as 'Nelly Trim', based on a local legend, and 'The Green Valley' were inspired directly by the Chaldon landscape.

With the publication of her first novel 'Lolly Willows' (1926) Sylvia's reputation as a highly original writer took flight. Her exquisitely told story of a young spinster's transformation into a witch delighted Theodore but with its *lightly worn erudition* she was already moving away from the allegorical style of his own work. Although Sylvia possessed a delicate sense of place, her *wayward imagination* was seldom confined by mere geography. She lived most of her life in Dorset but, unlike Theodore, few of her short stories have a west country setting and throughout the 1920s his influence is less discernable. The style of 'A Moral Ending' (1931) is still deeply derivative, a final tribute to the man whose own short story, 'The Key of the Field', had appeared in the same series for Furnival Books with a foreword by Sylvia. 'Opus 7' (1931), her long narrative poem about Rebecca Random's cottage at Love Green brought to a close her imaginative affair with Chaldon.

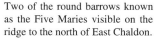

Two of the round barrows known as the Five Maries visible on the ridge to the north of East Chaldon.

Miss Green's cottage, home of Sylvia Townsend Warner and Valentine Ackland 1930 - 33.

The year 1930 was in many ways a turning point for Sylvia. She decided to abandon her biography of Theodore, a man who by his own admission *did nothing .... went nowhere .... met nobody*, she bought Miss Green's cottage opposite The Sailor's Return, *a small slate-roofed cottage with nothing to be said in its favour except that it was totally unpicturesque and stood by itself*, and she fell in love. Chaldon had already begun to fill up with friends and family drawn to the village by the presence of T F Powys. Llewelyn and his wife Alyse Gregory were living at Chydyock (see p229) with his sisters Kate and Gertrude. The sculptor Betty Muntz had followed Stephen Tomlin's directions and David Garnett had written his novel 'The Sailor's Return' (1925) while staying at the village pub. Among the influx of London visitors was Mrs Molly Turpin, a tall, elegant and rather boyish-looking young woman on the run from a disastrous marriage. She had helped prepare the manuscript of 'Mr Weston's Good Wine' (1925) for publication and wrote verse under her maiden name Valentine Ackland. She also admired Sylvia's poetry and after a shaky start the two became friends. Returning from a walk on the hills in February 1930 Sylvia confided in her diary:

It was clear moonlight, but a faint mist was on the shoulder of High Chaldon. At first it seemed to me that the mist was my sorrow and I stared, feeling that this would explain everything if only I could attend. The mist was me, transiently obscuring the outline of a lasting grief.

She felt lonely and unloved and bought Miss Green's on the understanding that Valentine would share it with her. The two moved in at the end of September when *Mrs Moxon lit our first fire, with a gimelled prayer cum incantation of good-will upon us*. Bedevilled by thoughts of their unworthiness both were still emotionally frail and unprepared for the feelings that were about to overwhelm them. The weather was wild and portentous:

A brilliant tearing gale of a morning. The Trinity (a group of trees on High Chaldon) *had lost all their leaves, the house sounded like engines, and we had to lock the front door to keep the gale out. We walked a very quarterdeck walk along the Maries, seeing the pheasants trying to rise into the gale, but flutter down again. Looking over the heath* (Winfrith) *we could see the wind .... a cloud of sea-spray and earth dust. In the afternoon I made a sackcloth rug like a fallen woman.*

A few days later Sylvia's fall was altogether more joyous. After lunch when she and Valentine walked to Beth Car *there was a strange stilled light over the landscape.* Once there they discovered that a servant girl at the vicarage had run away from her employer, a Miss Stevenson, who had a reputation for maltreating backward children. Enraged by the news they set out on the first of many crusades against injustice to remonstrate with the woman. Back at Miss Green's, exhausted by the confrontation, they retired to their respective bedrooms and lay talking until, moved by the *forsaken grave wail of her voice,* Sylvia climbed into Valentine's bed and *found love there.* Next day the two lovers *spent the morning lying in the hollowed tump of the Five Maries, listening to the wind blowing over* (their) *happiness.* Soon after the weather produced a spectacular storm that seemed to mirror the dramatic events of the last few days. Sylvia's diary records:

I walked up the Maries, seeing a terrific blue stormcloud westward over the sea. As I turned again to it a flash of lightning greeted me. It was the intensest scarlet. A blackbird shrieked, an owl hooted low, everything was afraid. Another flash, a pink one, and then, walking up the drove, pale and spirit-like in that strange light came Valentine to look for me. We got in just before the rain, and lay on my bed watching the storm.

Valentine Ackland (left) at Miss Green's and Sylvia Townsend Warner in 1937 at West Chaldon.

West Chaldon looking towards Holworth from High Chaldon.

Three years later they leased a *mouldering grange* on the Norfolk Broads while on a visit to Valentine's mother, but after 18 months their stay was cut short by the libel case brought against them by Miss Stevenson. Crippled by legal costs and with Miss Green's already let, they were obliged to rent 24 West Chaldon, a damp and dilapidated stone cottage owned by the Weld estate. Once installed they began a campaign against the privations of rural life and the agricultural wage. Sylvia delivered a sample of contaminated well water to the estate office in Lulworth while Valentine's articles on life in Chaldon appeared in the Left Review under the title of 'Country Conditions' (1935). They became active in local politics, joined the Communist Party and attended election meetings where Sylvia discovered a talent for heckling. In 1937 they travelled to Spain to work for the Red Cross during the Civil War but on their return the village seemed less appealing. Llewelyn Powys was already in a Swiss sanatorium, Theodore was bedevilled with tourists and the sanitary arrangements at West Chaldon had lost their charm long ago. With some reluctance the two women decided to rent a house on the banks of the Frome at Maiden Newton where they remained for the rest of their lives. It was 1949 before they could bear to visit Chaldon again, their return delayed by the news that Miss Green's had been destroyed by a German bomb at the end of the war:

The little snub-nosed squat victorian house
That preened in the sun through so many decades of peace,
Grey as a dove, and its slated salt-box roof
Sloped like the tail-feathers of a sitting dove,
All in a summer night scattered and gone
As a dove at a thunder-clap is flown!

At the blast it rose up from its foundation,
With a fluster it spread its wings of grey stone,
And went its piecemeal way into the dark, and is gone.

They arrived at a difficult point in their relationship with the reappearance of Valentine's American lover and as they wandered among the weeds and rubble where their love had taken root, the wreckage seemed painfully significant. Their love did survive and today they lie buried together in a corner of St Nicholas' churchyard and here, or up at the Five Maries, their spirits mingle with the ghosts at Chaldon Herring of Sylvia's poem:

Hush, my dear, hush!
Who are these that pass
Up shady lane?
Their feet don't brush
Any dew from the grass
And they are silent, too.

White Nose

Llewelyn Powys was brought up in a large, precociously gifted family at Montacute (see p78) where the Powys father combined his religious duties with an enthusiasm for the natural world common among late Victorian clergymen. All his children were encouraged to explore the woods and meadows around the village and this childhood mixture of freedom and intellectual company, tempered by orthodox Christianity and the formal education they received at Sherborne School, helped shape the very different literary achievements of all three brothers. In Llewelyn's case this found expression in anti-religious philosophical works, in the reflective mood of his dramatised autobiographical novels and the carefully modulated prose style of numerous essays inspired by the Wessex countryside.

From the sea stacks off Handfast Point westward to the windswept margins of Chesil Beach, the strange and beautiful *gull haunted* cliff-line is one of the most exhilarating stretches of coast in Britain. For the solitary walker, the sublime contours and rocky outcrops are an eloquent reminder of the sea's awesome power. Scattered between St Aldhelm's Head and Portland Bill the more bizarre rock formations - Bat's Head and Worbarrow Tout, Durdle Door, Blind Cow, the fossil forest at Lulworth and the oily shales of Burning Cliff - are celebrated in some of Llewelyn's finest prose, notably ***Earth Memories*** (1934) and ***Dorset Essays*** (1935). By superimposing his own mental map on the topography, Llewelyn claimed this enchanted coast as his personal terrain before offering it up in a series of exultant meditations on the glory of life and the insignificance of man.

Bat's Head from White Nose with St Aldhelm's Head in the distance.

Llewelyn at Chydyock with the Ankh, Egyptian symbol of life.

For Powys the towering chalk cliff known as White Nose was *the wildest, proudest headland of all the Dorset Coast*. He first discovered it as a child along the coast path from Weymouth where it was clearly visible from his grandmother's house in Brunswick Terrace. Years later, just when his reputation had become established with the completion of 'Skin for Skin' (1925), he returned from New York with his young American wife Alyse Gregory to live in one of the coastguard cottages perched on the edge of the cliff. John Cowper had recently agreed to another exhausting lecture tour in the States, but the wrench from his dearest elder brother was made easier by the prospect of being near Theodore and his sisters Kate and Gertrude who lived nearby at Chydyock.

No 5 Coastguard Cottages was a bleak outpost in winter suited only to the most puritanical recluse, a place where, according to Llewelyn, windows were often shattered by the most violent gales that blew seaweed right up the face of the cliff and sent *slates from our roof flying over the ploughlands behind the houses as lightly as though they were sycamore leaves. And then, as soon as ever the wind went down, a sea mist would suddenly descend upon us, enveloping us utterly*. At other times the silence was broken only by the eerie noise of the foghorn booming out across Weymouth Bay from The Shambles lightship *as though some huge antediluvian monster were out searching for its mate through the trough and bulging backs of the waves*. Each morning Llewelyn went out to the little stone hut with its upturned boat for a roof that had become his study. Here he worked or gazed out over the broad sweeping bay to the Isle of Portland tethered offshore and *stretching its bald bold turkey's head far out into the English Channel*. Llewelyn's decision to live on top of a cliff was made on practical grounds as much as his desire for solitude or an exhilarating view. Since the age of twenty five he had suffered from tuberculosis. The debilitating attacks often left him weak for long periods and, on the advice of doctors, he arranged for the revolving shelter he had slept out in at Weymouth to be re-erected in the garden at White Nose.

The enormous weight of chalk, slumped over a sticky layer of Gault clay, has come to rest in a confusion of *giddy ledges and castle rocks* known locally as the undercliff. It was Thomas Hardy, preferring the local name to the more archaic White Nothe or White Nore, who first likened its distinctive, broken profile to the Duke of Wellington's powdered nose. Llewelyn spent many hours alone in these *strange landslide glades* with nothing but the cliff foxes for company. He would sometimes catch a glimpse of one curled up on the rocks below or running across the foreshore at low tide, and he loved to watch a litter of cubs at play in the moonlight. The colony that patrolled the undercliff undisturbed was, he thought, a much bolder, more cunning breed than those persecuted in the Frome valley. He loved the wild intelligence of the animal as much as he admired the red deer on Exmoor and the bark of an old dog fox, carried on the frosty air of a November evening with ravens circling overhead, transformed the undercliff into a world of fairy tale where *groves* (are) *grown thick with ancient elders, whose skeleton branches are white as marrow bones, groves where the old ballad witch might well hold her step-children*.

In late spring the steep grassy slopes are covered with pink centaury whose healing properties were, according to legend, first divulged by Chiron the centaur. With this reminder of ancient Greece, Llewelyn considered the white cliff was *more classical than medieval in spirit as it rises against the blue sky, so light, so marble, so well-proportioned.* Access to the *strange secrets* of the foreshore *where the wild lavender blows* is by way of the old smugglers' path used by Elziver Block to outwit the militia in 'Moonfleet' (see p184). Once at the bottom the discovery of an ancient sea cave led Powys to imagine Dorset as the last island of Ogygia and the cave where the nymph Calypso captivated Ulysses. Dramatic in all weathers White Nose was, for Llewelyn, most resplendent in the evening light when:

the sea, as the sun went down, was transformed to flaming tossing gold and when we looked at the bastion of the White Nose we noticed the chalk was illuminated with an evil ecliptic light such as I have never seen before, and such in a single breathless heightened moment recorded beyond dispute the treacherous thinness of our dream life.

These words, written in 1925, anticipated with unerring accuracy the *treacherous thinness* of the dream world into which Llewelyn plunged three years later. On returning to America as visiting critic on the New York Herald Tribune, he soon became entranced by the languorous beauty of Gamel Woolsey. Despite one miscarriage, the young American poet was determined to bear Llewelyn's child and followed him to England a year later. The fisherman's cottage overlooking Ringstead Bay where she took lodgings was only two miles west of White Nose and, once installed, Llewelyn was soon striding along the cliff path to resume their passionate affair, oblivious to the pain it caused his wife Alyse.

Glebe Cottage with its thatch roof, looking very much as Llewelyn Powys and Gamel Woolsey knew it in the late 1920's.

The two lovers shared an interest in Romantic literature and, suffused with love, the little wooded valley where they walked soon became an enchanted grove. For Llewelyn, writing some years after the relationship had ended, it was already a legendary spot *with its stiles built of old oars, with woods gay with butterfly orchids, and with every field thick-spangled with elfin flowers.* Despite his sister Gertrude's conviction that their love *transcended all other loves, having something supernatural that could never be quenched,* Llewelyn's letters suggest an element of make-believe that lies at the heart of Romantic love. Ringstead, a place that exists in name only, provided the perfect setting. Deep in the woods, the chancel arch incorporated in Glebe Cottage, is all that remains of the medieval church and the irregularities in the adjoining meadow mark the site of the deserted village. Nothing is more romantic than the visible remains of a lost world, however slight, and the young couple were clearly susceptible to the magic of Ringstead.

The mythical beasts that inhabit the landscape of Gamel's poems are to be found wandering through her lover's dreams in which a white unicorn grazes in the moonlight outside a cottage guarded by a wyvern, while inside the couple make love. The scene reappears in Llewelyn's autobiographical novel 'Love and Death'. This celebration of the love that blossomed at Ringstead also mourns its demise following Gamel's marriage to Gerald Brenan. After the lyrical intensity of his early epistles Llewelyn's letters to Gamel, the Dittany Stone heroine of 'Love and Death', soon take on a *rather mannered self-indulgence* as though he was drawing on the experience to provide material for a novel that had been taking shape in his mind for several years. Alyse Gregory's journals for the same period carry a greater dignity and a more convincing reality in the way they express her anxiety at the thought of losing her husband. She did at times contemplate suicide but only ever suggested the depth of her despair in the novel 'Hester Craddock' (1931) at the point where the heroine abandons the man she loves in the arms of her sister and throws herself off Black Nore, leaving the reader to wonder how good a writer Alyse might have become had she not chosen to sacrifice a promising literary career in order to marry Llewelyn.

On the edge of White Nose and later at Chydyock, Llewelyn was often balanced precariously between life and death but, nursed by Alyse and his sisters, he survived frequent attacks of tuberculosis and threw himself into his writing with renewed energy. His work is charged with a rare vitality that reflects both his considerable charm, his enormous appetite for life and a heightened sense of his own mortality. Somerset Maugham thought that Llewelyn, of all the Powys brothers, *by living cheek by jowl with death .... learnt to be honest.* Friends and admirers were often struck by his appearance as he strode about the Dorset downs in rough tweeds, broad-brimmed hat and flowing cape *with the wind in his sandy-gold hair and a queer light in his grey-blue eyes.* In later life, with a wiry beard, his countenance became even more patrician. On first meeting Llewelyn in 1925 Valentine Ackland immediately recognised his *unique quality of being a demi-god, of being shining and dazzling, of being violently warm, as I imagine the old gods were.* Young female poets were particularly susceptible to his charms but Alyse, who knew

The view from Ringstead Bay to the coastguard cottages on top of White Nose.

him better than anyone, recognised the essence of his finest work. *He was from beginning to end in a perpetual enchantment over the visible world* in a way reminiscent of Richard Jefferies.

For Llewelyn religion was no more than *a heightened awareness of the poetry of existence*, or what he also called *the stream of earth life* revealed to man whenever he *realises the utter isolation of his soul*. At such times he is able to conjure the most fanciful legends. What matters, he argued, is not whether they are true or not, but that such strange and beautiful notions should have been imagined at all. The unicorn legend, reworked in his outstanding collection of essays **Earth Memories** (1935), is emblematic of man's need to travel imaginatively beyond the world of everyday truths. This magical beast, unburdened by daily toil, is free to roam in solitude through the wasteland of medieval romance. Llewelyn enjoyed walking at all times but especially in the half light of a summer's evening or at daybreak on a crisp autumnal morning. It was then, he believed, that man is able to *draw nearest to the heart of existence*, when he can best express his *secret yearnings* and become aware of the miracle of life in a *dry, salty plant of thrift on a cliff's ledge*. The unicorn was endowed with the power to purify water by dipping its horn below the surface, a miracle best performed before the arrival of the forest animals when:

... a halcyon calm will be upon the bay, and our outcast prayers of life-gratitude will rise again from the seashore sands, from bright buttercup meadows, from silent and familiar rooms, as easily, as naturally, as freely as birds on their migratory flights.

Although Llewelyn Powys' nature essays come from the same literary tradition as the diaries of Francis Kilvert and Dorothy Wordsworth's journals they read more like prose poems. 'Earth Memories' is full of revelatory exclamations that spring directly from nature quietly observed. Expressed in carefully modulated prose so different from John Cowper's volcanic outpourings, they display the consummate skill of a craftsman at the height of his power. His brother discerned an undercurrent in this writing *like the sound of wings in the air, of waves in the water, of fires on the heath* but was quick to point out that these meditations on the power and savagery of elemental forces are grounded in the reality of daily labour and human endurance.

'Dorset Essays' is deeply rooted in time and place, drawn from the author's childhood experience and his last years on the Dorset coast, but in 'Earth Memories', by uniting the overtly polemical themes of his earlier work and precise observations of the Wessex landscape, he illuminated his philosophy with images that transcend geographic reality. As 'The Pond' and other titles suggest, descriptions of place and natural phenomena are pared down to simple, concise language as Llewelyn's prose moves from detailed record to universal symbol. Many of the essays are the product of his invalid years on the downs at Chydyock where, unable to travel far, he found inspiration in the natural world around him. In the shelter brought from White Nose and re-erected in the lea of an ancient earthwork, he transformed the experiences into the *momentary consciousness* that distinguishes his most accomplished work.

In 'The Partridge' he celebrates the pleasure of planting lettuce seedlings on a summer evening when *a stillness lay upon the green valleys, delicate and profound.* The silence, broken by the cry of a partridge, makes him aware of this *hour of mystic grace* and in his heart he cries out *To be alive, only to be alive! Here is the praise, the wonder, and the glory!*. In 'A Butterfly Secret'

Llewelyn spent his last years at Chydyock in the wooden shed on the left where the sea air was considered to be good for his tuberculosis.

his thoughts turn to the *folded hills, whose rounded contours have the strength and simplicity of old Testament prose*. To what purpose, he asks, have the centuries passed since the barrow men worshiped their gods? The answer comes quite clearly on the night air - *there is no purpose*. For Llewelyn *every religion is as brittle as an empty snail shell in dry weather, as quick to disappear as cuckoo-spit in a summer hedge*. Life is its own justification. Resting on the grassy slope of a tumulus he contemplates the mating of two chalk blue butterflies and as he catches sight of the male's eye *lit up with a kind of arrogant exultation*, he knows like Blake, that *eternity is now*.

The vertical face of White Nose, behind it the broken profile from which the cliff takes its name.

'The Pond' is arguably Llewelyn's masterpiece in 'Earth Memories'. Located at the junction of two valleys a mile from his house, it appears but a rather ordinary feature in the landscape. The author visits it at intervals throughout the year hoping to receive *a whisper as to the secret life*. He witnesses the slow evolutionary process of orange-bellied newts, *those little ancestors .... who are privileged to experience the forgotten rhythm of saurian life* and the tadpoles turning into frogs that leap out onto dry land. As he sits quite still the reader begins to realise this is no common pond but *a mirror that reflects God's moving shadow* into which the ghost of a cow once disappeared. Eventually on a warm September evening the long-awaited messenger approaches. The moon hanging in the sky has sent its harbinger of truth and under its spell Llewelyn falls into a reverie to be awakened by a sound *sensitive and fresh as soft rain upon a leaf*. The moment of grace has arrived - *It was the hare drinking*. Robert Gittings knew Llewelyn Powys well and illustrated several of his books. His first impressions of the writer were shared by many of Llewelyn's admirers:

... close as he was to nature, one felt at times that he was entirely disembodied. There was something elfin about him. I shouldn't have been surprised if I had seen him disappear into the ground at any moment .... he seemed utterly content with his Dorset hills. All that his soul needed he could draw from them. They certainly gave him a grandeur of personality, a grandeur that seemed to spread about him like a wide aura of light.

Llewelyn lived close to death for so many years that he was able to teach others how to endure suffering and celebrate life, and he did so in prose containing moments of great beauty and rare insight. On one occasion after a severe attack his brother Bertie obtained permission from the Weld estate for Llewelyn to be buried on the downs. Several skeletons, arranged together in sitting positions and wreathed in antlers, had been unearthed when the Five Maries were excavated in the early 19th century and Llewelyn instructed that his own body be laid in a crouched position like an ancient Bronze Age warrior. In the event he survived for another five years and died in a Swiss sanatorium in 1939. After the war his ashes were buried on the cliff-top at White Nose beneath a slab of Portland stone inscribed with the words *The Living, The Living, He shall praise thee*.

Poxwell

Llewelyn and his brother Theodore were a familiar sight in the late '20s tramping the hills around East Chaldon in all weathers. One of their favourite walks took them westward from the Five Maries along the old ridgeway track as far as Poxwell before returning via Burning Cliff and West Chaldon. Arranged on top of an oval mound and measuring no more than fourteen feet across, the diminutive stone circle on the downs above Upton is Dorset's oldest and most enduring sacred place. Only three weather-beaten stones of any size now protrude above the barrow but Llewelyn was in no doubt about their antiquity. He shared the popular belief that the Poxwell or Puck's Well circle was an ancient Druidic temple. Both he and Theodore were sensitive to the

circle's *elemental force* and he would sometimes kneel and touch the ground
with his forehead in recognition of the old religion. On one occasion, walking
back from Weymouth at night with a parcel of fish for his brother, he entered
the circle and arranged the six herrings in a row in an act of appeasement, *their
plump sides in the moonlight more glittering than the frost.* On another
occasion he arrived with his brother one crisp New Year's Eve as though intent
on re-enacting some pagan ritual:

*Theodore entered the ring first, the shadow of his bowed figure - he had
taken his old cloak about him - appearing, as it fell across the deep-sunken
stones, like the shadow of some Biblical prophet, like the shadow of the
prophet, Amos! And with what curious, prophetic eyes he squinnied up at the
sky during those still, frosty moments!*

Poxwell stone circle.

8
The Hollow Land
Poole
and Purbeck

*In this sea line are cliffs of jagged rocks, sheer as a bastion wall,
as well as green lawns which creep lazily to the water's edge.
There are wide, open bays, and fissured sea-echoing chines.
There are round coves, inlets reaching through arched rocks,
level sands, and moaning caves. There are beaches of shingle, of
pebbles, of colossal boulders, and of the clay of crumbling banks;
precipices of every colour, from the white of chalk to the black of
shell; and walls of stone streaked with tints of yellow, buff or red.*

From ***Highways & Byeways of Dorset*** by **Sir Frederick Treves**

Bournemouth

Encouraged by opportunists like Sir George Tapps-Gervis who built the
Westover estate as early as 1836, the town began to take shape, but it was not
until the late arrival of the railway in 1870 that what Hardy called *the city of
detached mansions* started to spread with indecent haste across the surrounding
heathland, spilling over into the deep, wooded chines that lay in the direction
of Poole Harbour. As Angel Clare set out in search of Tess, *an outlying
eastern tract of the enormous Egdon Waste was close at hand, yet on the very
verge of that tawny piece of antiquity such a glittering novelty as this pleasure
city had chosen to spring up.*

Bournemouth was an example of the brand new Victorian seaside resort and
among those who sought the curative properties of the town's mild sea air, the
railway brought a flurry of literary visitors to Bournemouth in the late 19th
century. One of the first to arrive in 1875 was Francis Kilvert who recalled the
*wild sad sweet trysts in the snow and under the pine trees, among the sandhills
on the East Cliff and in Boscombe Chine.* Few stayed long enough to develop
any real affection for the place and it was left to Paul Verlaine, who stayed the
following year teaching French in a Catholic school, to convey the town's
peculiar residential atmosphere:

> *The long wood of Scotch firs twists down towards the shore
> A narrow wood of firs, laurel and spruce. All round,
> The town has, masquerading as a village more,
> strewn in among the trees, red bungalows galore,
> The whitewashed seaside villas on the lower ground.*

Although the town failed to inspire any literature worthy of the name it could boast a succession of celebrated writers who, by association, gave Bournemouth a reputation for adventure and intrigue it hardly deserved. Robert Louis Stevenson who moved here in 1884 hoping, like D H Lawrence, the sea air would ease his consumption, took an instant dislike to *that nest of British invalidism and British philistinism.* He wrote 'Kidnapped' during his stay and his thoughts were never far from Scotland. Before Stevenson and his wife left for Samoa he made the acquaintance of Shelley's son at Boscombe Manor. The poet's heart had reputedly survived the funeral pyre in Italy, a form of cremation not encouraged on the sands at Bournemouth, and had been retrieved by Mary Shelley, an act of devotion appropriate to the author of 'Frankenstein'. Wrapped in a page of Shelley's ode to Keats it was buried in 1889 alongside his wife and son in St Peter's churchyard. Swelled by the influx of summer visitors Bournemouth became a place for secret assignations where the whiff of scandal soon mingled in the sea air with the resinous scent of the ubiquitous fir tree. Dangerous liaisons occasionally lead to desperate remedies and the town is perhaps best known as the place where Tess put an end to her tormentor. Alec d'Urberville is murdered in the discreet surroundings of Mrs Brooks' *stylish lodging-house* where the scarlet blob on the ceiling grows rapidly into the shape of *a gigantic ace of hearts.*

The notoriety of Hardy's Sandbourne is seldom matched by the real guest-house world of the south coast's most respectable resort, where life revolves sedately around a succession of orchestral concerts and tennis tournaments. Bournemouth is a place where people go to die peacefully and without assistance, lulled to sleep by the sound of the waves in one of the town's many residential homes. The hotels stacked up on top of Paul Theroux's *toast-coloured crumbling cliffs* stand as a monument to the town's prosperity built upon those peculiar national institutions 'The Full English Breakfast' and 'The High Tea Trade'. But for many Bournemouth has also become synonymous with a particularly virulent strain of urban sprawl. As early as 1910 E M Forster was referring to *Bournemouth's ignoble coast* and forty years later **John Betjeman** arrived to reassess its character excited by the prospect of exploring an unrivalled selection of late Victorian churches:

Bournemouth is one of the few English towns one can safely call 'her'. With her head touching Christchurch and her toes turned towards the Dorset port of Poole she lies, a stately Victorian duchess, stretched along more than five miles of Hampshire coast. Her bed has sand for under-blanket and gravel for mattress and it is as uneven as a rough sea. What though this noble lady has lately disfigured her ample bosom with hideous pseudo-modern jewellry in the shape of glittering hotels in the Tel-Aviv style, her handsome form can stand such trashy adornment, for she is lovely still. Warm breezes caress her. She is heavy with the scent of pinus laricio, pinus insignis .... She wears a large and wealthy coat of precious firs. Beneath it we may glimpse the flaming colours of her dress, the winding length of crimson rhododendron, the delicate embroidery of the flower beds of her numerous public gardens which change their colours with the seasons. The blue veins of her body are the asphalt paths meandering down her chines, among firs and sandy cliffs ....

Poole Harbour

Caught up in the bohemian world of 1920s Europe, places meant less to the writer **Mary Butts** than the artistic circles in which she moved. Brought up on the edge of Poole Harbour she spent many hours gazing out across the water to the wooded slopes of Brownsea Island and beyond to the distant line of the Purbeck Hills, *a land it became* (her) *profoundest desire to know*. Her short, turbulent life was in many ways a defiant act of rebellion but she never lost sight of the Dorset landscape. Purbeck became a place of cherished memories, a sacred land beyond the wave of speculative development that was to sweep away all trace of her past. Butts' childhood had been full of ghosts and mythical heroes and her fiction combined a strong element of the supernatural with a well-defined sense of locality and orderly tradition threatened by an increasingly hostile world. Her autobiography **The Crystal Cabinet**, published just before her death, offers a fascinating insight into the mind of a highly imaginative but rather lonely child brought up at the turn of the century in the *wood and wind-lulled quiet* of a remote country house *rising gently out of the marsh*. Salterns remained Mary's home until just after her father's death when, at the age of 14, she was packed off to a desolate outpost on the Scottish coast to continue her education.

From the Arne peninsular, looking across the mud creeks of Poole Harbour to Round Island and the Purbeck Hills.

The dining room at Salterns 1920.

Captain Butts was a stern but kindly traditionalist who instilled in his daughter an intense dislike for all things vulgar, a man whose refined sensibility created the atmosphere of cultural well-being in which she thrived. Through his Norfolk family Mary could claim kinship with Rider Haggard and an 18th century bishop of Ely whose collection of early Ming vases adorned the drawing room. Her great grandfather, Thomas Butts, had been friend and patron to William Blake and his watercolours gave Mary an early taste for esoteric imagery, enriched by scenes from Arthurian legend that reflected Captain Butts' friendship with Rossetti. Draped with heavy curtains and lined with William Morris wallpaper, the principle rooms at Salterns provided a sumptuous setting for a selection of exquisite family heirlooms. Ivory toys and ebony boxes, musical instruments, polished brass that shone in the candlelight and chiming clocks delighted the romantic young girl, but most of all she loved to sit by the fire in her father's library and listen to tales from Homer.

Rebuilt in the late 18th century, Salterns was *the kind of house the Dorsetshire gentry lived in.* The grounds of about 20 acres had been laid out in a conventional manner with walled kitchen garden and orchard. A shrubbery and woodland walks flanked the croquet pitch and beyond, the lawn sloped down to the saltmarshes. The monkey puzzle and an enormous macrocarpa were the only alien features in an otherwise harmonious picture and years later Mary shed few tears when these ugly specimens were felled. The whole composition was framed on the landward side by a crescent-shaped plantation that stood between Salterns and the outside world.

Mary Butts
(1890 - 1937)

236

For the first ten years, until the arrival of her young brother, Mary had the grounds to herself. Inspired by 'The Heroes of Asgard', she populated the undergrowth with mythical beasts and re-enacted scenes from 'The Three Musketeers' in the outbuildings. The stump of an old oak became a magic island, a huge conifer the Tree of Yggdrasil and quartz pebbles found on the heath were turned into precious stones. Natural objects were not just anthropomorphic, they possessed a life of their own and all were sacred. Mary had always wanted a ghost for company and, undeterred by her father's insistence that the house was not haunted, she did eventually see a lady dressed in black disappear from the Lavender Walk. She was then sixteen and signs of a more sinister force were already apparent beyond the confines of Salterns.

Luscombe valley and a sizeable tract of heath still lay between the house and the advancing line of redbrick villas but, in the absence of legislation, its effectiveness as a green belt was already seriously compromised by the number of clay pits that scarred the countryside. The strange lunar landscape with its abandoned workings and pools of *chinese blue water* was a legacy of the potteries, a desolate and dangerous place. In this *Edgar Allen Poe country* stood an empty cottage on a spur of land jutting out into one of the lakes, its walls *cracked like the House of Usher*. Away from the coarse laughter of the men from Monkey Island who worked in the potteries, the old honey-coloured sandpits, full of brambles and birdsong, provided a safer and more exciting playground closer to home. *Civil in the sand and rude in the clay,* according to Mary, but when her favourite aunt was discovered face down in three feet of water by Witts Wood, the land seemed forever blighted. The heathland around Poole, once the scene of gypsy encampments, had been despoiled, reduced to a wasteland where tramps lurked in the bushes. There were signs of a violent struggle near the boundary fence, there was talk of suicide and Butts thought the open verdict on her aunt had probably been returned to spare the family.

The tide of new development on the shore of Poole Harbour.

Throughout her childhood Mary watched the *dreadful conjunction* of Poole and Bournemouth with a sense of rising panic as the restless *butcher-coloured scum of little houses* edged its way through the woods, engulfing the villages of Parkstone and Lilliput. In one sense the 'Tide' had already entered the house. Mary's mother, brought up in one of the *large comfortable houses of peculiar architectural dreadfulness* that had broken through onto the low ridge of hills above Salterns, had arrived with all the narrow-mindedness of her petty bourgeois family. But its *shabby, sun-steeped rooms* revealed a panorama of unrivalled splendour and by reciting each element in turn Butts lay claim to the landscape; the land was anointed and the view transfixed:.

From the far west, behind Poole, where Lytchett Clump humped itself on the horizon, to the mudflats of Holes Bay, to the masts and grey roofs of the port, to the silver dimness where the Wareham river began its scour .... Grange Hill, where Purbeck divides, and a huge down-spoke slides down the horizon to Flower's Barrow above Worbarrow and the western sea .... Round to the hub of the downs, to where Corfe Castle stands on its hill, with its towers ....

At the foot of the hills lay the great heath, and alongside it the Harbour's most mysterious reaches, Arne and Ower and Scudder and the black hook of Goathorn thrust into the flats among the little islands behind Brownsea.

Butts' mother, who revelled in the refined atmosphere at Salterns, was a sturdy introduction to the household but never fully came to terms with Captain Butts' unconventional and scholastic way of life. On his death she hastily piled up some of his more 'unseemly' books on the tennis court and burnt them. According to Mary, when her mother decided to marry a handsome young man from Brankstone Park the following year, *a period of illiteracy descended on Salterns. It became more fashionable, under my mother's sure touch, far more beautiful; but no more fascinating catalogues and great packages of books arrived, some splendid, some worn with antiquity. These ceased, and with them a life.* The precious Blake paintings, now on display in the Tate Gallery, were sold in order to pay off death duties and after the war the house itself was auctioned off, the trees felled and the grounds carved up into building plots. The Tide was rising fast until it reached the shore; time was running out and, gazing across *a flowing world, at flood ribbons of the tides' pure silver, a plain of green weed laced by oozing mud-channels at ebb*, Mary Butts realised what she must do to keep her father's secret alive.

Turning her back on a land despoiled by greed and ignorance she crossed the ferry to the dunes and the flower-studded hills *laid out like a god*. There on top of Nine Barrow Down she turned for the last time to see *the maggot-knot of dwellings that was once* (her) *home* before heading inland to transplant her ancestral home of revered tradition deep in the heart of Purbeck.

> *The Maiden caught me in the wild*
> *Where I was dancing merrily*
> *She put me into her cabinet*
> *And Locked me up with a golden key.*

From 'The Crystal Cabinet' by William Blake

Corfe Castle and the Isle of Purbeck, an enchanted land visible from Salterns that had beckoned to Mary Butts since childhood.

Badbury Rings

Situated in open countryside between Blandford and Wimborne, the earthworks known as Badbury Rings have assumed a special place in the landscape history of Dorset, from prehistoric ritual site to Roman route centre. In the 19th century the central enclosure was adorned by a clump of trees to provide the Banks' family with a suitably impressive landmark on their estate at Kingston Lacey. Earlier this century, several writers drew inspiration from the peculiar atmosphere that still lingered about the Rings. For **Mary Butts** they formed the most northerly landmark in the sweep of sacred country visible from her grandmother's home at Parkstone. She would often catch the train to Wimborne and walk out to the Rings along the avenue of beech trees beside the park. With each solitary visit the earthworks became charged with an ancient, supernatural power:

> *Up from the sea over the hill's high tower*
> *On breathless autumn days there whistles light*
> *A ghostly breeze. Their immemorial crown*
> *Makes audible in the gaunt tree-tops' height.*
> *Red glow the slender pine-shafts of the down*
> *   On Badbury Rings.*
>
> *Broad be the girdles of the Holy Wood*
> *Bare ramparts of lean grass close menacing,*
> *That all but trembles on our sight, who made*
> *Some passion of dim Gods therein out played*
> *Or the vast act of a forgotten King*
> *The imminent wonder, nameless luminous*
> *   On Badbury Rings.*

In the heightened awareness of these moments she came to recognise the essential truth that rescued her from the ideas of Jung and Bernard Russell or what she called *the group-consciousness of the post war generation*. Safe in the cup that held her Butts knew that progress towards a more spiritual life was constantly thwarted by the advance of an increasingly ugly, material world, and the struggle between these opposing forces preoccupied much of her work. In 1922, while staying with friends near Kimmeridge, she returned to the Rings:

I lay stretched out on the ground, and understood that the Rings' signature is written in its quiet .... made audible by the sound in the grove. I saw the fir-tree tops on their red shafts and the bunches of needles that pass sideways. They have the sensual, distinct beauty of Japanese or Chinese silk-paintings.

Aware perhaps of Hardy's levity with the nearby tower in Charlborough Park (see p130) Butts indulged in her own kind of topographical restructuring. Enchanted by the Rings she admitted to an *aesthetic restatement* of her experience there. In ***Ashe of Rings*** (1925) the earthworks re-emerge in Purbeck as a powerful force at South Egliston beside the ancestral home:

Rings lay in a cup of turf. A thin spring sun shone on its stones. Two rollers of chalk down hung over it: midway between their crest and the sea, the house crouched like a dragon on a saucer of jade.

Badbury Rings by Paul Nash 1935.

In 1935 the painter **Paul Nash** visited the Rings while gathering material for his Shell Guide to Dorset. Always alive to the sculptural possibilities of landscape and with a delicate sense of place his response was, like Butts', both immediate and lasting:

It has the dread peculiarity of a crown of dense trees planted in concentric circles. I have read of enchanted places, and at rare times come upon them, but I remember nothing so beautifully haunted as the wood in Badbury Rings. Long afterwards I read of the tradition that King Arthur's soul inhabited a raven's body which nested there .... Beyond the outer plateau the rings heave up and round in waves 40 feet high. A magic bird in a haunted wood, an ancient cliff washed by a sea changed into earth.

Studland

With its mixture of brick and stone cottages clustered round a beautiful Norman church and the natural advantages of its position, Studland is in many ways the perfect place for a holiday. The village lies at the foot of the Purbeck hills with heathland stretching away to the mudcreeks of Poole Harbour. Studland Bay is wide and sandy, sheltered by chalk cliffs and the monolithic sea stacks off Handfast Point, with sweeping views across to Bournemouth and the Isle of Wight. The transition from agricultural community to coastal resort for the rich and discerning began in the early 19th century with the construction of Manor House, a marine villa, for the Rt Hon Geo Banks, but it was the end of the century before Studland acquired its reputation as a writers' retreat. Hill Close, on the western outskirts of the village, was designed by Voysey in 1896 for the poplar Edwardian playwright Alfred Sutro and a young **T F Powys** arrived from Suffolk five years later. Unlike his brothers, Theodore had been educated at Aldeburgh on the Suffolk coast but attempts to persuade him to follow his father into the church had come to nothing and Theodore eventually chose farming as a career. The agricultural experiment was short-lived and he left East Anglia to pursue his bookish inclinations in Dorset with the help of a small annual allowance. He remained at Studland for the next three years writing and enjoying the contemplative life until, tired of the summer tourists, he took his stick and set out in search of some forgotten village where he would be altogether free from distractions

Llewelyn and Bertie Powys relished the prospect of spending time with their elder brother and holidays at Studland became a blessed release from the strictures of family life at Montacute. The three passed the time bathing, exploring the heath, climbing Toad Rock and trudging for miles over the Purbeck hills. 'Booze Nights' were the week's highlight, the beer being conveyed from the village inn to Theodore's rented cottage in a wheelbarrow. Once unloaded they would sit around drinking, talking or reading Rabelais and other authors disapproved of at home. Adolescent memories of Studland, where Llewelyn first experienced the pangs of young love, were recalled years later in his 'Dorset Essays' (1935). The insistent cry of the gulls about Old Harry rock and his first sight of deer on Studland Heath were just two of many happy recollections. Before leaving Montacute, the two brothers had promised to attend church each Sunday but Llewelyn, who was already shrugging off his religious upbringing, failed to appreciate the architectural delights of St Nicholas' church. To Llewelyn it was *squat like a grey toad in a field of oblong emmet butts*. After the service his *wayward inclination* led him straight out to where Puck Stone and Agglestone rock fought like giants on Godlington Heath. The Agglestone, a lump of ferruginous sandstone exposed on top of a low hill in the manner of a Dartmoor tor, impressed him more than it did Paul Nash who later complained; *it is the subject of the usual tiresome legends concerning the Devil, who is supposed to have thrown it at someone or something and, as usual, misjudged the distance.*

St Nicholas church Studland.

The legendary Agglestone.

Following the death of her father **Virginia Woolf** seldom returned to the family retreat in Cornwall, preferring Manorbier in Pembrokeshire and Studland where she spent several holidays before the outbreak of war. She first rented a cottage here in 1909 enjoying what for her was the almost unique experience of looking after herself. She recorded the delights of taking in the milk and cooking eggs before a dip in the sea, where she swam far out *until the gulls played over my head, mistaking me for a drifting sea anemone.* She was back in the village the following spring with her sister and Clive Bell but this time under doctor's orders to rest. After three weeks of sea air and good weather she was feeling much better but back in Fitzroy Square headaches and insomnia returned with the distractions of London life. Virginia's last visit was in September 1923 with Leonard Woolf when they stayed in a ducal home on the road to the ferry. The Knoll, later a hotel, was the seaside retreat of the Duke of Hamilton and had been placed at their disposal complete with servants. Guests included Maynard Keynes and Lydia Lopokova, the Russia dancer he later married. Virginia's sense of place was usually hierarchical and the presence of Lydia gave her the opportunity to indulge her capacity for malicious gossip. *Lydia's habits are, of course, not ducal* she reminded Jacques Raverat in a letter before relating the incident of the Used Sanitary Towels, her last offering from the Dorset coast.

Time has not been kind to Studland, or the literary biographer. Virginia Woolf and T F Powys were contemporaries but the Powys circle and the Bloomsbury group had few points of contact and the two never met. The nearest they came to a meeting was probably in Studland if, as Theodore would have agreed, a five year interval is a near miss. One can only speculate on what, if anything, might have passed between two of this century's most remarkable literary figures.

The Purbeck Hills

Midway through **Howards End** (1910), Margaret and Helen Schlegel leave London for their annual visit to Aunt Juley in Swanage, having been forced to relinquish their apartment in Wickham Place. Swanage with its *bourgeois little bay though dull, was stable*, but on arrival Margaret is greeted by a letter from Henry Wilcox offering the sisters a lease on his Ducie Street property and summoning her back to the city to discuss terms that include a rather business-like proposal of marriage. While awaiting her return, Aunt Juley has arranged a picnic on the downs. For **E M Forster** the landscape unravelling beyond Poole Harbour was the essential English countryside, unspoilt and enduring, that he had grown to love on visits to his mother's friend in Salisbury (see p62):

If one wanted to show a foreigner England, perhaps the wisest course would be to take him to the final section of the Purbeck hills, and stand him on their summit, a few miles to the east of Corfe. Then system after system of our island would roll together under his feet. Beneath him is the valley of the Frome, and all the wild lands that come tossing down from Dorchester, black and gold, to mirror their gorse in the expanses of Poole. The valley of the Stour is beyond, unaccountable stream, dirty at Blandford, pure at Wimborne - the Stour, sliding out of fat fields, to marry the Avon beneath the tower of Christchurch. The valley of the Avon - invisible, but far to the north the trained eye may see Clearbury Ring that guards it, and the imagination may leap beyond that onto Salisbury Plain itself, and beyond the Plain to all the glorious downs of central England.

Corfe Castle by Paul Nash 1935.

In 'Howards End' the car becomes the supreme symbol of a new, mechanised civilization corrupted by the pursuit of profit and epitomised by people like Henry Wilcox. Forster warned *the fields will stink of petrol* and years later he lamented how much of the countryside had been destroyed since the novel's publication. By then the lanes had become clogged with cars, the rivers polluted and the wildlife poisoned by pesticides. When writing the novel he was aware of the encroaching tentacles of the capital, a place that offered stimulation but, unlike the countryside, little sustenance. From Purbeck the view is already tainted:

Bournemouth's ignoble coast cowers to the right, heralding the pine trees that mean, for all their beauty, red houses and the Stock Exchange, and extend to the gates of London itself. So tremendous is the City's trail!

Arriving back in Dorset, Margaret joins the party and Helen becomes seized with *panic and emptiness* at the news of her sister's engagement. But despite Henry's distrust of emotion and imagination, despite his acquisitiveness and lack of respect for tradition, Margaret is convinced she will grow to love him and still retain her independence. *Only connect the prose and the passion, and both will be exalted* becomes her creed and the epigraph for a novel concerned with the possibilities of reconciliation. Turning again to the landscape, Margaret confirms her belief that the liberal classes could not enjoy the benefits of civilisation, least of all the luxury of a view like the one before them, without the enterprise displayed by generations of Wilcoxes. But this time the movement is reversed, the tide is returning: *The water crept over the mud-flats towards the gorse and the blackened heather. Branksea* (Brownsea) *Island lost its immense foreshores, and became a sombre episode of trees.* The land pulsates with life, the litany of places becomes a rising chorus reverberating across the hills. *Over the immense displacement the sun presided .... England was alive, throbbing through all her estuaries, crying for joy through the mouths of all her gulls, and the north wind, with contrary motion, blew stronger against her rising seas.* But, Forster asks, does England belong to the Wilcoxes who have made her or, echoing Lancaster's famous speech from Richard II, to the Schlegels who have *seen the whole island at once, lying as a jewel in a silver sea, sailing as a ship of souls .... towards eternity?*

* * * * *

In more recent years this stretch of the Dorset coast has been subjected to the critical gaze of two American travel writers well acquainted with the idiosyncrasies of English life. With some help from British Rail and the local bus network, **Paul Theroux** completed an ambitious hike round the coastline of Britain in the summer of 1982 collecting material for ***The Kingdom of the Sea*** (1989). Alighting from the Sandbanks ferry he was immediately struck by the proliferation of pornographic material and what he thought were naked perverts in the heather, unaware that much of the beach is reserved for nudists. The flat expanse of Studland heath, eroded by copulating couples and choked with litter, cast a disturbing shadow over the day:

In the remotest parts of this wild place there were girlie magazines .... I supposed that lonely men had taken them here, crept into the dunes by the sea and examined them, feeling safe and hidden.

Ballard Down and the chalk stacks off Handfast Point.

I was uneasy on this part of the coast path. It was not only the violence of the magazines. It was the wind, the dry grass, the desolation, the solitary standing men. It was one of a number of places on the coast where I expected to happen upon a dead body - a torso, decomposed, with missing limbs.

Theroux plodded on through Studland and over Ballard Down without a backward glance, heading for the next dreary boarding house in Swanage. Read ***Notes from a Small Island*** (1995) by **Bill Bryson** and you gain a fresh perspective on the same journey. As he set out from the ferry in glorious autumnal sunshine the three miles of sandy beach proved less revealing. Bryson had the place to himself and even managed to shrug off an attack by two black mongrels on the hill towards Handfast Point with his usual mixture of good-humoured indignation. His forbearance was rewarded by a stunning view from the top of Ballard Down. The description may lack Forster's informed sense of geography but, untainted by the author's emotional appeal to national sentiment, Bryson's view of his adopted country is equally rapturous:

For miles around the Dorset Hills rolled and billowed, like a shaken-out blanket settling onto a bed. .... It was beautiful beyond words, one of those rare moments when life seems perfect. As I stood there, spellbound and quite alone, a bank of cloud drifted in front of the sun, and through it there poured magnificent spears of shimmering light, like escalators to heaven. One of them fell at my feet and for one moment I could almost swear I heard celestial music

P D James
(1920 -)

Kimmeridge

For a man who walked the coastline of Britain expecting to stumble upon a mangled corpse in each new cove, Theroux was in surprisingly buoyant mood as he strode westwards along the Kimmeridge Ledges:

The sun and wind made the long grass flicker like fire ... There were pastures on the cliffs, and just to the left of the overgrown path two hundred vertical feet of gull-clawed air to the sliding surf, and the whole ocean beyond. This was the most beautiful stretch of coast I had seen so far, and I was alone on it .... I always felt I was safe - everything would be fine - if I stayed on the coast.

Theroux had clearly not read **P D James'** crime thriller ***The Black Tower*** (1975), a sad omission given his predilection for mutilated bodies. In it the author's sleuth arrives at Toynton Grange, a home for the disabled on the Dorset coast, only to discover that his old friend Father Baddeley is dead and that one patient has already plunged to his death in a wheelchair. What for Adam Dalgliesh begins as a period of quiet convalescence, soon turns into another murder enquiry as the detective becomes embroiled in the life of this enclosed community. Soon after his arrival Dalgliesh approaches the black tower in an atmosphere of impending doom:

Clavel Tower above Kimmeridge
Bay with South Egliston beyond.

The view, spectacular and frightening, made him catch his breath .... below, the cliff tumbled into a broad fissured causeway of boulders, slabs and amorphous chunks of blue-black rock which littered the foreshore as if hurled in wild disorder by a giant hand .... As he looked down on the chaotic and awe-inspiring waste of rock and sea and tried to picture what the fall must have done to Holroyd, the sun moved fitfully from behind the clouds and a band of sunlight moved across the headland lying warm as a hand on the back of his neck, gilding the bracken, marbling the strewn rocks at the cliff edge. But it left the foreshore in shadow, sinister and unfriendly. For a moment Dalgliesh believed that he was looking down on a cursed and dreadful shore on which the sun could never shine.

Smedmore, home of the Tory historian Sir Arthur Bryant after the war, was used as the model for Toynton Grange in P D James' crime thriller *The Black Tower*

In a disclaimer James apologises for presuming to erect her own architectural follies along the Purbeck coast, but the framework of reference persists. Toynton Grange, rebuilt in 1843 following a fire that destroyed the Elizabethan manor house, is a thinly disguised approximation to Smedmore, the Georgian enlargement of William Clavell's original Jacobean house just a mile south east of Kimmeridge. The village, with its cluster of stone cottages and dull Victorian church, is the most likely model for Toynton. Perched on a low headland at the entrance to Kimmeridge Bay, Clavel Tower is the author's most blatant appropriation. Refaced with thin blocks of dark bituminous shale it becomes the black tower from which the novel takes its title and the setting for its gruesome climax. Built in 1820 as an observatory by Smedmore's eccentric incumbent the Revd John Clavell, the tower now stands empty and neglected. Nicholas Pevsner was in no doubt about its original purpose:

A scholarly mixture of motifs, as befits a folly: round the bottom a colonnade of Tuscan columns of the primitive type favoured by French painters such as David for their backgrounds, and round the top false machicoulis and a parapet pierced with quatrefoils.

The author's tower is a recognisable hybrid with the circular base of its Kimmeridge prototype surmounted by an octagonal cupola *like a pepperpot pierced with eight glazed slit windows* salvaged from Horton's brick observatory north of Wimborne. Set in the wall is a plaque that records the death in 1887 of Wilfred Mancroft Anstey for whom the black tower was built on completion of Toynton Grange. Anstey, a more sinister eccentric than his real life contemporary, had walled himself up in his own folly to await the second coming, and starved to death. Dalgliesh has been in Baddeley's cottage long enough to realise the old man was murdered and, as he ponders the evidence on his way over to the Grange, he becomes engulfed in *a sudden physical invasion of white obliterating clamminess*. The dense sea mist:

... hung on his hair, caught at his throat and swirled in grotesque patterns over the headland. He watched it, a writhing transparent veil passing over and through the brambles and bracken, magnifying and altering form, obscuring the path .... the sound of the sea swelled and became all-pervasive, disorganized, menacing, seeming to advance on him from all sides. It was like a chained animal, now moaning in sullen captivity, now breaking free to hurl itself with roars of impotent rage against the high shingles.

Just as Dalgliesh thinks he is lost, Anstey's folly rears up out of the mist. Resting his face against the tower he hears quite distinctly *the spine-chilling scrape, unmistakable, of bone ends clawing against the stone* that seems to be coming through the wall, unaware that this same macabre sound will shortly come to his rescue.

Tyneham

Mary Butts' love affair with the Isle of Purbeck grew from family holidays spent sailing round the Dorset coast and it was perhaps inevitable that her solitary excursions along the chalk ridge should end by the sea at Arish Mell. Skirting Worbarrow Bay she came to Tyneham valley, a forgotten landscape of unrivalled beauty cradled between Whiteway Hill and Gad Cliff. From below at South Egliston *the sacred wood runs its closed fan to the sea*. This was old country of the Dorset squirearchy with whom Butts felt such a close affinity. The Welds still lived in Lulworth Castle, while the Bonds divided their loyalties between Creech Grange and Tyneham's late 16th century manor. The house was impressive although Butts was more interested in its occupation by a single family for the last 300 years than the antiquity of the building itself.

In 1916 the Royal Tank Corps took up a rather ominous position outside Lulworth but when Butts began writing the only military-style invasion to have reached the *green transparent land* of Tyneham was the annual scout camp from Eton College. *Ashe of Rings* (1925), the first of her three Purbeck novels, was published in the same year as 'Bindon Parva', a collection of

The village inn, East Lulworth.

stories by George A Birmingham whose fictional village lay in the same *hollow among the downs*. The vicar of Bindon Parva is possessed of clairvoyant powers and believes that strong emotions are absorbed by a building *charging the very stones with a certain energy*. His choice of location and his theory of architectural consecration bore a close resemblance to Butts' theme of family history, and its almost magical effect on his characters suggests a familiarity with her work ('Ashe of Rings' had been serialised in the Little Review in 1919).

As Butts develops the tension between her group of displaced aesthetes and the ancestral place in which they seek renewal, her alchemy begins to work and the landscape around Tyneham is lit up in the amber glow of the author's memory where, as the critic Patrick Wright suggests, *the view thickens to form an aspic around its cherished object*. The myth of Tyneham as emblematic of traditional values threatened by a debased urban culture had begun to emerge long before its inhabitants were persuaded to evacuate the village on the strength of a broken promise. Populated by a few ageing rustics in the aftermath of war, Butts' *Hollow Land* is no longer a working landscape. Her sacred valley becomes home to a colony of indolent artists blown out by the whirlwind of Parisian cafe society and traumatised war poets who manage to retain the refined sensibility necessary to interpret the language of place:

Tyneham valley in early morning light from Whiteways Hill with St Aldhelm's Head beyond.

Tyneham House shortly after Ralph Bond had been forced out by the War Office.

Nothing came to trouble the continuity of his dream. The sheen on the new grass, the expanse of sky, now heavy as marble, now luminous; the embroidery that a bare tree makes against the sky, the iridescent scum on a village pond, these were to be his remembrances, the assurance of his reality.

In this atmosphere of sensory contemplation the world is made real by the distinction and naming of natural objects. This incantation of information becomes a redemptive therapy in which Butts' characters are little more than static figures who know the wisdom of the hills. History is inward looking, a chronicle of one family's past set in a palimpsestuous landscape cut off from the real world and accessible only to those initiated by birth and breeding. The search for meaning in a transient world of nature was, for Butts, a measure of the cultured mind and she was always careful to distinguish it from the more popular *cult of nature*. Pursuit of the picturesque, with its origins in the Romantic poets, had reached its most debased form in the taste for spectacular scenery acquired by an urban population propelled by Shell and enticed into the countryside by a burgeoning tourist trade. Solitary walks by people like Richard Jefferies, the Powys brothers and Mary Butts in search of secret knowledge produced an inspired legacy of rural literature that was its own justification. But the recreational fashion for hiking among the urban proletariat was roundly castigated by Butts. Her essay 'A Warning To Hikers' (1932), in which the city stereotype is berated for his unsuitable clothes, his litter and disregard for a way of life sanctified by time and privilege, reads like a landowners' charter in the current 'Right to Roam' debate.

The urban hiker, ignorant of *the magic of person and place,* is just part of the same materialist 'dis-ease' unleashed, according to Butts, by the ravages of war-torn Europe; a tide of machines, rapacious developers and caravan tourists about to sweep down her precious valley and obliterate its sacred geography. The threat appears far more serious than the tanks lined up on the far side of Whiteway Hill and in her poem 'Corfe', Butts invokes the Almighty to mount a rearguard action against the infidel.

> *Make many slugs where the stranger goes*
> *Better than barbed wire the briar rose;*
> *Swarm on the down-tops the flint men's hosts*
> *Taboo the barrows encourage ghosts.*
>
> *Arm the rabbits with tigers' teeth*
> *Serpents shoot from the soil beneath*
> *By pain in belly and foot and mouth*
> *Keep them out of our sacred mouth*

In Butts' last novel, ***Death of Felicity Taverner*** (1932), the forces of 'progress' are represented by Nick Kralin, a Bolshevik Jew in exile from pre-revolutionary Russia. Butts' brief marriage to John Rodker, a left wing Jew, ended acrimoniously and there are autobiographical overtones in Kralin's marriage of convenience to the heroine, a woman of reduced circumstances. Having driven Taverner from her ancestral home Kralin draws up an ambitious scheme to exploit the timeless beauty of the estate by building a monstrous holiday village. He then attempts to blackmail the family into selling him the land by threatening to publish his wife's erotic and occult writing. Taverner has already died in mysterious circumstances but her presence continues to dominate the book. She is the presiding spirit of the place, *the hills were her body laid down*, and the guardians of her memory, while endeavouring to discover the circumstances of her death, are drawn to defend the green translucent land against the *grey thing*; the cancerous growth lodged in the heart of their Hollow Land. Triumph over evil can only be secured by the annihilation of Kralin and the task is allotted to a White Russian emigre who sees in Kralin the same grey power that had overthrown the established order in his own country.

After a nervous breakdown Mary Butts returned from Europe in 1930 with the painter Gabriel Aitken. Her mystical vision of Dorset was shaped not in a blood-red Parkstone villa but in one of the cadaverous grey bungalows that had already begun to disfigure the Cornish coast, a cruel irony not lost on the author. From Salterns to Sennen Cove Butts' wheel had come full circle, and lay dashed to pieces by another wave of speculative development. Her headstone in Sennen churchyard, adorned with the line from Blake, *I strove to seize the inmost form*, looks out in vain towards the legendary land of Lyonesse while the Armed Knight lies at the foot of Lands End, vanquished by the spectre of rampant greed on Albion's most distant shore. Butts never courted the wider reading public and her novels read more like esoteric texts that document the destruction of a lost kingdom. Her particular brand of occult mysticism allied to her belief in an aristocratic social order was more fashionable in the 1920's but by the time she reached maturity as a novelist a decade later these same ideas had become less palatable. Once dismissed as an obscure 'period' writer Butts' fiction has become the subject of renewed interest and is now more readily available in this country at a time when the destruction of sacred sites continues unabated.

Butts would have been horrified by the desecration of her Hollow Land that followed its occupation by the military. Forced out by the War Office in 1943, Ralph Bond had fought doggedly against any form of modern intrusion, ensuring that his estate remained more like a wildlife sanctuary than an efficient agricultural unit. As the last of seven generations to inhabit Tyneham House he had done his best to continue the tradition of paternal feudalism established by the family when it first acquired the property in 1686. There are Bond memorials in the church and the National Board School stands as a monument to the family's sense of moral responsibility. In 1892 Goldsmith's poem 'The Deserted Village' was set for examination, a seemingly unremarkable entry in the school log book that now stands as a chilling reminder of Tyneham's more recent fate.

Tyneham valley 1927, the *Hollow Land* of Mary Butts' novels.

With one eye on the car park at Lulworth there are those who argue that the tanks have saved Tyneham from a worse fate of the kind predicted by Mary Butts. To many others the transformation of Tyneham into a ghost village, the destruction of an ancestral home and a traditional way of life is a more heinous crime. By now the debate has become obscured by the Tyneham myth but Patrick Wright's acclaimed book, 'The Village That Died for England' (1995), does much to disentangle the barbed wire from the briar rose, shedding valuable new light on Tyneham's elevation to position of national shrine.

Tyneham inspired Lilian Bond's elegy to a lost village and a way of life destroyed by the military.

The cult of Tyneham, inflamed by Attlee's broken pledge, began shortly after with a rallying cry from the Tory historian Sir Arthur Bryant. Knighted for his patriotic version of English history, Bryant seemed well-qualified to set the betrayal of Tyneham in the wider context of nationhood. It was the defence of places like Tyneham, he argued, that men had been fighting for, not their destruction. Written on St George's Day 1949 from Smedmore, the manor house a few miles east of Tyneham chosen by Butts as the ancestral home of Felicity Taverner, Bryant's call reverberated around the Purbeck hills and when Lilian Bond had finished her elegiac 'Tyneham-A Lost Heritage' (1956) she immediately turned to him for the preface. Inscribed with Hilaire Belloc's, *The corner of a corner of England is infinite and can never be exhausted*, Bond's recollections distort the view down the valley of her Edwardian childhood. In a world of shabby gentility the landscape is enriched by a language that strains to appease the sense of violation and betrayal felt by the author. The library, flooded with late afternoon sunlight, is filled with *that mellow sense of ancient buildings*, the garden with rare and exotic plants. The valley echoes to the sound of sheep bells and *the rhythmic sighing of the blade* from the woodyard while overhead the buzzard and the peregrine keep watch over their domain. The village is a model of sobriety, honesty and social deference in a time when *servants thought no shame of following their age old calling.*

This view from the terrace across Bond's earthly paradise bears more than a passing resemblance to Mary Butts' world at Salterns. Both exist in the same frame of time and are informed by the same intelligence, but as Wright is quick to point out, Tyneham is the reverse image of East Chaldon (see p222), *the spartan virtues of one being the injustices and deprivations of the other.* The death of Imber village, a desolate spot on Salisbury Plain lamented by its few inhabitants, has never caught the public imagination in quite the same way, but the Wiltshire gentry had always shunned the Plain for the more sheltered reaches of the Wylye Valley. Readers of Bond's 'Tyneham' are left to consider whether *the allegorical fables of malign encroachment* would have persisted for so long or found such a sympathetic audience but for the efforts of its most eloquent advocates.

Jacket design (1933) by Gabriel Aitkin

The spoils of victory have been divided up; the 17th century pulpit from St Mary's church is now at Lulworth Camp, the east front of Tyneham House, dismantled by the Ministry of Works in 1967, was removed to Athelhampton House and its 16th century porch now adorns the manor house at Bingham's Melcombe. Tyneham's distant past has been exploded, its history reconstructed and its architecture rearranged. Living history has become both a legendary world and a poignant symbol of an England that has vanished. Today in the visitor centre the MOD presents a carefully constructed view of itself as custodian of our natural heritage while the urban hiker treads warily along the coastal path.

The mouth of Lulworth Cove with its *Pillars of Hercules.*

Lulworth Cove

Lulworth or Lulwind Cove, as Hardy called it, is the most perfect of the many strange rock formations along this stretch of coast. Embraced by jagged headlands, *the pillars of Hercules to this miniature Mediterranean*, and shut in by towering chalk cliffs, this watery amphitheatre has become the setting for several curiously connected literary events. In September 1820, having accepted an invitation from Shelley to join him in Italy, **Keats** set sail from London with the painter Joseph Severn. Heading down the channel the 'Maria Crowther' was becalmed off Dorset and they put into shore at Lulworth where Keats spent his last day in England clambering over the rocks. Two years earlier he had fallen deeply in love with Fanny Brawne and that evening on board ship, knowing he might never see her again, he wrote his last poem 'Bright Star', a poem that ends in death. The young poet was by then seriously ill with consumption and died in Rome the following year at the age of 26. When **Hardy** came to write ***Far From The Madding Crowd*** (1874) he decided to use the theatrical possibilities of Lulworth Cove as the setting for Sergeant Troy's ill-fated dip in the ocean, but it was 1920 before the publication of his poem 'At Lulworth Cove A Century Later' commemorated the centenary of Keats' brief visit. Two strangers discuss a third gazing up into the evening sky:

Good. That man goes to Rome - to death, despair;
And no one notes him now but you and I:
A hundred years, and the world will follow him there,
And bend with reverence where his ashes lie.

Having paid his last respects at Fanny's grave, Troy heads south out of Weatherbury (Puddletown), intent on putting as much distance as possible between him and the scene of his misery. Crossing the Frome valley he began the long, slow climb to the top of the downs where his spirits are lifted by the spectacular view out over a *broad steely sea.* Descending to the shore he undresses and plunges in but, not content with the smooth waters of the cove, *to get a little ocean swell* (he) *presently swam out between the two projecting spurs of rock* where he is caught by strong currents and swept out to sea. His rescue on the point of exhaustion by a boat that takes him into Budmouth (Weymouth), brings about a full recovery and Troy eventually works his passage to America. In the meantime his clothes are discovered by a coastguard and news is brought to his estranged wife Bathsheba that her husband is presumed drowned.

Rupert Brooke
(1887 - 1915)

At the beginning of this century another handsome young poet with dazzling reputation came to Lulworth intrigued by one of the series of oddly named outcrops along the Dorset Coast (cf Swyre Head, Durdle Door, Bats Head and Worbarrow Tout). **Rupert Brooke** was then at Cambridge and, like many of his contemporaries, had just discovered the delights of long country walks. In the summer of 1907, while staying with aunts in Bournemouth, Brooke was pouring over a map of the region when 'Mupe Rocks' caught his attention. *Have even we made a better name* he enthused to a friend. Having decided on Lulworth just a mile west of the rocks, he packed his books, reserved rooms above the village Post Office and set off for the Isle of Purbeck. On arrival the young poet immediately succumbed to some kind of food poisoning and spent the first few days *throwing up, indeed, all I had eaten for weeks and also my immortal soul and several political convictions*, but he recovered sufficiently to write *today I am weak but cheerful, I can sit up and take a little Plato.* Before long the completion of 'Pine Trees and the Sky: Evening' signalled a return to health and the more serious business of writing verse. The following incident, recounted soon after in language suitable to the occasion, illustrates perfectly the ability of certain places to nurture the most astonishing literary associations:

On Tuesday, we sat on seagirt rocks and read J Keats, when I leapt from rock to rock J.K. fell from pocket into swirling flood beneath; and ere aught could be done, was borne from reach on swift current. We rushed to the harbour, chartered a boat, and rowed frantically along the rocky coast in search of it .... At length we spied it close in, by treacherous rocks .... we beached our barque (at vast risk) half a mile down the coast and leapt lightly over vast boulders to the spot. At first we re-saw it not. Then Hugh's small but acute left eye saw it in the midst of a roaring vortex. There was a pause. With a hurried misquotation from Diodorus Siculus I cast off my garb and plunged wholly naked into that fury of black waters and white foam - enough J.K. was rescued in a damaged condition. All (except my stomach) is well.

It was several years later before Brooke discovered the Keats connection with Lulworth while reading a collection of the poets letters and it confirmed the village for him as the ideal place for literary gatherings since his introduction to the Bloomsbury group. He returned to Lulworth for New Year in 1912 with Lytton Strachey and the artist Henry Lamb, staying this time at Churchfield House, only to find his relationship with Ka Cox, the Fabian student he had met in Cambridge, rocked by her love for the young painter. His rejection precipitated a nervous breakdown from which he never fully recovered when, in 1915, he was dispatched to the Dardanelles and died of food poisoning at the age of 28. Like Keats he was buried *in some corner of a foreign field / that is forever England* on the Greek Island of Scyros.

Looking west from Flower's Barrow towards Mupe Rocks.

Bibliography

Ackland, Valentine, *For Sylvia*, Methuen, 1986.

Ackroyd, Peter, *First Light*, Penguin, 1993.

Adeane, Louis, Mary Butts, *World Review*, Mou 1951.

Allsop, Kenneth, *In the Country*, Hamish Hamilton, 1972.

Ashdown, Douglas, *William Barnes*, Dorset Books, 1996.

Aubry, James R., *John Fowles : A Reference Companion*, Greenwood Press, 1991.

Babb, Howard S., *The Novels of William Golding*, Ohio University Press, 1970.

Barnes, William, *The Dorset Engravings*, Dorset Nat. Hist. and Arch.Soc., 1986.

Beauman, Nicola, *Morgan : A Biography of E.M.Forster*, Hodder and Stoughton, 1993.

Bell, Quentin, *Virginia Woolf Vol.1 1882-1912*, The Hogarth Press, 1973.
    Virginia Woolf Vol II 1912-1941, The Hogarth Press, 1973.

Betjeman, John, *Collected Poems*, John Murray, 1980.
    Coming Home, Methuen, 1997.
    Summoned by Bells, John Murray, 1960.

Bird, Eric, and Madlock, Lilian, *Writers on the South-West Coast*, Ex-Libris Press, 1994.

Blaen, Angela, *Maiden Castle and the Celtic Calender,* Powys Review, No 15, 1984-5.

Blondel, Nathalie, *Mary Butts : Scenes from the Life*, McPherson and Co, 1998.

Boyd, S J, *The Novels of William Golding*, The Harvester Press, 1988.

Bryson, Bill, *Notes From a Small Island,* Black Swan, 1996.

Butts, Mary, *Speed the Plough and Other Stories*, Chapman & Hall,1923.

Cavaliero, Glen, *John Cowper Powys : Novelist*, Oxford, 1973.
    Sylvia Townsend Warner : An Appreciation, Powys Review, No 5, 1979.
    The Powys Family and Dorset, Powys Review, No 7, 1980.
    The Rural Tradition in the English Novel, Macmillan, 1977.

Chandler, John, *Wessex Images*, Alan Sutton, 1990.

Cheetham J.H., and Piper J., *Wiltshire : A Shell Guide*, Faber and Faber, 1968.

Clark, Leonard, *Alfred Williams : His Life and Work*, David and Charles, 1969.

Clew, Kenneth, *Kilvert's Langley Burrell*, 1981.

Coates, C A, *John Cowper Powys : In Search of a Landscape*, Macmillan, 1982.
    Gerda and Christie, Powys Review, No 5, 1979.

Collins, H.P., J*ohn Cowper Powys : Old Earth-Man*, Barrie and Rockcliff, 1966.

Crompton, Don, *A View from the Spire*, B.Blackwell, 1985.

Daiches, David and Flower, John, *Literary Landscapes: A Narrative Atlas*, Paddington, 1979.

Davies, Stevie, *Boy Blue*, The Women's Press, 1987.

Day Lewis, C., *The Buried Day*, Chatto and Windus, 1960.

de Selincourt, Aubrey, *Dorset : Vision of England*, Paul Elek, 1947.

Delaney, Frank, *Betjeman Country*, Paladin, 1985.

Diffey, T.J., *John Cowper Powys and Thomas Hardy*, Powys Review No.12, 1982-3.

Drabble, Margaret (ed), *The Genius of Thomas Hardy*, Weidenfield and Nicolson, 1976.
    A Writer's Britain, Thames and Hudson, 1979.

Draper, R P (ed), Hardy: The Tragic Novels, Macmillan Casebook Series, 1975.

Dugdale, Giles, *William Barnes of Dorset,* Cassell.

Eagle, Dorothy and Stephens, Meic, *The Oxford Literary Guide to Great Britain and Ireland*, O.U.P., 1993.

Elwin, Malcolm, *The Life of Llewelyn Powys*, The Bodley Head, 1945.

Falkner, J.M., *Moonfleet*, Wordsworth, 1994.

Farjeon, Eleanor, *Edward Thomas : The Last Four Years*, O.U.P., 1973.

Forster, E.M., *The Longest Journey*, Penguin, 1989.
    Howards End, Penguin, 1989.

Foss, P.J.,*Llewelyn Powys: Towards a Reconsideration*, Powys Review, No 6, 1979-80.

Fowles, John, *The French Lieutenant's Woman*, Jonathen Cape, 1969.
    Lyme Regis Camera, Dovecote Press, 1990.

Furbank, P.M., *E.M.Forster : A Life, Vol 1 1879-1914*, Secker and Warburg, 1977.

Gibson, J. and Johnson, T., *Thomas Hardy Poems*, Macmillan, 1979.

Gittings, Robert, *The Younger Hardy*, Penguin, 1978.
    The Older Hardy, Penguin, 1980.

Golding, William, *A Moving Target*, Faber and Faber, 1982.
>   *The Hot Gates*, Faber and Faber, 1965.
>   *The Pyramid*, Faber and Faber, 1967.
>   *The Spire*, Faber and Faber, 1964.

Gregor, Ian, *The Great Web : The Form of Hardy's Major Fiction,* Faber and Faber, 1974.

Grigson, Geoffrey (ed), *The Faber Book of Poems and Places*, Faber and Faber, 1980.

Hallett, T., *Ramsgard to Blacksod:The Setting of Wolf Solent*, Powys Review, No.24, 1989.

Hardwick, Michael, *A Literary Atlas of The British Isles*, David and Charles, 1973.

Hardy Thomas, *The Return of the Native*, Penguin, 1978.
>   *The Mayor of Casterbridge*, Penguin, 1978.
>   *Tess of The D'Urbervilles*, Penguin, 1978.
>   *The Distracted Preacher and Other Tales*, Penguin, 1979.
>   *The Well Beloved*, Macmillan, 1925.
>   *The Woodlanders*, Penguin, 1981.

Harman, Claire, *Sylvia Townsend Warner : A Biography*, Chatto and Windus, 1989.

Hassall, Christopher, *Rubert Brooke : A Biography*, Faber and Faber, 1964.

Hawkins, Tim, *Dorset : Photographers' Britain*, Alan Sutton, 1991.

Hillier, Bevis, *John Betjeman : A Life in Pictures*, John Murray, 1984.
>   *Young Betjeman*, John Murray, 1988.

Hooker, Jeremy, *Writers in a Landscape*, University of Wales Press, 1996.

Hopkins, Kenneth, *Llewelyn Powys,* Macdonald, 1952.
>   *The Powys Brothers : A Biographical Appreciation*, Warren House Press, 1972.

Hudson, W.H., *A Shepherd's Life*, Methuen, 1910.

Hughes, Ian, *A Poor Ragged Maiden : The Textual History of Maiden Castle*, Powys Review, No. 12, 1982-3.
>   *Allusion, Illusion, and Reality : Fact and Fiction in Wolf Solent*, Powys Review

Humfrey, Belinda, *Recollections of the Powys Brothers*, Peter Owen Limited, 1982.
>   *John Cowper Powys's Wolf Solent : Critical Studies*, University of Wales Press, 1990.

Hunter, William, *The Novels and Stories of T F Powys*, Trigon Press, 1977.

Huxtable-Selly, Susan, *Mysticism, Trivia and Sensations : Observations on Weymouth Sands*, Powys Review, No.11, 1982-82.

Ingrams, R., and Piper J., *Piper's Places,* Chattos and Windus/The Hogarth Press, 1983.

James, Henry, *English Hours*, O.U.P., 1981.

James, P.D., *The Black Tower*, Penguin, 1975.

Jefferies, Richard, The Society, *Richard Jefferies, A Spirit Illuminated,* Swindon, 1987.
>   *The Story of My Heart*, Longmans, 1894.
>   *Wildlife in a Southern County*, Nelson.

Jones, Bernard, *John Meade Falkner 1858-1932*, Dorset Worthies No 18.

Kay-Robinson, Denys, *Hardy's Wessex Re-appraised*, David and Charles, 1972.

Keith, W.J., *The Archaeological Background to Maiden Castle*, Powys Review, No 22, 1988.
>   *The Rural Tradition*, Harvester Press, 1975.

Kilvert, Francis, *Kilvert's Diary*, Penguin, 1977.

Kinkead-Weekes, M., & Gregor, I., *William Golding:A Critical Study,* Faber & Faber, 1967.

Krissdottir, Morine, *John Cowper Powys & The Magical Quest*, Macdonald and Janes, 1980.

Lane, Denis, *The Elemental Image in Wolf Solent*,

Lea, Hermann, *Thomas Hardy's Wessex*, Macmillan, 1977.

Lee, Hermione, *Virginia Woolf*, Chatto and Windus, 1996.

Legg, Rodney, *Literary Dorset*, Dorset Publishing Co, 1990.
>   *Steep Holm, Allsop Island*, Dorset Publishing Co, 1992.

Lock Charles, *Maiden Castle and the Violation of Form*, Powys Review, No 21, 1987-88.
>   *Weymouth Sands & the Matter of Representation:Live Dogs, Stuffed Animals & Unseated Stones*, Powys Review, No 23, 1989.

Looker, S, and Porteous C, *Richard Jefferies : Man of The Fields*, Country Book Club, 1966.

Low, Anthony, *Dry Sand & Wet Sand:Margins & Thresholds in Weymouth Sands*, Powys Review.

Lukacher, Ned, *Wolf Solent's Metaphoric Legends*, Powys Review, No 6, 1979-80.

Bibliography

Mabey, Richard (ed), *Landscape with Figures: An Anthology of Richard Jefferies' Prose*, Penguin, 1983.

Marsh, Jan, *Edward Thomas*, Elek Books, 1978.

Mitchell, J., Lawrence, *The Visionary World of T F Powys,* Powys Review, No 7, 1980.

Moran, Margaret, *The Vision and Revision of John Cowper Powys's Weymouth Sands*, Powys Review, No 11, 1982-3.

Morris Jan (ed), *Travels with Virginia Woolf*, The Hogarth Press, 1993.

Nash, Paul, *Dorset : A Shell Guide*, Faber and Faber 1935.

Olivier, Edith, *The Love Child*, Virago, 1981.

O'Sullivan, Timothy, *Thomas Hardy : An Illustrated Biography*, Macmillan, 1977.

Page, Norman (ed), *William Golding : Novels 1954-67*, Casebook Series, Macmillan, 1985.

Pevsner, Nikolaus, *Wiltshire, The Buildings of England,* Penguin, 1963.
   and Newman, John, *Dorset, The Buildings of England*, Penguin, 1972.

Pitt-Rivers, Michael, *Dorset : A Shell Guide*, Faber and Faber, 1966.

Powys, John Cowper, Autobiography, Macdonald, 1967.
   Diaries 1932-33: A selection on the writing of Weymouth Sands, Powys J,. Vol II, 1992.
   Remembrances : Weymouth Sands, Powys Review, No 11, 1982-3.
   Wolf Solent, Macdonald, 1951.
   Maiden Castle, Macdonald, 1937
   Weymouth Sands, Macdonald, 1934.

Powys, Llewelyn, *A Baker's Dozen*, The Bodley Head, 1934.
   Earth Memories, The Bodley Head, 1934.
   Dorset Essays, Redcliffe Press, 1983.

Powys, T F, *Mr Weston's Good Wine*, Chatto and Windus, 1927.
   Mockery Gap, Chatto and Windus, 1925.

Rands, Susan, *Maiden Castle:Symbol, Theme & Personality,* Powys Review, No 15, 1984-5.

Rodman, J.S., *Setting Weymouth Sands*, Powys Journal Vol I, 1991.

Roulstone, Micheal, *Llewelyn Powys*, Powys Review, No.2, 1977.

Seymour-Smith, Martin, *Thomas Hardy*, Bloomsbury, 1994.

Sorley, Charles, Hamilton, *The Collected Poems*, Cecil Woolfe, 1985.

Stinton, J., *Chaldon Herring:The Powys Cricle in a Dorset Village*, The Boydell Press, 1988.

Street, A.G., *Farmer's Glory*, O.U.P., 1983.

Style, Colin, *On Hardy's Sacred Ground: John Cowper Powys's Weymouth Sands*, Powys Review, No.17, 1985.

Swift, Graham, *Ever After*, Picador, 1992.

Tanner, Robin and Heather, *Wiltshire Village*, Collins, 1939.

Theroux, Paul, *The Kingdom by the Sea*, Penguin, 1984.

Thomas, Edward, *Collected Poems,* Faber and Faber, 1936.
   The South Country, J M Dent, 1984.

Thomas, Helen, *As It Was and World Without End*, Faber and Faber, 1956.

Thorpe, Micheal, *Writers and their Work* : John Fowles, Profile Books, 1982.

Tomalin, Ruth, *W.H.Hudson : A Biography*, O U P, 1984.

Warner, Sylvia Townsend, *Collected Poems,* (ed) Claire Harman, Carcanet New Press, 1982.
   Diaries, (ed) Claire Harman, Chatto and Windus, 1994.
   Letters, (ed) Claire Harman, Chatto and Windus, 1982.

Weinstock, M B, *The History of Fleet Village*, 1971.

Wessex Journal, *Kenneth Allsop : The Man who re-invented Rural England*, 1996.

Whistler, T., *Imaginations of the Heart: The Life of Walter de la Mare*, Duckworth, 1993.

Williams, John, *Theodore Powys and the Devil*, Powys Journal, Vol II, 1992.

Wilson, Angus, *John Cowper Powys as a Novelist*, Powys Review No 1, 1977.

Wright, Patrick, *On Living in an Old Country*, Verso, 1951.
   The Village That Died for England, Jonathen Cape, 1995.